Praise for *Unintended Consequences*

"*Unintended Consequences* is full of substance, it is one of the must-read books of the year, and once I finish it I will be giving it a second read through right away."
—Tyler Cowen, Professor, George Mason University; Columnist, *The New York Times*; Author of *Marginal Revolution*

"*Unintended Consequences* reveals the author's intelligence and skill at elucidating economics." —*Bloomberg Businessweek*

"Conard's defense of private enterprise deserves the attention of policymakers in Washington." —*Publishers Weekly*

"Edward Conard provides a provocative interpretation of the causes of the global financial crisis and the policies needed to return to rapid growth. Whether you agree or not, this analysis is well worth reading."
—Nouriel Roubini, New York University; Chairman, Roubini Global Economics

"*Unintended Consequences* presents a fascinating and refreshing view of our financial system and how the reactions of Congress and regulators to the near meltdown of 2008 may make our nation less competitive and our banking system less stable. Anyone interested in the future of our financial system needs to read this."
—Judd Gregg, Former Chairman of the Senate Budget Committee

"This is a wonderful book, filled with wisdom by a guy who really knows what he's talking about. It is must reading for both business-men and politicians."
—John C. Whitehead, Former Co-chairman, Goldman Sachs & Co; Former Deputy Secretary of State

"*Unintended Consequences* will be the most talked about economic book in 2012. When Ed Conard points the spotlight at recent economic history, his uncanny ability to cut through the confusion provides something totally unexpected: a fresh, nonpartisan perspective on what is right and wrong with America."

—Kevin Hassett, Director of Economic Policy Studies,
American Enterprise Institute

"Edward Conard identifies the root causes of the Financial Crisis. Washington policymakers will debate Edward Conard's analysis for years to come."

—Emil W. Henry, Jr., Former Assistant Secretary of the
Treasury for Financial Institutions

"Edward Conard has written a provocative and important book about the economy that challenges conventional wisdom about the Financial Crisis, the trade deficit, government policy, and the path to prosperity. His insights into the kind of risk taking we need to spur innovation and job creation are particularly salient, given the inevitable flight from all risk coming out of the crisis. I hope policymakers and business leaders will pay close attention to Conard's framework."

—William A. Sahlman, Senior Associate Dean,
Harvard Business School

"Finally, common sense! Voters, politicians, and policymakers should take a careful look at this counterintuitive explanation of the contemporary economy and the Financial Crisis. It dispels misconceptions that hamper the recovery and replaces them with insights essential to accelerating it. Even sophisticated economists will find this valuable reading."

—Bruce C. Greenwald, Coauthor of *Globalization*, Professor of
Finance, Columbia University, Graduate School of Business

"Edward Conard's book represents the most cogent and persuasive analysis of the Financial Crisis to date. It is deeper and likely more accurate than what we have seen so far from journalists, academics, and particularly former government officials."

—Andrei Shleifer, 1999 John Bates Clark Medal winner;
Former Editor, *Quarterly Journal of Economics*;
Professor of Economics, Harvard University

"Edward Conard's keen business insight and sharp eye on economic forces explain structural strengths and weaknesses of the American economy. While some of his proposed solutions are controversial, the U.S. economy can recover its mojo if policy makers understand Conard's diagnosis."

—Glenn Hubbard, Dean, Graduate School of Business,
Columbia University; Former Chairman,
President's Council of Economic Advisers

"The world needs to do more work to understand the recent crisis and its aftermath. Ed Conard has written a compelling book that challenges conventional wisdom and provides an important contribution to the debate about what we must do to build the economy and increase prosperity. It is an intelligent and fresh look at where we've been and where we need to go. It should be widely read."

—Robert Steven Kaplan, Professor, Harvard Business
School; Author of *What to Ask the Person in the Mirror*

"Virtually everyone who reads *Unintended Consequences* will feel the pain of knowing that we may never get EVERYONE to read it. The clarity of Edward Conard's explanation of where we are, how we got here, and what we do now is profound."

—Bill Bain, Founder, Bain & Company

Edward Conard was a partner at Bain Capital from 1993 to 2007. He served as the head of Bain's New York office and led the firm's acquisitions of large industrial companies. He sits on several boards of directors including the board of Waters Corporation. He is also a visiting scholar at the American Enterprise Institute. Prior to Bain, Conard worked for Wasserstein Perella, an investment bank that specialized in mergers and acquisitions, and Bain & Company, a management consulting firm, where he headed its industrial practice. He is a graduate of Harvard Business School and the University of Michigan.

www.EdwardConard.com
www.facebook.com/EdwardConard
Twitter@EdwardConard

UNINTENDED CONSEQUENCES

WHY EVERYTHING YOU'VE BEEN TOLD
ABOUT THE ECONOMY IS WRONG

EDWARD CONARD

PORTFOLIO / PENGUIN

PORTFOLIO/PENGUIN
Published by the Penguin Group
Penguin Group (USA) Inc., 375 Hudson Street,
New York, New York 10014, USA

USA | Canada | UK | Ireland | Australia | New Zealand | India | South Africa | China
Penguin Books Ltd, Registered Offices: 80 Strand, London WC2R 0RL, England
For more information about the Penguin Group visit penguin.com

First published in the United States of America by Portfolio/Penguin, a member of Penguin
Group (USA) Inc. 2012
This paperback edition published 2013

THE LIBRARY OF CONGRESS HAS CATALOGED THE HARDCOVER EDITION AS FOLLOWS:
Conard, Edward.
Unintended consequences : why everything you've been told about the economy is wrong /
Edward Conard.
p. cm.
Includes bibliographical references and index.
ISBN 978-1-59184-550-8 (hc.)
ISBN 978-1-59184-630-7 (pbk.)
1. United States—Economic conditions. 2. United States—Economic policy.
3. Finance—United States.
I. Title.
HC103.C7348 2012
330.973—dc23
2012006013

Printed in the United States of America
10 9 8 7 6 5 4

Set in ITC New Baskerville Std
Designed by Pauline Neuwirth

ALWAYS LEARNING   PEARSON

For my wife and daughter

CONTENTS

INTRODUCTION

WAS OUR COUNTRY'S economic success over the last twenty-five years built on false pretenses? Did we simply borrow and spend too much money? Are we now paying the price for that unsustainable spending spree?

In the aftermath of the Financial Crisis in late 2008 and early 2009, many commonly held beliefs have emerged to explain its causes. Wall Street bankers* stand accused of using low down payments, teaser rates, and other predatory tactics to seduce home owners into buying homes they couldn't afford. Critics charge that bankers used fraudulent credit ratings to sell these risky mortgages to unsuspecting investors, bundling pools of risky mortgages into securities in which 80 percent of the cash flows received the lowest-risk, AAA ratings—ratings that agencies have long since downgraded. These risky loans and their subsequent defaults, they claim, would have bankrupted our financial infrastructure had it not been for taxpayers' bailouts. If taxpayers must provide guarantees to lenders, shouldn't they demand fair compensation for their guarantees?

Many of the same people assert that bankers put our financial

---

* The book uses the terms "banking," "bankers," and "Wall Street" loosely to encompass both commercial banks that accept deposits and investment banks that do not. My usage of the terms aligns most closely with common usage. Where differences are relevant, the text delineates different types of financial institutions.

infrastructure at risk for their own gain by allegedly funding loans with too much short-term debt and engineering their way around prudent banking regulations while the Bush administration looked the other way. All the while, Wall Street raked in unprecedented pay. Critics blame misaligned incentives and sheer incompetence for this recklessness. Don't we need extensive regulations to protect us from a repeat of this behavior?

Meanwhile, American households stand accused of borrowing recklessly to increase consumption. Over the last twenty years, debt* as a percent of gross domestic product (GDP) rose from 250 percent to 350 percent. Personal saving rates declined from a historical average of 10 percent in the 1970s and early 1980s to essentially zero prior to the Crisis. We seem addicted to financing increased consumption, while the trade and fiscal deficits skyrocket. Have we mortgaged our children's future as a result?

Others believe the Federal Reserve spurred this borrowing by holding interest rates too low after the 2001 recession. They blame cheap credit for artificially driving up real estate prices, which lulled borrowers and lenders into a false sense of confidence and increasingly reckless behavior.

At the same time, the trade deficit exploded as income inequality grew dramatically. Some economists claim that low household saving rates and a corresponding lack of investment eroded U.S. competitiveness. Overheated consumption supposedly tightened our industrial capacity utilization, which drove valuable manufacturing jobs offshore. Critics claim Americans have become a nation of hamburger flippers and that open trade borders and cheap offshore labor have held down the wages of domestic workers. According to the *New York Times*, 99 percent of the U.S. population went without pay raises for decades as their standards of living declined. Meanwhile, the incomes of the top 1 percent grew 300 percent.[1] Income inequality increased substantially. The evidence seems mighty damning.

To add insult to injury, the tax policies of the Bush administration

---

* The sum of government, business, and financial debt.

appear to have allowed reckless risk takers and the beneficiaries of open trade borders to keep an unfair share of these seemingly ill-gotten gains while ordinary citizens suffered. In the end, the prior decade—2000 to 2010—produced no gains in asset values, employment, or standards of living, the worst decade-wide performance since the Great Depression. Meanwhile, critics claim the government funded tax cuts by scrimping on health care, education, and investments to slow global warming. Fifty million Americans don't have health insurance. Shouldn't politicians raise taxes on the rich to redistribute their ill-gotten gains?

All these factors seemed to converge and cause the economy to collapse under its own weight. The inability of banks and households to continue financing more and more debt appeared to tighten credit and slow consumer demand. As soon as that happened, presumably, asset prices fell and investors panicked, exacerbating the decline. Something had to give, didn't it?

Do free markets optimize on their own, or can private investors put our economy at risk for their own gains? Nothing less than the credibility of capitalism is at stake.

Science judges hypotheses, not by what they explain, but by what they fail to explain. When anomalies pile up, experts reject the hypothesis that engender them. The various hypotheses explaining the Financial Crisis are riddled with anomalies. For instance, if the United States has become a nation of consumers rather than investors, why has productivity soared? Productivity growth was lackluster for decades prior to the commercialization of the Internet. But if the answer is simply "the Internet," why didn't productivity also improve in Europe and Japan? Since 1991, France's GDP per worker, adjusted for purchasing power, has fallen from 91 percent of that of the United States to 78 percent; Germany's from 86 percent to 73 percent; and Japan's from 86 percent to 74 percent.[2] These countries had access to the same technology and possessed similarly educated workforces; why didn't they perform as well? And if the United States simply has a more entrepreneurial culture, why couldn't that culture produce differentiated results prior to the Internet?

With historically high productivity gains, how does the trade deficit demonstrate a lack of competitiveness? If the United States has become a nation of hamburger flippers, why were half the jobs created since the 1980s created at the highest and most technical end of the wage scale—doctors, lawyers, scientists, supervisors, writers, and teachers?[3] And if households aren't saving—or worse, borrowing to consume—why has household net worth risen even at post-recession asset values?[4]

If predatory bankers took advantage of home owners, why did the requirement for down payments decline? Smaller down payments shifted risk from home owners to lenders. If banks used securitization to offload troubled loans onto naïve investors, why did they retain 40 percent of those loans on their balance sheets? Can any investors honestly claim they didn't know that nomoney-down loans to borrowers with undocumented incomes were both risky and common? If mortgage defaults are the primary cause of the recession, why were banks rendered insolvent long before home owners defaulted? If banks used innovation to avoid regulations, why did they choose to hold less risky AAA-rated securities on their balance sheets instead of higher-yielding A-rated securities, which regulations allowed them to hold with the same level of capital adequacy reserves? If moral hazard—where risk takers capture the benefits of risk taking without full exposure to its consequences—motivated bankers, why did the CEOs of the top banks personally lose billions of dollars?

If the risks were easy to spot, why did top financial regulators, even liberal regulators like Robert Rubin, former Treasury Secretary during the Clinton administration, resign his board seat after having admonished Citigroup to increase its risk? Why did former Obama economic adviser and Harvard University president Larry Summers likewise undertake enormous investment initiatives to expand Harvard's campus when its endowment rose in value? Those investments now lie fallow. Why did Nobel laureate and then–World Bank economist Joseph Stiglitz and former Obama budget director Peter Orszag coauthor a paper[5] that concluded,

"The risk to the government from a potential default on GSE* debt is effectively zero"? Fannie Mae and Freddie Mac are now bankrupt.

If the Bush administration turned a blind eye to banking regulations, why did it substantially tighten capital adequacy requirements in 2001? Why did it introduce and fight for legislation to rein in Fannie Mae and Freddie Mac? Why was it slow to transition the United States to international banking standards, which loosened capital adequacy requirements? If loose monetary policy is the primary cause of the Crisis, why are loan defaults predominantly confined to subprime mortgages† and not spread more broadly?

A full explanation of the workings of the economy and the Financial Crisis must account for these apparent anomalies. The commonly held beliefs do not; this book endeavors to provide explanations that do.

I've split this explanation into three parts: "What Went Right," "What Went Wrong," and "What Comes Next." The names of the first two parts require no explanation. The third part makes recommendations for safeguarding the economy, accelerating its recovery, reducing unemployment, and maximizing long-term economic growth. The reasons for including the second and third parts are obvious. I start with "What Went Right" because I feel it's important that, in order to avoid making changes that do more harm than good, we must first establish agreement about what worked well with our economy prior to the Financial Crisis.

In the wake of the Financial Crisis, we have heard an endless stream of criticism of what many claim is an obviously flawed economic model. These critics make improvements sound easy to identify and implement, and yet anyone who has ever tried to get rich by finding economic improvements quickly discovers just how

---

* Government-sponsored enterprises, principally Fannie Mae and Freddie Mac, two quasi-private companies that guarantee the repayment of residential mortgages on behalf of homeowners.

† The book uses the term "subprime" to include subprime, Alt A, and home equity loans except where further differentiation is needed.

difficult this is. It's nearly impossible. Well-intended but misguided advocates make improvements seem easy by naïvely overlooking unintended consequences.

New York Times columnist Paul Krugman, for example, argues that the economy can thrive with greatly scaled-back financial markets because it thrived in the 1960s without them.[6] But the 1960s economy also thrived without computers. Would eliminating computers serve us better today? Obviously not. Krugman's logic is flawed.

Former Federal Reserve chairman Paul Volcker dares anyone to give him "one shred of neutral evidence that financial innovation has led to economic growth."[7] Yet New York University economics historian Thomas Philippon provides evidence that the financial industry grew (as a percent of GDP) in the late 1800s in response to the need by railroads and heavy industries for outside capital. It grew again in the 1920s when electrification accelerated economic growth, and companies like GE, GM, and P&G completed their initial public offerings. It stabilized at a historically low 4 percent of GDP after World War II when large, profitable cash flow–rich corporations with less need for external financing dominated the postwar economic landscape. But then it grew again in 1990 when 50 percent of investment shifted to small companies whose profits provided only a third of the needed financing.[8] In sum, it grew when the economy needed it to grow. Surely, the same is true today.

It's hardly surprising to find that, throughout history, growth of the financial sector happened for real economic reasons. Darwinian survival of the fittest largely governs the economy. It tests real-world alternatives against fierce competition for scarce resources—food and sex in the case of biology, customers and capital in the case of economics. It pits new ideas against existing alternatives that prevailed in the face of the same competition. Survival of the fittest ruthlessly prunes away less capable alternatives, ensuring that only the most valuable and robust remain. That's not to say evolution isn't filled with kludge, but rather that surviving alternatives prevail for valuable reasons. We should be highly skeptical of proposals that claim to offer improvements, and scrutinize them carefully for unintended consequences.

Unfortunately, when we dig into the underlying causes of economic success we find the world of economics deeply divided and inherently political. Advocates for stronger incentives for risk taking and those for income redistribution each work backward from their conclusions to find a set of indisputable beliefs upon which to build their arguments. Such beliefs, whether true or not, are easy to find; the economy is so complex that it's impossible to definitively isolate the effect of any one factor. As a result, academics and economists have fought each other to a draw on virtually every issue. Take the critical issue of the effect of taxation on savings, for example. In his comprehensive survey of the literature,[9] Stanford economist Douglas Bernheim concludes, "As an economist, one cannot review the voluminous literature on taxation and saving without being somewhat humbled by the enormous difficulty of learning anything useful about even the most basic empirical questions." Unfortunately, the same is largely true of all of economics. We must use empirical evidence to evaluate the beliefs that divide economics and decide for ourselves which set of beliefs seems most plausible.

I have searched for a fair and comprehensive summary of both sides of the issues, but couldn't find one. Here is my attempt to provide it. I have endeavored to piece together a mosaic of academic studies to explain how the economy works; why the United States has outperformed its high-wage rivals; what caused the Financial Crisis; and what improvements might better protect our economy without damaging its growth. I've tried to dispel commonly held misconceptions, provide facts, and fairly represent both sides of the argument.

This is not a book that takes a couple of insights and expands them into 300 pages. Quite the opposite; it covers the entire scope of the economy in order to propose unexpected links between disparate economic objectives. It will reward you with a sophisticated understanding of the contemporary economy. It will load your gun with unbiased facts and direct you to cutting-edge research on the most important issues confronting our economy. My hope is that it will change your view of the economy and of economic policy.

No set of conclusions will persuade everyone. My goal is to present provocative conclusions that fair and thoughtful opposition will respect. Even if you don't agree with them, they will inoculate you against superficial claims and proposals filled with unintended consequences.

PART I

WHAT WENT RIGHT

CHAPTER ONE

A BRIEF HISTORY OF THE U.S. ECONOMY

THE PERFORMANCE OF the U.S. economy over the two decades prior to the Financial Crisis was much stronger than commonly perceived. Over the last two decades, the productivity of the U.S. economy has grown nearly as fast as it did after World War II, when it enjoyed unique advantages over the rest of the world. Many of those advantages have eroded gradually over time. Europe and Japan rebuilt their infrastructures following the war; they educated their workforces just as the United States did; and they built manufacturing industries with worldwide economies of scale. Nevertheless, U.S. economic performance relative to other advanced economies has accelerated over the last two decades. It's true that economies like China's are growing faster than ours, but comparing the United States to China instead of Europe or Japan is misleading. Yes, we can grow more quickly if we accept drastically lower wages, but who wants to increase growth that way? Relevant comparisons must be similar enough that they reveal relevant differences. A brief overview of economic history helps to put these comparisons into perspective.

1950s AND 1960s: THE HALCYON DAYS

A unique set of circumstances accelerated the growth of the U.S. economy in the 1950s and 1960s. The world economy suffered a decade-long depression in the 1930s that stifled capital invest-ment. Following the Great Depression, a devastating world war diverted U.S. investment away from the private sector, which sus-tains long-term growth. The war effort may have provided spill-over benefits to the economy, but the economy also emerged in the 1950s with twenty years of underimplemented innovation.

World War II destroyed Europe's and Japan's infrastructure. This weakened their ability to compete with the United States, and it took decades for these advanced economies to catch up. This left U.S. companies with an open playing field for growth.

Meanwhile, the commercialization of television and advertising, newly built U.S. interstate highways, and automated manufac-turing allowed American companies to create nationwide mass markets for their products. Because international trade was under-developed at that time, the United States was essentially a closed economy. U.S. manufacturers benefited from enormous econo-mies of scale relative to a divided Europe and a technologically underdeveloped Japan. Only their ability to find and exploit untapped opportunities limited the growth of American corpora-tions.

The advanced education of the American workforce acceler-ated the growth of the post-World War II economy. Decades ear-lier, the United States had been the first nation to educate all its citizens publicly. Europe and Japan were slow to follow. In 1955, the United States enrolled 80 percent of its fifteen- to nineteen-year-olds in school full time compared to only 10 percent to 20 percent in Europe. And most European students were studying for vocations that prepared them to do jobs better suited to the past rather than rigorous academic subjects that would allow them to take their economies into the future.[1] In the United States, where high schools were more academically oriented, the GI Bill allowed more Americans to attend college. In the 1950s and 1960s, workers with college degrees propelled the transition of the U.S. economy from simple farming to sophisticated manufacturing.

The 1950s and 1960s were also favorable to wage growth in the United States. While opportunities were expanding domestically, the workforce was constrained by both a baby bust in the difficult 1930s and 1940s and by the loss of half a million young working-age Americans in the war. In the 1930s, the U.S. population grew by only 7 percent, compared to 19 percent in the 1950s. At the same time, the half million war casualties were mainly men who comprised a greater percentage of the full-time workforce in a population that was only about 132 million—less than half the size it is today. Eventually immigration and the entry of women into the workforce would put downward pressure on men's wages. In the 1950s and 1960s, however, an explosion of great corporate jobs, together with a restricted supply of labor, produced healthy wage growth. Real wages grew 2.8 percent per year from 1959 to 1973, but then declined to 1.2 percent per year until the early 1990s.

While it's true that the United States enjoyed twenty years of prosperity following World War II without the benefit of computers or highly developed financial markets, that doesn't mean today's economy would grow as fast without these tools. The United States was prosperous for a unique set of reasons that are impossible to duplicate today, including a decade-long depression, the destruction of the rest of the developed world's infrastructure, a failure of potential foreign competitors to educate their people, and a highly restricted supply of workers. For the sake of mankind, let's hope those conditions aren't repeated! It seems to me that anyone who makes comparisons between today's economy and that of the 1950s and 1960s without fully disclosing their differences is deceiving their readers.

1970s AND 1980s: GROWTH OF COMPETITION

The 1970s and 1980s provide a more relevant comparison for evaluating the current economy. By then, a handful of factors ended the halcyon days of the 1950s and 1960s.

After the postwar catch-up, advanced economies saw their growth slow and their unemployment rise. Productivity growth—the relevant measure of an economy's growth—stalled (see Figure 1-1). The most talented U.S. workers were fully educated. Europe and Japan caught up to the United States by educating their workforces.

FIGURE 1-1: U.S. Productivity Growth Relative to Other Developed Economies

COUNTRY	GROWTH IN OUTPUT PER WORKER (Percent per year)		
	1948–1972	1972–1995	1995–2007
France	4.6	1.6	1.4
Germany	5.7	1.7	1.1
Japan	7.7	2.4	1.2
United Kingdom	2.4	2.0	2.6
United States	2.3	1.2	2.0

SOURCE: PENN WORLD TABLE, 2012.

Declining protectionism and the commercialization of containerized ocean freight facilitated international trade. As worldwide markets offered economies of scale to all successful producers, competition—principally from the Japanese—caught U.S. manufacturers off guard, eroding their market share and scale advantages.

Free trade weakened labor unions' monopolies on the supply of labor for industries such as steel, auto manufacturing, and airlines and limited the wage premiums they collected from consumers. The higher pay of union jobs represents nothing more than an unfair tax on consumers. Higher priced goods that cover the higher cost of union labor transfer money from poorer nonunion consumers to highly paid union labor. This transfer has never been economically sustainable without government-mandated labor laws and closed trade borders that prevent non-union competition. If some manufacturers can shift a portion of their manufacturing to lower-cost non-union suppliers—if the government opens borders to allow non-unionized imports, for example—then prices will fall to match the lower cost of labor. Consumers benefit from lower prices. In the 1970s and 1980s, foreign competition gained a toehold in the markets. Prices fell and consumers captured the savings. The United States only lost high paying union jobs because unions lost their ability to tax consumers.

At the same time, baby boomers and women flooded the workforce. This put downward pressure on wages. By the late 1980s, immigration into the United States began to increase, and by 2009, 50 million immigrants and their U.S.-born children lived here.[2] This also put downward pressure on wages, especially the wages of white men who were previously the predominant source of labor.

When markets were growing in the 1950s and 1960s and companies were scrambling to fulfill unmet demands, competition was less significant. But as growth slowed, competition intensified. In his book, *The Great Inflation and Its Aftermath*,[3] journalist Robert Samuelson contrasts the competitiveness of the 1980s and early 1990s to the unfettered boom of the 1950s and 1960s by comparing Alfred Sloan's landmark 1963 book, *My Years with General Motors*,[4] to Intel CEO Andy Grove's 1996 book, *Only the Paranoid Survive*.[5] Sloan's book contains chapters with titles like "The Concept of the Organization," "Co-ordination by Committee," and "The Development of Financial Controls." In a world where building and organizing a business is the major hurdle to success, the specter of competition is barely on his radar. Grove, on the other hand, writes, "I believe in the value of paranoia." He adds, "The more successful you are, the more people want a chunk of your business . . . until there is nothing left." He warns that firms have to overcome "strategic inflection points" that alter "the way business is conducted." Samuelson points out that Grove exhibits none of Sloan's confidence. Instead, Grove focuses exclusively on competition.

As competition grew for products that enjoyed worldwide economies of scale—autos, steel, machine tools, etc.—job growth from the largest companies with the highest paying jobs began to slow. Large companies with the most promising investment opportunities generally pay the highest price for labor. Economies of scale and entry barriers, which create the need for large competitors, also reduce competition, often to only a handful of companies. In the early stages of an industry's life cycle, when markets are growing, these obstacles to competition allow large companies to earn higher profits. This, in turn, allows them to pay higher wages. Smaller companies often compete in fragmented industries without the benefit of scale or entry barriers. That's why competition is fragmented. Competition is more intense, and competitors squeeze costs, including wages, to survive.

Although the United States did not keep statistics on net job creation by firm size until 1996, statistics since then indicate a decline that began earlier. From 1996 on, the full-time U.S. workforce grew from 105 million to 120 million workers. Close to 60 percent of those new jobs originated in small firms with less than five employees. Yet these firms represent only 5 percent of U.S. employment. Small firms with between five and hundred employees created another third of the new jobs. On the other end of the spectrum, large firms with over 500 employees, who employed almost half the U.S. workforce in 1996, added only 523,000 new jobs. While employment in large firms with over 500 employees grew by seven million people over the ten-year period, almost all of that growth came from smaller firms that grew larger—like Google and Facebook—and not from firms that were already large.[6]

Without an abundance of small firms growing larger, the 1970s and 1980s took on the slow-growth characteristics of large companies. In the face of an influx of forty million new full- and part-time workers since the 1980s, the U.S. economy gradually shifted to a more entrepreneurial mode.

It's hardly surprising to find that these turbulent developments have taken their toll on employees. As Robert H. Frank and Phillip J. Cook's 1995 book, *The Winner-Take-All Society*, points out, employee tenure has declined and churn has increased. More than ever before, employers compensate employees with bonuses and incentive pay based on the success of their business. 401(k) plans that expose employees to the risk of financial-market fluctuations have replaced defined benefit pension plans that companies—even the auto companies—can no longer afford. Some populists blame lawmakers, business leaders, and capitalism itself for unfairly exposing workers to the risks of a more competitive world. But it is likely that our leaders have little if any influence over these changing conditions. Competition simply evolves and grows more intense over time.

To make comparisons to a less competitive past without recognizing the changing landscape is misleading. We can demand that equity capital, and not employees, bear these additional risks. But we should recognize the consequences this shift would entail for employment. In the 1970s and 1980s, when equity bore these risks, growth slowed and unemployment rose.

1990s TO 2008: THE RISE OF INNOVATION

As the world grew increasingly competitive, one might have expected growth to slow, wage growth to flatten, and the risk of unemployment to rise. But the opposite happened in the 1990s and beyond. The U.S. economy began to grow faster than those of Europe and Japan, its advanced competitors. Relative standards of living rose. U.S. innovation grew and U.S. productivity growth accelerated. Beginning in the early 1990s and lasting through 2008, productivity increased from 1.2 percent per year to 2.0 percent per year, almost a 70 percent increase (see Figure 1-1).

Most of the increase in U.S. productivity came from an increase in know-how and not from an increase in the capital invested per worker or an increase in the education of the workforce, the other sources of productivity improvements. Productivity improvements from know-how grew twice as fast as they had in the 1970s and 1980s.[7]

It's hardly coincidental that this increase in know-how coincided with the commercialization of the Internet and email. Most ideas come from novel combinations of preexisting ideas,[8] from "ideas having sex with one another."[9] The more people communicate, the more likely they are to discover valuable connections between ideas. It's no surprise that the centers of trade—Athens, Florence, London, Hong Kong, New York—have been at the vanguard of innovative ideas throughout history. The Internet is today's communication hub.

While it's no surprise that innovation grew with Internet and email usage, it's peculiar how radically U.S. productivity began to improve relative to Europe and Japan. Both had access to the same technology. They had equally educated workforces. With higher saving rates, Germany and Japan certainly had the capital necessary to invest in the discovery, commercialization, and use of these innovations. Both nations, however, poured capital into the United States. While U.S. workers dug in and went to work, their peers in Europe slowed their work effort (see Figure 1-2).

FIGURE 1-2: U.S. Hours Worked per Worker Relative to Other Developed Economies

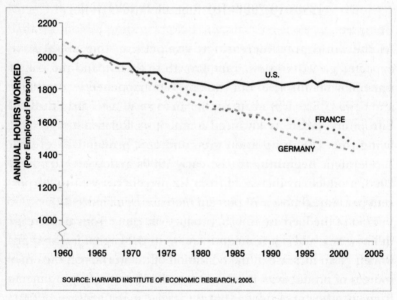

SOURCE: HARVARD INSTITUTE OF ECONOMIC RESEARCH, 2005.

It's true that U.S. workers work more hours, which contributes to greater productivity per worker. But since 1995, U.S. output per hour worked has outgrown other industrialized economies as well (see Figure 1-3).

This accounting of output per hour underrepresents true U.S. productivity gains relative to Europe and Japan. The United States expanded its workforce participation from 63 percent of all working-age adults in 1982 to 67 percent in 2007.[10] This brought a host of marginal workers into the workforce, many of whom

FIGURE 1-3: U.S. Hourly Productivity Growth Relative to Other Developed Economies

COUNTRY	CUMULATIVE PRODUCTIVITY GROWTH (1996–2001)		
	CHANGE IN OUTPUT PER WORKER	CHANGE IN HOURS PER WORKER	CHANGE IN OUTPUT PER HOUR
France	5.2%	−4.0%	9.2%
Germany	1.0	−8.5*	9.5
Japan	6.4	−2.1	8.5
United Kingdom	7.2	−1.0	8.2
United States	11.4	−2.2	13.6

*Major statistical revision in 2000

SOURCE: GREENWALD AND KAHN, *GLOBALIZATION: THE IRRATIONAL FEAR THAT SOMEONE IN CHINA WILL TAKE YOUR JOB*, 2009.

were previously unemployed. During the same period, Europe's participation languished at 58 percent.[11] Europe achieves a significant part of its productivity gains by excluding less-productive workers from its workforce.

From Figure 1-4, you can see that France achieved per-hour productivity on par with the United States. It did this, however, by limiting work to only the most productive workers. It achieved high productivity by suffering high unemployment and by excluding women and young workers. To create new jobs, France limited the hours worked per worker and retired its workforce early. In 2007, at the peak of the economic cycle, only 40 percent of male French workers fifty to sixty-five years old participated in the workforce! But even then, France couldn't create enough jobs to fully employ its young adults who suffered twice the unemployment as their U.S. counterparts in 2007—20.2 percent unemployment versus 10.5 percent. Many studies have shown that because on-the-job training and specialization are a critical determinant of productivity, students who graduate from college in a recession and fail to gain top-notch employment early in their careers suffer lower wages throughout their lives.[12] It seems that France, like most European countries, competes and grows by eating its young.

FIGURE 1-4: Effect of Economic Policies on Employment (2007-2008)

COUNTRY	GDP per Capita	GDP per Hour Worked	Annual Hours per Worker	Unemployment	Workforce Participation 55–64 year old men	Unemployment 19–25 year olds	Workforce Participation Women	10 year Annualized GDP Growth Rate
France	$33,400	$53.40	1561 hrs	8.6%	40.4%	20.2%	51.5%	1.7%
Germany	35,600	50.70	1433	8.7	57.2	11.9	51.6	1.5
Japan	34,200	38.00	1785	3.0	68.4	7.6	47.9	1.0
UK	36,100	45.20	1670	5.4	59.3	14.4	56.5	2.4
US	46,800	54.90	1794	4.6	62.8	10.5	59.3	2.4

SOURCE: U.S. DEPARTMENT OF LABOR

Germany suffered the same high level of unemployment as France but kept its young employed by spreading the pain of its slow-growth policies to the core of its workforce—the workforce raising its families! The higher employment of Germany's youth came at the expense of higher core unemployment, slower growth, and even fewer hours worked per worker than France. The Japanese kept everyone working (except women), but they accomplished this through low productivity and poor growth. Britain's policies were more akin to those of the United States, but again with lower productivity and higher unemployment of its young.

Obviously, governments and businesses can enhance productivity per hour and per worker by pruning less productive workers and putting them on the dole. But who wants to increase productivity by filling the country with unemployed citizens? Worse, when highly skilled workers are underemployed, lower-skilled workers who depend on their leadership (and consumption) for increased employment are hurt.

In contrast, the United States provided—at least until the Crisis—viable employment for its youth, its marginally employed, its near-retirees, and its women, many of whom work part-time and temporarily exit the workforce in mid-career to raise children. As a group, these workers have below-average productivity. Also, a large share of the forty million new American workers employed since the mid-1980s have been low-skilled, younger-than-average Hispanic immigrants, largely lacking high-school degrees and with poor English language skills. Obviously, this group currently has lower productivity than the average U.S. worker.

In addition to immigration and the increased employment of marginal workers, the U.S. workforce now has lower aptitude and subject matter test scores than its advanced competitors. Test scores have a significant impact on productivity. Nevertheless, the U.S. workforce is more productive than its industrialized competitors. Today, U.S. GDP per capita, adjusted for purchasing power, is 30 percent to 40 percent higher than in other developed economies, taking into account our less productive demographic mix of workers (see Figure 1-5).

FIGURE 1-5: Effect of Science Test Scores on Productivity

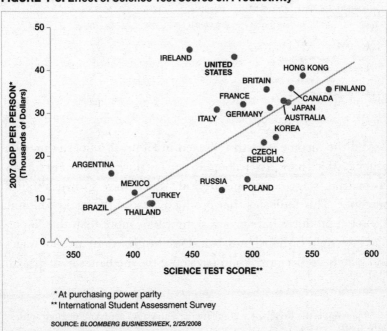

* At purchasing power parity
** International Student Assessment Survey

SOURCE: *BLOOMBERG BUSINESSWEEK*, 2/25/2008

Despite misconceptions to the contrary, not only has U.S. productivity increased, but incomes have increased as well. Since 1980, median incomes have grown for every demographic of the U.S. workforce (see Figure 1-6). At the same time, the composition of the U.S. workforce has shifted to demographics with lower incomes. Median incomes have increased 30 percent, on average, across all demographics.* Wages reflect productivity. This suggests that productivity gains might be greater than they appear to be because the reported statistics fail to account for shifts to demographics with lower productivity.

FIGURE 1-6: Growth of U.S. Income by Demographics

DEMOGRAPHIC	1980*		2005		REAL INCREASE IN INCOME
	PERCENT OF WORKERS**	MEDIAN INCOME	PERCENT OF WORKERS**	MEDIAN INCOME	
White Men	42%	$30,700/yr	37%	$35,200/yr	15%
Non-White Men	7	19,300	12	22,300	16
White Women	43	11,200	39	19,600	75
Non-White Women	8	10,200	12	16,500	62
Total***	100%	$19,900/yr	100%	$25,700/yr	30%

*2005 Dollars
**Includes Part-time Workers
***Weight Average

SOURCE: U.S. CENSUS BUREAU

And the income growth reported in Figure 1-6 doesn't include benefits, which have grown about 15 percent since 2001—substantially faster than wages over this period, which have grown about 3 percent.[13] This indicates that productivity and the real economic income it produces have grown significantly more than the 30 percent growth in cash incomes. Nor does the growth in median wages and benefits reflect growth in pay above the median, where growth

---

* 30 percent is the weighted average increase in wages across all demographics since 1980.

in pay has been significantly higher. Half the jobs created by the United States between 1983 and 2005 were created at the highest end of the wage scale—doctors, lawyers, managers, scientists, etc. Prior to 1983, these jobs represented only 23 percent of the workforce.

This surge in productivity has had an astonishing impact on U.S. growth. In addition to increasing its standards of living relative to Europe and Japan, the U.S. economy has grown 63 percent since 1991, net of inflation, while France grew only 35 percent over the same period; Germany, only 28 percent; and Japan, 16 percent.[14] Since the early 1980s, the United States increased its workforce by 40 percent, or 40 million workers—not counting the tens of millions of offshore workers the U.S. economy employed in Mexico, China, and Southeast Asia, as well as workers it employed in Germany and Japan—while Germany and France grew their workforces by less than half as much. No high-wage economy has done more for workers.

Skeptics claim the growth of the economy came from increased consumption funded by an unsustainable one-time increase in debt, since debt obviously can't continue to rise relative to income forever. They point out that household saving rates have fallen to historic lows while households accumulated a growing mountain of debt (see Figure 1-7 and Figure 1-8). They claim this debt-fueled consumption temporarily inflated asset values, and when the increase in debt slowed, asset prices fell, causing the Financial Crisis.

But we should recognize that consumption does not grow productivity, nor does it increase wealth. Only successful investment and innovation can do those things. Since 1991, the market value of U.S. companies has soared from about 60 percent of GDP historically to over 100 percent, even at post-recession values (see Figure 1-9). Investors clearly believed the value of companies had increased. It's true that market values are fickle and may not always reflect true values. But market values have proven to be the most reliable indication of value that we have.

We speak of a "housing bubble" as if it were a foregone conclusion that prices were irrational. Real estate, both commercial and residential, captures a significant share of the wealth and income of its tenant. As tenants grow more prosperous, they compete

FIGURE 1-7: U.S. Household Saving Rates

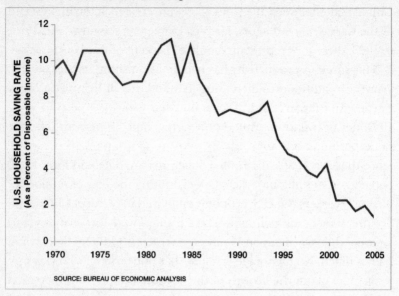

FIGURE 1-8: U.S. Debt Relative to GDP

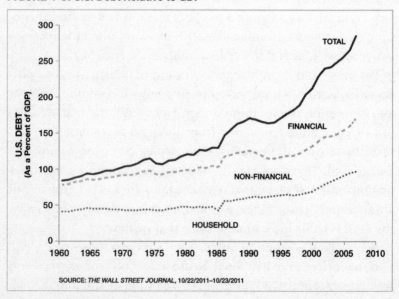

FIGURE 1-9: U.S. Stock Market Capitalization Relative to GDP

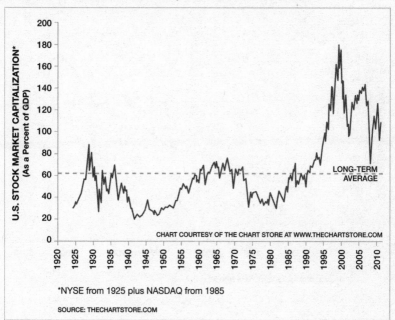

*NYSE from 1925 plus NASDAQ from 1985

SOURCE: THECHARTSTORE.COM

against one another for the most sought-after locations, and bid up prices. Despite U.S. prosperity outpacing the rest of the high-wage world, U.S. housing prices grew more slowly than most other countries.[15] And housing only doubled in value from the mid-1990s to its peak in 2007 while the Dow grew 370 percent over the same period—from 3,800 in 1995 to 14,000 in 2007. The price of oil rose sevenfold, from $18 to $125 a barrel. Ironically, residential housing was one of the worst performing asset classes.

Despite low saving rates, real household net worth, even at the nadir of the Financial Crisis, grew 60 percent since the early 1990s. Even with the European sovereign debt crisis looming over world markets, household net worth rebounded soon after the Financial Crisis to the same level it had reached at the peak of the Internet boom in 2000 (see Figure 1-10).

To exaggerate the case that there is too much debt, proponents of this argument often add financial debt to the sum of household,

FIGURE 1-10: Real U.S. Household Net Worth

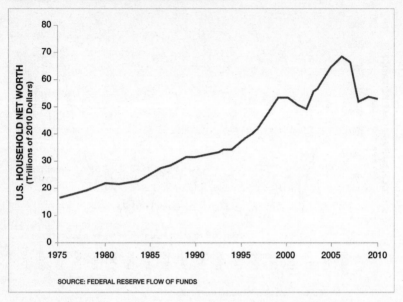

SOURCE: FEDERAL RESERVE FLOW OF FUNDS

business, and government debt. This double counts the total amount of debt. A bank, for example, borrows from its depositors and lends to a home owner. That creates two liabilities—the bank's loan from the depositor and the home owner's loan from the bank. Simply adding the bank's and the home owner's borrowing together double counts the true debt outstanding. There's just one loan—the home owner's mortgage, ultimately borrowed from the bank's depositors.

Modern finance exaggerates this mistake. Today, in its simplest version, a home owner borrows from a mortgage broker that borrows from a bank that borrows from a securitized investment vehicle (SIV) that borrows from a money market fund that borrows from a depositor. That replaces the home owner's loan with five intermediate loans. If you just add up the debt, you get an apparent two- to threefold increase, but nothing has changed. Wealth still equals one house. And ultimately, there is still just one loan— the home owner's mortgage. When the Federal Reserve creates its quarterly balance sheet for the U.S. economy, it doesn't make this mistake. It logically nets all the double counting.

In truth, total U.S. debt, with double counting properly removed, has risen less than most other advanced economies. In the United States, government, business, bank, and household debt combined is 290 percent of GDP, about the same as frugal Germany's combined debt, which is 285 percent of GDP. France has grown its combined debt to 340 percent of GDP, and Japan and the United Kingdom to nearly 500 percent of GDP.[16]

Proponents of the too-much-debt argument also ignore the fact that interest rates have fallen substantially over the last thirty years, making the ongoing cost of debt much cheaper. Many people forget that long-term interest rates have fallen continuously, from 14 percent in the early 1980s to 4 percent today. As a result, debt has logically risen as the cost has fallen proportionately. Also, if a renter buys a home, debt and interest expense rise relative to income, but a decline in rent offsets this increase. A more relevant measure of household debt is the Federal Reserve's financial obligation ratio (FOR), which measures both mortgage payments and rental payments (as well as property taxes and auto and consumer debt payments) as a share of disposable income. The FOR rose only from 17 percent in the 1990s to 18.75 percent at its peak in 2007, about a 10 percent increase.[17] This is not nearly as reckless an increase as critics of debt who focus only on gross debt have led us to believe.

Advocates of the too-much-debt argument intentionally ignore the fact that, as a nation, two-thirds of our debt—both household and government debt—is owed to ourselves. That's right; we pay the interest and principal to ourselves. You can't get rich or go broke lending money to yourself. Try it and see. You go broke by spending too much and investing too little.

Unfortunately, finance doesn't trump the laws of physics. In the real world, we can't teleport things back from the future to increase spending today. One household can borrow against its future earnings from another household, spend too much today, and go broke in the future trying to pay back the loan. Some households did exactly that. They used no-money-down subprime mortgages to borrow against the inflated value of their home, and spent the proceeds on other things. Now they are saddled with debt and must reduce their consumption. But one household can only borrow and spend if another household reduces its consumption in order to lend. Overall, the two must balance. If the first household fails to pay back their loan, the second one suffers. Again, the future gains and losses must balance. There's no free lunch.

It's true that the United States can borrow from offshore lenders and, like the individual borrower above, consume rather than invest the proceeds—and then face a poorer future as a nation when we have to pay back China instead of ourselves. But the amount we have borrowed from offshore lenders is small in comparison to the increased value of our assets. From 1991, nominal household assets have increased $40 trillion while household and government debt has increased $15 trillion. Offshore investors loaned us half that increase in debt. Eliminating the assets that arise from counting domestic borrowing as both an asset and a debt (offshore investors hold the asset from offshore loans) shows that household assets rose four times more than offshore borrowings.* Far from leaving our children a legacy of debt, we left them a legacy of assets to pay for that debt.

CONCLUSIONS

To criticize today's economy because it is not what it was in the 1960s is neither a fair nor a useful comparison. The 1950s and 1960s offered a cornucopia of almost impossible-to-repeat opportunities that temporarily lifted the U.S. economy. The 1970s and 1980s provide a more relevant comparison. Revitalized global competitors pulled even and slowed U.S. growth. Yet despite the success of these advanced competitors, the United States distanced

---

*   [$40T–$7.5T]/[$15T–$7.5T]

itself from the rest of the advanced world with the advent of the Internet.

Why did the United States capitalize on the Internet to accelerate productivity more effectively than Europe and Japan? Both had access to the same technology, similarly educated workforces, and the necessary investment capital. Yet the United States ran the table on Internet innovations, creating companies like Google, Facebook, Microsoft, Intel, Apple, Cisco, Twitter, Amazon, eBay, YouTube and others. Europe and Japan scarcely contributed.

Delineating the differences is critical to our continued success. As we take actions to avoid the next Financial Crisis, we must avoid damaging those things responsible for our success. If we blame the wrong causes and pursue poorly thought-out solutions that cause unintended consequences, we may easily damage the very factors driving our success.

CHAPTER TWO

THE ROLE OF INVESTMENT

PROPONENTS OF INCOME redistribution and opponents differ greatly in their explanations of the success of the United States relative to other countries. Opponents argue that the discovery and commercialization of innovation is no different than any other investment. To achieve rare success, investors must risk capital to fund an inordinate number of failures. And like any game of chance, payoffs for success incentivize investors and employees to take risks and suffer their losses.

Proponents of income redistribution point to the steadiness of long-term economic growth and the loose correlation between tangible investment and innovation as evidence that changing levels of investment and risk taking play only a secondary role in innovation. They believe innovation bubbles up randomly in the normal course of business. They are skeptical of the power of financial incentives and instead emphasize the importance of culture. They claim that U.S. investors and employees are eager to take risks regardless of the incentives, while Europeans and the Japanese are reluctant, no matter the incentives. From this perspective, incentives don't play much of a role in the development of culture. Rather, happenstance blessed the United States with a more entrepreneurial culture. Economists with these views see minimal costs to the economy

from redistributing income from wealthy investors to poorer consumers.

Because of these differing views, opponents of income redistribution push for lower marginal tax rates to incentivize risk taking
and accelerate the accumulation of investment. They worry about
the long-term effect on the culture from higher taxes watering
down incentives and from the redistribution of income from rich
investors to poor consumers slowing the accumulation of capital,
especially risk-bearing equity. Economists with these views tend to
oppose income redistribution.

INVESTMENT PRODUCES INNOVATION

It's true that the discovery of knowledge is partly random, and this
random component is large enough for progress to ebb and flow,
no matter the level of investment. A breakthrough like the Internet will accelerate growth no matter what level of investment
ensues. But the notion that knowledge advances only randomly,
without much need for investment, is dubious at best. If substantial
investment didn't accelerate the rate of innovation, why wouldn't
companies nix their R&D budgets? Surely, investment accelerates
the rate of innovation.

The more time and resources investors and entrepreneurs
devote to searching randomly for innovation, the more likely
they will be to find it. It's like putting together a jigsaw puzzle; the
puzzle won't assemble itself. This random "puzzling" requires
time that the economy could devote to other endeavors. An
increase in investment by one economy relative to another will
likely affect their relative rates of discovery and implementation.
When successful, risky investments to discover and implement
innovation will grow the economy faster than less risky investments that enlarge existing capacities in response to slowly growing demand.

We see this exact phenomenon with lean manufacturing, an

innovative process technology popularized by Toyota and other companies that has produced substantial productivity improvements. Even though the workers in an organization have many ideas for improvement, it still takes the concerted effort of well-trained experts to mine the ideas, identify and prioritize the most effective ones, and drive their implementation—and this takes talent that could be devoted to other endeavors. Productivity may grow 1 percent to 2 percent per year, on average, but that's because businesses make the same amount of investment every year to advance it.

Successfully commercializing good ideas is as important as discovering them and requires similarly risky investments of time and resources. As Thomas Edison reminds us, "Genius is one percent inspiration and ninety-nine percent perspiration." Even if Facebook and Google had randomly stumbled upon great ideas, they still had to invest inordinate amounts of money and overcome high levels of risk to commercialize those ideas. Their efforts prevailed against great odds. Facebook grows at the expense of MySpace despite enormous investments on both their parts. Google similarly defeated Yahoo, which defeated AOL, which defeated Prodigy, not to mention all the forgotten start-ups that failed. Success represents lucky investments in almost certain failure.

In *The Age of Turbulence*,[1] Alan Greenspan reminds us that the U.S. economy has grown sevenfold in real terms since World War II, while physical inputs, like steel and oil, have risen only twofold. Most of the growth came from intellectual capital, not from the expansion of factories and machinery. Investments that create innovation cover anything and anybody that make a company more productive. This includes product and process engineers, computer programmers, and strategic planners and marketers, to name but a few—anyone with a good idea and the skill and determination to implement it. Today, cutting-edge economies like that of the United States invest largely by paying the salaries of talented thinkers who invent and redesign new products and processes.

INNOVATION GROWS THE ECONOMY

Innovation grows the economy in two ways. It reduces the cost of existing products and discovers new products that are more valuable than existing ones. In both cases, the economy can use the same amount of resources to create more value.

Lowering the cost of a product frees up resources for other uses. It also increases the relative value of existing products and yet-to-be-discovered products. An increase in their value increases demand for existing products, investment to discover new products, and, eventually, demand for the newly discovered products. This increased demand puts idle resources back to work.

Consider an isolated farming community where one hundred subsistence farmers each spend a year growing just enough food to survive. The introduction of an innovative technology—a tractor, for example—allows one farmer to grow all the food for all one hundred farmers. A Luddite* might fear that the other ninety-nine farmers will fail to find alternative work, and starve to death. But that turns out to be absurdly unlikely. Even if the farmer could maintain the price of food at a man-year's worth of labor, the value of the tractor would only be equal to what the farmer could buy with his profits—a hundred man-years of work. If all the farmer could buy was his increased leisure, the tractor wouldn't have much value—surely not enough to give him the wherewithal to buy it in the first place!

Before the tractor, when food was prohibitively expensive to produce, alternative uses for a year of a man's labor were less valuable than the year's worth of food a worker needed to produce in order to survive. So no one could afford to divert resources to produce or buy these alternatives. With the cost of food lowered to one one-hundredth of a man-year, the alternative uses for labor become relatively more valuable. So any endeavor that can produce more

---

* The Luddites destroyed mechanized looms in 1811 Britain, fearing the looms would permanently decrease employment.

than one one-hundredth of a man-year of value—the value of food—with a man-year's worth of work is now worth pursuing. These other endeavors turn out to be just about anything—teaching, cooking, doctoring, and so forth. The farmer uses the output from the tractor—the food—to hire the workers idled by the tractor. The value of their labor relative to the value of food—food that's now much less valuable—determines the value of the tractor.

In the real world, not everyone ends up working for the farmer. The farmer can't maintain the price of food at a man-year of labor. Competition among farmers with tractors drives the price of food down to nearly its cost of production. This makes it impossible for the tractor-owning farmer to capture much of the value from the tractor. Who captures the value from the tractor? Not the farmer who competes with other farmers for unskilled tractor-driving wages; his return comes largely from avoiding the cost of not investing. Not the tractor manufacturers who compete fiercely with one another on price. Not the landowners—tractors make it easier to plow more difficult land—and not investors, such as banks, that compete with one another to supply the capital at perhaps a 7 percent return. The consumer captured almost all of the value through lower food prices.

Lower prices often express themselves not as lower prices but as higher quality goods at the same price, as lower "quality-adjusted" prices. Because of the difficulties of measuring changes in quality, economists generally disregard quality improvements and assume away ebbs and flows in their rates of change. In 1955, when President Eisenhower suffered a heart attack, his doctors sent him home for bed rest with a bottle of oxygen. Today he would receive triple bypass surgery, stents in his arteries, a pacemaker, and a lifetime regime of cholesterol-reducing, blood-thinning, pressure-regulating drugs. Have prices per unit of value increased or decreased? No one really knows for sure, despite claims of rising prices. With innovation and productivity accelerating after 1995, one can only surmise that quality improvements have likely accelerated. Quality is, after all, an intangible good.

Sometimes, workers capture the value of innovation and

productivity gains through higher wages. Ultimately, higher wages and lower prices are the same because workers are both wage earners and consumers. In the simple farming economy discussed above, real wages are the amount of food one can buy with an hour of work. Previously, a year's worth of food was worth a year's worth of labor. Now it's worth one one-hundredth of a year of labor. It doesn't matter whether prices have fallen or wages have risen. They are two sides of the same coin. In a more complex economy, a basket of goods represents output. With increased productivity, prices fall and real wages rise.

As tangible or intangible investment per worker increases, one might logically expect capital to capture an increasingly greater share of the output from the combination of labor and capital. But that hasn't happened. Figure 2-1 shows that as the U.S. economy has grown more capital-intensive over time, labor has continued to capture about 70 percent of GDP as wages. The same is true across economies with varying degrees of capital intensity.[2] Labor continues to capture 70 percent of the return from investment.

FIGURE 2-1: U.S. Labor's Share of Income

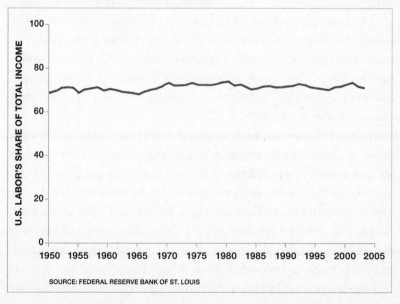

In addition to capturing the value of investment through lower prices and higher wages, consumers also capture the value of products over and above their price. Obviously, consumers wouldn't buy products if they weren't worth more than the price they had to pay. A car, for example, is worth much more than its price. Economists call this "buyers' surplus." GDP measures the value of goods at their prices, not at their value to purchasers. If consumers capture 70 percent of GDP as wages and 100 percent of the buyers' surplus, it is clear they capture a very large share of the value created by investment—perhaps 90 percent or more. In the case of Google, for example, users and society capture the enormous benefits of Internet searches in exchange for a small loss of privacy.

Innovation continues to drive the cost of products down and their value up. Darwinian survival of the fittest prunes away product offerings with low value-to-price ratios. Cars drive out horses and buyers' surplus grows. Fierce competition between producers drives price down to cost plus a competitive return on investment.

Competition forces all profitable competitors to invest in valuable innovation or face extinction. Take email and the Internet, for example. Companies must use these tools to survive against competitors who also take advantage of them. Because every competitor invests, none of them gain an advantage relative to the other. Without such an advantage, competition drives prices to costs. Investors largely earn a return on their investment by avoiding the loss of their profitable business. The use of an innovation like email grows the economy, but consumers end up capturing almost all the value.

We can see these same dynamics at work in agriculture. As agricultural productivity has doubled since the 1940s, expenditures on food as a percent of GDP have fallen proportionately from over 20 percent of disposable income to less than 10 percent today (see Figure 2-2). Obviously there are many pushes and pulls around the decline in food expenditures as a share of income. Today, for example, food expenditures include the cost of dining out, which has risen from 20 percent to 40 percent of food expenditures. At the same time, costs have fallen in the rest of the economy.

Nevertheless, food costs have fallen dramatically. In comparison, western European countries, like France, spend about 15 percent of their income on food; lesser-developed countries, like Russia and China, spend over 25 percent. In the United States, savings from lower-cost food provided much of the resources needed to grow demand for manufactured goods. Today, similar productivity gains in manufacturing are driving growth in services.

FIGURE 2-2: U.S. Food Expenditures Relative to Disposable Income

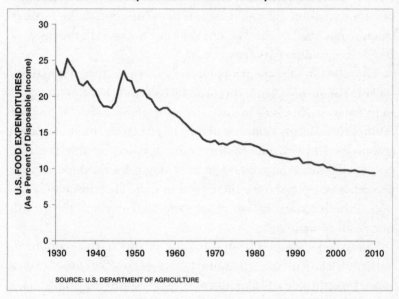

SOURCE: U.S. DEPARTMENT OF AGRICULTURE

The reduction in food expenditures displayed in Figure 2-2 allows us to approximate the magnitude of the value captured by consumers relative to producers. Overlooking the pushes and pulls, consumers captured the difference between 24 percent and 10 percent of disposable income—income that is approximately seven times larger today than it was in 1950. In other words, consumers kept 14 percentage points of their income—income that was seven times bigger. That's a lot! Producers, on the other hand, benefited less. Their profits, after depreciation and before interest and taxes, remained stable at about 10 percent of revenues, or 10 percent of what consumers spent. Producers captured 10 percent of a much smaller portion of a much larger pool of disposable income. If you do the math, you find that the split of value (before corporate taxes) between consumers and producers created by agricultural innovation and investment is in the range of 20:1 in favor of consumers.*

The split of value between offshore producer economies and the U.S. buyer economy is similar. Again, for the sake of simplicity, assume the U.S. economy saves about the difference between $17-an-hour unskilled domestic labor and the cost of 75-cents-an-hour offshore labor by moving production offshore. The offshore producing economy captures something akin to the seventy-five-cents-an-hour cost of labor, plus a small profit. The ratio of value to cost is in the range of 20:1 before transportation expenses.†

These estimates are probably very conservative. They don't include the surplus value captured by consumers before the costs were reduced; they only include the value of price reductions. Nor do they include any value created by the freed-up and redeployed resources. Nor do they capture value created outside the U.S. economy. Other countries might use Google, for example, or copy U.S. know-how to reduce their costs as well. The commercialization of the Internet and email, for example, increased the growth rate of all economies.

These two examples from disparate sectors of the economy—agriculture and offshore manufacturing—probably converge on a similar magnitude of value to consumers relative to producers—approximately 20:1—because all product offerings are in competition with one another for an incremental dollar of customer demand. Consumer choices are driven largely by the ratio of value to price. A return of this magnitude constitutes a hurdle rate for successful new alternatives. And when we consider the value-to-price ratio of recent innovations like personal computers, spreadsheets, word processing, email, and Internet search, which have created enormous value but have very low prices, it's easy to speculate that the ratio may be growing larger. With a value-to-price

---

* $[[24\% - 10\%] \times 7] / [[10\% \times 10\% \times 7] - [10\% \times 24\%]]$

† $21.7 = [\$17.00 - \$0.75] / \$0.75$

ratio in the range of 20:1, we see just how robust economic Darwinian survival of the fittest really is. Surviving entities must produce enormous value for consumers over and above their price in order to survive against competing alternatives.

This one-sided split of the returns from capital between investors and labor (i.e., consumers and wage earners) is the reason radical proponents of income redistribution, like Paul Krugman,[3] seek to regulate the allocation of capital through the political process rather than through free markets. Because of the split, presumably many investments are valuable to society but not to investors. Why let the small returns to private investors determine the allocation of capital critical to the welfare of mankind? Proponents of this position reason that even if the political process is inefficient, it should be more efficient than letting the tail wag the dog.

For the same reason, proponents of free markets are concerned that regulations will reduce profitability and return on investment, especially in circumstances in which producers can't pass the cost of regulation to consumers, who capture almost all of the value from investment. Because investment creates enormous value for consumers and wage earners, small reductions in profits and subsequent investment can have a big impact on wages, employment, and the price of goods. This reduction in profitability can unwittingly destroy more value than well-intended regulations create.

EQUITY INVESTMENT AND RISK TAKING ARE LESS THAN OPTIMAL

How do we know whether increased investment will grow the economy and produce benefits for workers and consumers? At some point, can't we oversaturate the economy or sectors of the economy with too much investment? Wasn't that the case with housing before the Financial Crisis? Didn't we create a wasteful surplus of housing?

It is widely recognized that the link between investment and productivity has been strong, and that relationship has held across an extraordinarily broad range. As Figure 2-3 illustrates, a country's

GDP per worker is proportionate to the amount of capital invested per worker. At the top of the spectrum, the United States and Japan invest heavily and, as a result, their GDP per worker is high. At the bottom, less-developed economies, like Nigeria, invest less capital per worker, yielding a lower GDP per worker. In America, workers dig with mechanized backhoes. In Nigeria, they still largely dig with shovels.

FIGURE 2-3: Effect of Investment on Productivity

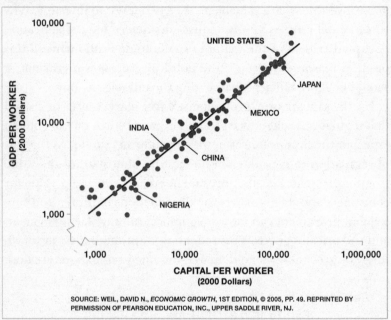

SOURCE: WEIL, DAVID N., *ECONOMIC GROWTH*, 1ST EDITION, © 2005, PP. 49. REPRINTED BY PERMISSION OF PEARSON EDUCATION, INC., UPPER SADDLE RIVER, NJ.

A broad range of investment continues to drive productivity because investment and risk taking, as a whole, are far below the optimal level. The work of Nobel Prize-winning economist Edmund Phelps presents compelling empirical evidence that capital for investment is in chronically short supply. Phelps's argument, greatly simplified, points out that an economy that allocated all its output to investment would grow, but without producing any goods for consumption, whereas one that consumed all its output would quickly grind to a halt. An economy somewhere in between provides just enough capital per worker to maximize all future consumption. At that optimal point, the ratio of investment per employee would logically remain constant—otherwise investment per employee would be moving away from the optimal point, which would be suboptimal. In order to remain at that optimal point, capital must earn a real return equal to the growth rate of the workforce—in highly developed economies, 1 percent to 2 percent per year. At that rate of return, the amount of capital per worker would grow in line with the workforce and maintain its optimal ratio.

As we will see in the next chapter, the trade deficit leaves the United States with a surplus of risk-averse short-term savings available to fund investment. Nevertheless, the United States continues to face a shortage of equity needed to underwrite the risk associated with making those investments. Risk averse short-term capital will only fund investment if equity underwrites the risk. As a result of these circumstances, it's more accurate to say the United States and the rest of the world have a shortage of equity and risk taking rather than a shortage of capital more broadly. As such, equity in the United States and worldwide earns about 7.5 percent per year,[4] indicating that equity and the risk taking it underwrites are in short supply and well below the optimal level.

It's not surprising to find equity in chronically short supply. At any given time, an economy has only a certain number of trained workers, limits to the state of its know-how, and a fixed amount of tangible production capacity. The availability of these resources limits production. Limited production can produce output for either consumption or investment. Because of these limits, an economy must lower consumption in order to increase the amount of equity it devotes to investment. Unfortunately, most workers, whether by choice or necessity, consume virtually everything they earn—no matter what elevated returns are available to equity investors.* They fiercely oppose reductions to their consumption,

---

* Many workers save through pension contributions but divest these savings by borrowing against their household equity to increase consumption; hence, the near-zero household savings rate prior to the Crisis, despite richer households saving a substantial share of their income.

and they vote for politicians who promise to raise their consumption by providing them with government services and benefits in excess of their level of taxation—namely, by taxing rich equity investors instead. Deficit spending reduces constraints to government spending and consumption even further. By resisting decreases in consumption—consumption paid for by taxing successful equity investors and redistributing their income—workers limit equity available for increased investment. A chronic shortage of equity leaves investment opportunities ripe for the picking.

That's not to say that investment and risk taking are one-dimensional—far from it. An economy can make poor investments and take imprudent risks in one sector—housing investment and mortgage risks, for example—without other parts of the economy (or the economy as a whole) extending beyond the point of optimality. Risk and return can be difficult—impossible, in some cases—to estimate. So, in a large population of risk takers, there will always be some risk takers who mistakenly expect more payoff than is likely to occur. This group may continue making risky equity investments well beyond the point of optimality, even as the risks increase and the returns decline.

In fact, Carmen M. Reinhart and Kenneth Rogoff's facetiously titled *This Time Is Different: Eight Centuries of Financial Folly,*[5] presents 800 years of evidence that rapid growth in capital, principally from offshore investors—what the authors describe as a "capital flow bonanza"—have systematically increased the chances of economies misallocating resources. Economies must run many experiments to find productive investment opportunities. That takes time. If capital from offshore sources governed by constraints that transcend the local economy grows faster than the rate of successful experimentation, that capital has a tendency to flow into unproductive endeavors.

Government subsidies can also drive risk taking beyond the point of optimality. Low-cost government-subsidized flood insurance, for example, encourages building in flood zones that might otherwise be uneconomical. Government-subsidized mortgages artificially inflate the demand for owner-occupied housing, especially among poor households that would otherwise represent uneconomical credit risks. These subsidies over-allocate investment to one sector—subprime housing, for example—at the cost of underinvestment in other sectors.

Regardless of the presence of these suboptimal pockets, economies, including the U.S. economy, suffer from large shortages of equity overall and the risk taking that equity underwrites. As a result, increases in investment and risk taking yield large returns, on average, through productivity gains and economic growth.

MONETARY POLICY FACILITATES INCREASED RISK TAKING

Seen from this perspective, printing money doesn't magically stimulate the economy. Only risk taking does. Monetary policy allows risk taking to grow when a lack of credit limits risk taking and the economy has excess capacity available to produce the increased growth. An owner of future cash flows (assets) may seek to increase the amount of risk he is taking by splitting his future cash flows into tranches so that he can exchange the low-risk first-to-be-repaid tranche (debt) with a risk-averse saver for the saver's current production (the saver's income). The seller of the low-risk cash flow uses that production (or the proceeds from the sale to buy production) to take risk that the current risk-averse owner of the production is unwilling to take. Putting that hoarded production to use expands the economy. An expansion of credit is merely a by-product of this increase in risk taking.

If the amount of available credit is restricted, risk takers may be unable to make these trades with risk-averse savers because they cannot add to the amount of first-to-be-repaid tranches of financial assets. Constraints on credit may occur if banks have already loaned all the available deposits. Printing money adds to lendable deposits. Constraints on credit can also occur if banks have used all their equity to meet the government's capital adequacy requirements for their existing loans. In that case, banks would not have the equity necessary to make additional loans. Lower short-term interest rates increase the spread banks earn by borrowing short-term savings and making long-term loans. This increases bank profits and grows their equity. Relieving credit constraints will grow the economy, if the economy has the capacity to produce the increase in demand.

Increases or decreases in optimism tend to create self-reinforcing feedback loops that monetary policy can either allow or restrict. As risk takers grow increasingly optimistic, asset values rise. As asset prices rise, investors and consumers grow increasingly willing to take more risks. As their willingness to bear risk expands, the economy's capacity to take risk grows. As risk taking grows, the economy expands. As the economy expands, investment grows and the value of assets rises relative to the economy.

This self-reinforcing feedback loop is often mistaken as monetary policy itself growing the economy, but this is not the case. If the Fed relieves constraints to the expansion of credit—when there is no pent-up demand for increased risk taking—credit will sit unused and the velocity of money will slow. This happens in recessions when investors and consumers grow risk-averse and hoard their output. In such circumstances, relieving credit constraints has little if any effect on the economy. Keynes described this as pushing on a string.

If increased consumption or investment is constrained by the production capacity of the economy—if unemployment reaches its lower boundary, as it did prior to the Financial Crisis, for example—an expansion in demand will simply increase the price of production rather than the volume. Under those conditions, if the Federal Reserve relieves credit constraints, an increase in risk taking merely pushes against capacity constraints and increases prices. Investment might grow, but only if consumption declines to offset it, and vice versa. Inflation largely offsets and nullifies the increased risk taking to hold the constrained economy in equilibrium. But inflation reallocates resources in disruptive and unpredictable ways, which unnecessarily increases uncertainty and destroys value. Offshore production capacity can help to relieve production constraints, but a portion of the value from increased risk taking may be lost to the growth of the offshore economy rather than the domestic economy.

Monetary policy exerts influence on the economy through other, less-significant channels, chiefly by widening the spread between long- and short-term rates, which can induce risk taking by redistributing ownership away from risk-averse savers. Unexpected inflation can also redistribute ownership, principally from lenders and investors to borrowers and consumers and from the private sector to the public sector. But the crux of the matter is this: printing pieces of paper doesn't grow the economy; increased risk taking does. If simply printing money could grow the economy, we should print lots of it. If only it were that easy!

INVESTMENT IS UNDERSTATED

Conventional accounting obscures the cost of innovation by grossly underreporting the level of investment required to drive innovation. Our antiquated 1940s manufacturing-based accounting rules expense the salaries of creative thinkers and leaders as intermediate costs of production, rather than capitalizing them as investments. Only recently have accounting rules allowed the capitalization of software development costs. Still, only 30 percent of companies capitalize rather than expense these costs.[6]

Accounting rules demand highly restrictive measures of investment to ensure comparability between accounting results. In the MCI WorldCom accounting scandal of 2002, for example, the company capitalized costs that companies traditionally expense. This gave MCI the appearance of higher profit margins and larger capital investments than its competitors. A fast-growing company with higher profit margins that is pouring more money into investment than its competitors looks more attractive to investors and garners a higher stock price. Accounting rules prevent this lack of comparability by erring on the side of expensing rather than capitalizing costs, especially employee-related costs. While this practice may be appropriate for accounting purposes, we cannot use these accounting methods to calculate the true cost of innovation.

Survivor bias exacerbates the masking effect of this mistaken accounting on the true cost of investment and further obscures the link between investment in risky innovation and its return. Survival of the fittest sets a high bar for success. Like the hit-driven music industry, one breakthrough requires hundreds of small, forgotten, and ruthlessly pruned failures. Failed investments in intellectual capital are expensed and forgotten—decoupled from the cost of the resulting success. Without clear linkages between the value of success and the hidden cost of failure, investment appears dramatically understated. Innovations seemingly arise randomly, without the need for many failed experiments. Economic statistics don't recognize the large cost of failure as investment.

Conservative measurements such as those employed in a 2006 Federal Reserve study, "Intangible Capital and Economic Growth,"[7] show significant increases in intangible investments. According to the Fed's estimates, intangible investments rose from about 7 percent of non-farm business output in the late 1970s to 10 percent in the early 1990s to about 14 percent today (see Figure 2-4). These investments rose dramatically in the 1990s when productivity accelerated.

Over the same period, traditional business investments in factories and machinery (but excluding commercial and residential real estate) grew from about 5.5 percent of GDP following World War II to about 8 percent today, ebbing and flowing with economic cycles. Adding both tangible and intangible investments together shows business investment grew from 15 percent of GDP after the war to a level approaching 25 percent today.

It's no surprise that intangible investment rates in Germany and France were only 60 percent to 70 percent of those in the United States in 2006 as a percent of GDP. Only the United Kingdom, which has grown as fast as the United States over the last two

FIGURE 2-4: U.S. Intangible Investment Relative to Non-Farm Output

*Adjusted to include intangibles

SOURCE: CORRADO, HULTEN, AND SICHEL, "INTANGIBLE CAPITAL AND ECONOMIC GROWTH," 2006

decades, has invested in intangibles at a rate comparable to the United States. The less advanced economies of Italy and Spain are investing at half that rate.[8]

It is likely that these simple estimates understate true investment. For the sake of defensibility, the studies measure only highly discernable expenditures such as company-related product development costs, computer-related investments, advertising, and employee training costs. But in reality, expenditures that increase the productivity of the most talented employees are much broader than that. To a large extent, almost everyone engaged in finance, for example, thinks about the value of future cash flows and how to maximize them. They make decisions about the allocation of financial assets that set the prices for various risks. These prices influence the allocation of investment. Again, economic statistics expense all these costs.

Email and web-based content also represent uncounted investment. We bombard each other with emails. This content changes our perspectives, influences our behavior, and saves us time. Users generate much of this content in their spare time, for no charge. GDP statistics don't count this as investment or cost. One might be skeptical about whether this expenditure represents investment or consumption, but productivity has soared in its wake.

In addition to talented workers thinking about how to improve future outcomes, there are other forms of overlooked investment. Immigration has freed many talented workers from household tasks and increased their availability for more productive activities—namely, work. Similarly, the logistics of home delivery— the picking, packing, and delivery of single units—reduces time spent shopping and increases time available for work. As mentioned in Chapter 1,* the most talented U.S. workers now spend more time working while the hours of their European peers and the rest of the workers in both of these economies have declined.

The productivity of the most talented workers is also growing faster than the economy as a whole. Most of the innovation and investment over the last three decades has increased the productivity of the most talented workers. Calculators and personal computers replaced slide rules. Word processing replaced typewriters and Wite-Out. Spreadsheets allowed for extensive "what if?" scenario planning and sensitivity analysis. Oracle, SAP, and other sophisticated software provided managers with X-ray vision into their companies' operations. The Internet and search engines allowed instantaneous access to a wealth and breadth of information far beyond anything that could be practically accessed in a library. Email allowed for asynchronous communication and increased communication via distribution lists. Cell phones, Black-Berrys, and now smart phones replaced landlines and extended the number of productive hours in each workday. With 5 percent of the workforce producing over a third of the output, increases in this group's productivity have a big impact on the economy overall.

---

* Chapter 4 provides further details about changes in hours worked relative to level of income.

Pundits often wonder why median wages have failed to rise in proportion to increased levels of productivity, as they have in the past, but the answer is obvious. The median wage is the highest wage of the lowest 50 percent of workers. Productivity growth has occurred predominantly at the top of the wage scale. It's no wonder pay is growing increasingly unequal.

Above the median, the wage premium for the most talented workers grew despite a large surge in the productivity-enhanced supply of knowledge workers (see Figure 2-5). An increase in supply should drive down wages, but pay rose because the value from deploying this talent was greater than their pay. As a result, the demand for talented thinkers grew faster than the rapidly growing productivity-enhanced supply. The growing wage premium shows that the growing supply of more educated employees didn't drive the shift in the economy to thought-oriented professions. Quite the opposite; unmet opportunity demanded it.

We can also see the increase in intangible investment in the changing composition of U.S. jobs since the mid-1980s. Again,

FIGURE 2-5: U.S. College Graduate Wage Premium

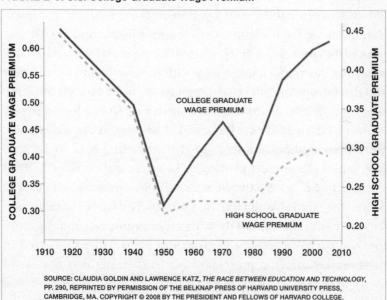

SOURCE: CLAUDIA GOLDIN AND LAWRENCE KATZ, *THE RACE BETWEEN EDUCATION AND TECHNOLOGY*, PP. 290, REPRINTED BY PERMISSION OF THE BELKNAP PRESS OF HARVARD UNIVERSITY PRESS, CAMBRIDGE, MA. COPYRIGHT © 2008 BY THE PRESIDENT AND FELLOWS OF HARVARD COLLEGE.

half of all the new jobs created over the last twenty-five years have been in thought-oriented professions. Such jobs made up only a quarter of total employment in the 1980s. This shift does not include the infrastructure of employment that grew to support them—household help, restaurant employees, home delivery, and the like.

It's also clear why the income of the top 1 percent of the United States is growing faster than that in Europe and Japan, despite their having access to the same technologies. U.S. innovators have produced Intel, Microsoft, Google, Facebook, etc. The rest of the world has contributed next to nothing. Successful innovation creates highly productive communities around these companies. These communities train people to innovate and commercialize related ideas. Imagine trying to create the next generation of Internet technology in Rome or Athens, with no supporting resources or inside knowledge. The emails exchanged between productive Americans, and the ideas they produce, are more valuable than the ones exchanged within the business communities of Europe and Japan.

Equity investors clearly recognized the changing composition of business profitability and investment. U.S. stock market capitalization soared from a long-term average of 60 percent of GDP to a peak of 145 percent in 2007, and still exceeds 100 percent of GDP today (see previous chapter) even with the slow economic recovery and the European debt crisis hanging over our heads. At the same time, non-financial corporate net worth rose from a low of 70 percent of GDP in 1993 to a peak of 114 percent in 2006 and 2007, more than a 60 percent increase, before falling back to 102 percent at its nadir at the end of 2008. To increase their value and net worth, companies must make successful investments and retain a portion of that value as increased profits. The latter is a tall order. Competition is fierce and the portion of profits retained by investors is small. As a result, the growth in net worth, as reflected in stock market values, represents only a fraction of the true value of these investments to society.

CONCLUSIONS

Stepping back, we see innovation is no different from any other investment. Perhaps there is greater randomness in the production of new ideas than there is in growing corn or manufacturing widgets; but, on average, the key to finding good ideas is to have many ideas. The quantity of ideas, both good and bad, comes from systematic investment. As with any other investment, the economy must divert scarce resources—in this case, talented labor—from production for current consumption to the search for and implementation of new ideas. Much of this investment results in failure.

Antiquated accounting, combined with survivor bias, obscures the link between investment and innovation by expensing rather than capitalizing investment in innovation, especially the cost of failure. This gives the false impression that innovation bubbles up randomly in the normal course of things, without the need for investment. But more careful accounting shows that, in fact, U.S. business investment has risen significantly along with productivity.

From this perspective, it seems clearer that the growth in U.S. productivity and asset values since the early 1990s stems from an increase in investment relative to consumption. In the end, we achieved hard-won improvements the old-fashioned way—by earning them. Business saved on behalf of households. Business and the economy shifted resources from production for consumption to investment in innovation.

Increased investment explains why U.S. productivity accelerated. It does not explain, however, why the United States capitalized on these investment opportunities faster than other advanced economies. Several additional puzzle pieces reveal these differences.

CHAPTER THREE

THE ROLE OF THE TRADE DEFICIT

AN ASTUTE READER may recognize that U.S. investment rose as household savings declined to near zero prior to the Financial Crisis. How was that possible? Several factors allowed the United States to continue growing consumption and investment simultaneously despite nearing capacity constraints and full employment prior to the Crisis. Most importantly, the U.S. economy cut costs—through both domestic productivity gains and imports—and shifted the resources to business investment and to the domestic service sector. Business grew more profitable, productivity soared, and the value of U.S. assets rose relative to GDP. Antiquated accounting masked the increase in investment.

As the U.S. economy moved production offshore, balanced trade would have required the United States to produce goods for export. Instead of selling goods to offshore producers to balance trade, we sold them assets (ownership rights to future cash flows split into debt and equity; in this case, the United States sold debt to offshore producers). This also allowed the United States to use freed-up production resources to increase domestic investment. We also redeployed freed resources to the domestic service sector.

Increased and more productive investments grew U.S. assets faster than the sale of assets to buy and consume imports. While debt owed to foreign economies grew, assets owned by Americans grew even more. Household net worth increased. As long as we continue to produce assets faster than we sell them, the trade deficit can grow forever. As long as the United States continues to earn a higher rate of return on investments than its cost to borrow cheap foreign capital, this can remain the case, and likely will remain so for the foreseeable future.

Because official measurements of household savings exclude the rising value of unsold assets, households only appear to have borrowed from offshore producers to fund the increased consumption of offshore goods. In reality, households owned businesses that made investments on their behalf and grew more valuable as a result. These businesses grew more profitable and poured money into investment. Antiquated economic statistics fail to recognize this increased investment. Real estate captured a significant share of this rising prosperity as tenants grew more prosperous and bid up the price of real estate.

For the sake of clarity, let's imagine a hypothetical economy that invested all of its output rather than consuming a portion of it. That economy would produce only assets—that is, future increases in cash flows. The economy's workers and asset owners would have to sell or borrow against the growing value of their assets from offshore lenders to buy goods for consumption produced offshore. Otherwise, they would have to reduce investment to produce goods and services for consumption. It would appear as though this economy was borrowing to fund increased consumption when, in fact, it allowed the economy to fund increased investment. Anyone who overlooked the high investment rate and subsequent growth of assets would fret about the growing debt and trade deficit. Ironically, they would admonish the participants to consume less and save more. In the aftermath of the Financial Crisis, they might even say, "I told you so."

Now imagine that those offshore workers were willing to work for free. If their labor was free, how much of it should we buy? All of it. At seventy-five cents an hour, it is effectively free. At that price, surely we can find better uses for our own labor, just like the farmers with the low-cost tractor. Our illustrative economy would not only benefit from producing innovation that was more valuable than producing goods for consumption or export, but it also would benefit from lower cost consumption and from redeploying labor, too.

Anyone who overlooks these trade-offs—the value of producing innovation rather than goods for consumption, and the savings from buying rather than producing goods for consumption—might fail to see that, over the long run, redeploying our labor from production for consumption to investment increases rather than decreases domestic employment. In fact, the increase is so large that the United States employed tens of millions of immigrants and offshore workers. No economy has done more for the poor. In a recession, when there is a lull in risk taking and unemployment rises and wages fall, skeptics might mistakenly claim that low-cost offshore producers were stealing our jobs and lowering our wages.

Despite accelerating investment, productivity, and growth prior to the Financial Crisis, skeptics claim that the growing trade deficit represents a lack of U.S. competitiveness. Far from demonstrating a lack of competitiveness, the trade deficit facilitated an increase in U.S. investment. As an economy shifts production to investment, it must increase offshore borrowing to maintain consumption. Otherwise, it would have to lower consumption to fund investment.

OFFSHORE CAPACITY GROWS THE U.S. ECONOMY

While the Internet increased the productivity of the most talented workers, businesses poured money into intangible investments. Assets—the net present value of future cash flows—skyrocketed in value from expected growth in future profits. The U.S. stock market grew from 60 percent of GDP historically to 140 percent prior to the Crisis. Households flush with increased wealth reduced savings and borrowed against the rising value of their assets—chiefly residential real estate—to increase consumption. Business investment and household consumption competed for scarce resources. Capacity utilization tightened. U.S. unemployment fell to a historic low of 4–4.5 percent and the price of the most constrained resource—talent—rose to historic highs.

As the economy neared full capacity, a further rise in expenditures—whether for consumption or investment—should have required an offsetting reduction elsewhere in the economy, notwithstanding gradual growth in capacity from investment and innovation. One household must reduce expenditures and save so that another can borrow and spend. Investment must decline so consumption can rise, and vice versa. Where households seek to sell assets—in this case, debt—to increase consumption, selling pressure should drive down the price of assets relative to the price of production. Increasing demand for production should drive up the price of production. Return on investment should decline as the price of assets decline relative to the price of production. The growth of investment should slow more than consumption until the economy reaches equilibrium. Prior to the Crisis, the opposite happened.

A growing trade deficit mitigates this dampening effect on investment. It allows offshore economies to provide constrained resources—labor and capital—to meet the growing demands of the U.S. economy for both increased investment and consumption. This can only happen if offshore producers choose to buy U.S. assets (ownership rights to future cash flows) with their proceeds from the sale of goods instead of U.S. goods. In other words, this can only happen if we run a trade deficit rather than balanced trade. If trade is balanced, we must use the U.S. capacity gained by moving production offshore to produce goods for export rather than for increased domestic investment.

Once an offshore economy chooses to accept our employment and produce goods for the United States, it must decide whether it will buy U.S. goods, buy U.S. assets, stuff the dollars in its mattresses, or sell/loan the surplus dollars to another entity, typically another country. Let's look at each of its options in turn. Since the Asian Financial Crisis of the late 1990s, there are no entities taking enough long-term currency exchange-rate risk to make lending or selling dollars to countries other than the United States a relevant option for surplus exporters. Prior to the Asian Financial Crisis, Southeast Asia borrowed dollars from dollar-rich surplus exporters, like China, and used the dollar-denominated loans to purchase U.S.-manufactured capital goods. They used these capital goods for investment in their domestic economies. When the exchange rates of their local currencies fell, they had difficulty paying back loans denominated in dollars. As a result, they fell into financial distress. Today they seek to grow domestic employment through exports rather than through successful domestic investment. They no longer have a need to borrow dollars. Nor do other countries, except the United States. Aside from during the Financial Crisis, when the world temporarily fled to Treasuries, who has a shortage of dollars today? Certainly not the Chinese, the Southeast Asian Tigers, the Japanese, Germans, or oil exporters. They are all flooded with dollars. And even if a surplus exporter did use their dollars to buy goods or assets from another country, the other country faces the same decision about how to redeem their dollars as the original owner did.

Obviously, exporters don't choose to buy an equal amount of U.S. production. If they did, there wouldn't be a trade deficit. Nor can we hope to buy imports with mattress stuffing—by offshore producers holding uninvested dollars that pay no interest. They're not that stupid.

As a result, exporters intent on running surpluses, like the Chinese, Japanese, and Germans, are left with one alternative: to use their surplus dollars to buy their trading partners' assets. Countries can't run trade surpluses with the United States unless their citizens are willing to defer consumption and hold U.S. assets—no exported savings, no exported surpluses of goods. It's simple arithmetic; the flow of dollars out of the United States to buy imports must flow back to the United States to buy U.S. exports or assets. To the extent they don't buy exports they must buy assets (see Figure 3-1). Slightly more dollars flow back to the United States than the trade deficit because dollars invested overseas by U.S. investors must also flow back to the United States to buy goods or assets—mainly assets.

FIGURE 3-1: U.S. Foreign Borrowings Relative to the Trade Deficit

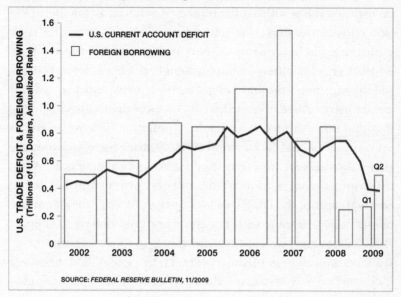

SOURCE: *FEDERAL RESERVE BULLETIN*, 11/2009

The willingness of countries to run trade surpluses by deferring consumption and exporting capital allowed the United States to move production offshore to countries that did not demand to purchase U.S. goods in return. And the reciprocal flow of offshore dollars back into the U.S. economy allowed households to borrow against the growing value of their assets—to sell debt—without putting downward pressure on the price of assets relative to the price of production. In fact, an abundance of offshore buyers for debt lowered interest rates, which helped to increase the value of assets.

At the same time, offshore production capacity allowed households to increase consumption without needing to compete with business for onshore production. Competing demand would have bid up the price of domestic production. Instead, low-cost offshore production reduced the price of production. This accelerated rather than dampened the demand for U.S. investment and consumption.

Let's not kid ourselves about just how cheap offshore labor really is. We not only pay substantially less per hour, we also avoid the costs we would incur if these workers immigrated here. We don't pay for their medical expenses when they show up in the emergency room without insurance. We don't pay for their pension costs if they don't save for retirement. We don't pay for their children's public education. Nor do we pay for their out-of-wedlock children, their unemployment benefits and workers' compensation, their slip-and-fall torts, their wear and tear on our public infrastructure, and the cost of their drunk driving, drug use, and other crimes. We outsource pollution, its adverse effects on our health, and its clean-up costs. Neither the employees nor their employers are here to vote and seek political handouts. When offshore producers "dump" incremental production below full cost, we capture the benefit of lower prices. When foreign governments subsidize trade with tax credits or hold dollars to support their currencies, we capture the value of those subsidies, too. It's true, we can't tax offshore workers, but low-skilled, low-wage U.S. workers pay less taxes than the government services they consume.

The products driven offshore are also those where the savings from unskilled labor are large enough to offset both the cost of transportation and long transportation lead times. These are predominantly price-sensitive, low-margin, undifferentiated commodity-like products. The manufacturing of these products is typically less profitable, more capital intensive, more cyclical, and slower-growing than the rest of the U.S. economy, which has grown substantially faster than manufacturing since World War II. From the perspective of the Chinese economy, cyclical undifferentiated manufacturing is more attractive than Chinese alternatives—highly unpredictable, weather-dependent, low-productivity peasant farming. In the United States, manufacturing was more attractive than its economic alternatives, too . . . a hundred years ago!

The use of lower-cost offshore resources not only frees up additional domestic resources for alternative uses, it also increases the relative value of those alternative uses—just like the farmer's tractor and any other productivity improvement. Contrary to popular belief, there is no difference between low-cost offshore sourcing and domestic productivity improvements; both lower costs, free up resources, and increase the relative value of alternative uses for resources. Just as lower food costs powered the growth of manufacturing after World War II, today the growing availability of low-cost offshore goods powers the growth of investment and domestic services. The economy redeployed talented workers to innovation and deployed less-skilled labor to the growing local service economy with jobs that paid less-skilled workers the same $17 an hour wages that manufacturing had previously paid, notwithstanding the taxes collected from consumers on behalf of unionized labor. Low-cost offshore goods increased the relative value of these jobs, and, as a result, demand for these domestic services grew; so much, in fact, that we employed 20 million immigrants without a drop in unskilled wages even as we employed tens of millions of offshore workers.

Lower production costs and higher asset values encouraged increased business investment and risk taking. With the ability to borrow cheaply against their assets—namely, their homes—to increase consumption, investors eagerly embraced increased risk taking and the reinvestment of business profits over the payout of dividends. Business was free to put the economy's scarcest resource—highly skilled U.S. labor—to work in search of innovation rather than using it to supervise the production of goods for domestic consumption or exports.

Increased business investment and the redeployment of labor to more valuable alternatives grew the U.S. economy 60 percent since the early 1990s, while Europe and Japan only grew 20 percent to 30 percent.* The additional U.S. growth clearly did not come only from the increased capacity of the trade deficit and its lower costs. An additional 6 percent or more of capacity contributed by offshore production† is small relative to the economy as a whole, and cannot account for the magnitude of the U.S. economy's relatively faster growth alone. A 6 percent increase in capacity, however, is

---

* France grew 35 percent over the same period, Germany only 22 percent, and Japan 16 percent.

† Imports, net of exports, divided by GDP.

large relative to the twenty-something percent of U.S. GDP invested by business. It's the compounding effect of increased investment and its effect on productivity that grew the economy over time to produce big differences in GDP.

WORLD SAVINGS AND DEMAND FOR EMPLOYMENT INCREASE U.S. CAPITAL

In addition to lowering costs and relaxing capacity constraints, the United States also benefits from the desperation of exporters to gain U.S. employment by holding dollar-denominated assets. Had the U.S. demand for capacity pulled a reluctant supply of labor and capital from foreign suppliers, U.S. interest rates would have risen and/or exchange rates would have fallen.[1] But this has not been the case; interest rates have fallen and exchange rates have remained relatively stable. Declining interest rates prior to the Crisis suggest that the desire of offshore economies to increase employment and hold U.S. assets must be greater than our demand for increased consumption. Americans aren't addicted to debt; the rest of the world is addicted to our employment.

It's obvious that China, Germany, Japan, and other countries have proactively pursued trade surpluses to increase employment by holding dollar-denominated U.S. investments as a matter of policy. They have even subsidized exports—both directly and indirectly—through monetary policy in order to hold down their exchange rates. Their desperation for employment and their eagerness to hold U.S. assets has benefited the U.S. economy by reducing the cost of goods and capital.

Circumstances added to the supply of low-cost offshore labor and capital. Following the Asian Financial Crisis in the late 1990s, for example, Southeast Asia cut investment in its local economies by almost a third and consequently stopped borrowing dollars to buy U.S.-manufactured capital goods (see Figure 3-2). This slowed U.S. exports (see Figure 3-3). Beginning in 1998, the U.S. trade deficit rose as the growth in U.S. exports flattened and

FIGURE 3-2: Effect of the Asian Financial Crisis on Non-China Asian Investment

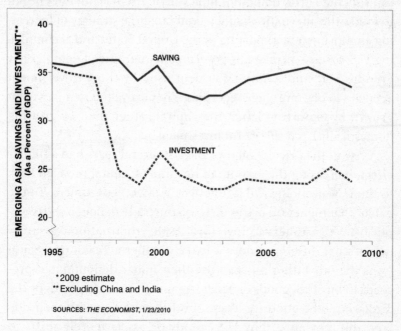

* 2009 estimate
** Excluding China and India

SOURCES: *THE ECONOMIST*, 1/23/2010

FIGURE 3-3: Effect of the Asian Financial Crisis on U.S. Exports

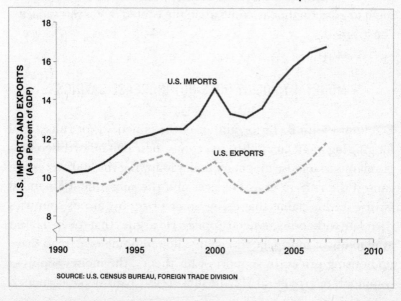

SOURCE: U.S. CENSUS BUREAU, FOREIGN TRADE DIVISION

slowed relative to imports. With high saving rates but without high investment to grow domestic employment, Asian economies began to follow the alternative Chinese and Japanese strategy of increasing employment by exporting to the United States and accumulating U.S. assets—principally government-guaranteed debt, largely Freddie Mac and Fannie Mae debt used by those government agencies to buy mortgage securities. They drove their employment growth by exporting labor and capital rather than by growing domestically from successful investment.

A rise in the price of oil over the last several years had a similar effect, increasing the amount of investment capital recycled back to the U.S. economy. Oil is, in effect, a tax on consumers. To the extent that higher oil prices increase the trade deficit, it shifts output from consumers to investors. Aside from national security issues, what difference does it make whether a Texan or a Saudi owns the oil? Either one can use their dollar-denominated proceeds to buy U.S. goods or assets. Again, if either the Saudi or the Texan buys the goods or assets of other countries with their dollars, the burden to buy U.S. goods or assets merely shifts to the seller. With the decline in Asian investment, and a rise in the price of oil, the trade deficit exploded. This allowed U.S. investment to grow further at a time when the United States was capacity-constrained.

MONETARY POLICY DOES NOT INCREASE SAVINGS

Economist John B. Taylor, author of the famed Taylor rule, a tool for guiding monetary policy, interprets these dynamics differently. He claims that loose monetary policy following the 2002 recession caused the run-up in asset prices and the subsequent Financial Crisis.[2] Taylor claims that rising home prices in various countries correlate with loose monetary policy. He argues that the increased availability of mortgage financing allowed home owners to drive up housing prices. In support of his theory, the money supply—commonly referred to as M2, the sum of cash, bank deposits, money-market funds, and overnight "repos" (repurchase agreements)—did appear to rise relative to nominal GDP in 2002 and 2003 (see Figure 3-4). From 2004 onward, however, M2 gradually tightened, yet asset prices continued to grow relative to GDP.

FIGURE 3-4: M2 Relative to Nominal GDP

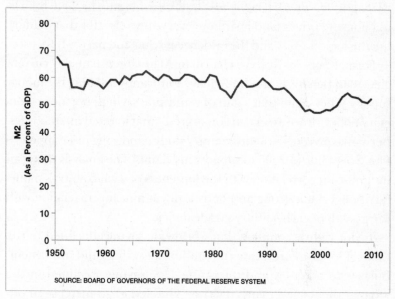

SOURCE: BOARD OF GOVERNORS OF THE FEDERAL RESERVE SYSTEM

It's true there is momentum in asset prices—a rise begets a rise as investors come to expect a rise—but it seems unlikely that monetary policy was a significant contributor. Conventional monetary theory provides little explanation for why asset prices rose substantially relative to GDP. There is no money tied up in financial assets. The ultimate sellers of assets* must use the proceeds to consume or invest. A money-based rise in the price of assets should produce a near-proportional increase in nominal GDP, whether by increasing output, prices, or both. At best, the Fed narrowly controls short-term interest rates, not long-term rates. Economic

---

* Many asset sellers are simply trading one financial asset for another, where buying and selling net to zero.

theory suggests short-term interest rates have only marginal effects on asset values. The drop in short-term rates in 2003 had little if any effect on long-term interest rates. Only real changes in the long-term expectations of investors, real changes in the share of income saved, or real increases in investment and risk taking explain rises in the price of assets relative to GDP. "Hard money" demagogues on the right are quick to blame the Fed for rising housing prices (and just about everything else, for that matter), but the logic is fuzzy and the evidence is scant and narrowly focused.

Former Federal Reserve chairman Alan Greenspan and current chairman Ben Bernanke both deny significantly inflating the money supply.[3] They claim that a glut of worldwide savings, not loose monetary policy, drove an expansion of credit that lowered interest rates. Bernanke presents a twenty-country study of housing price appreciation from 2001 to 2006 to support his claim.[4] The analysis shows an insignificant correlation with the looseness of each country's monetary policy but a strong and statistically significant correlation with the growth of each country's trade deficit.

Taylor rightly counters that worldwide savings declined in the wake of lower interest rates to equilibrate savings and investment. But, more precisely and relevantly, U.S. savings declined in the wake of the Asian Financial Crisis. That led to an increase in offshore savings flowing back into the United States, as Greenspan and Bernanke correctly asserted.

Greenspan puzzles over the fact that "between 1971 and 2002, the Fed-funds rate and the mortgage rate moved in lock step." He notes: "Between 2002 and 2005, however, the correlation diminished to insignificant."[5] A lack of correlation at that time would be consistent with the slowing of U.S. exports and increase in capital imports. Greenspan acknowledges that Fannie Mae and Freddie Mac, rather than merely guaranteeing mortgages, were buying 30 percent to 40 percent of the market for subprime and Alt-A loans using implicitly guaranteed government financing, largely financed by offshore investors.[6] Buying a large share of mortgages with offshore funds would contribute to the decoupling of mortgage markets from whatever influence monetary policy might have had on them.

RISK-AVERSION MAKES THE USE OF
OFFSHORE CAPITAL ATTRACTIVE BUT DANGEROUS

The concern that surplus exporters like China may no longer wish to lend money to the United States unwittingly assumes a contradictory scenario where the Chinese continue to run a trade surplus to maximize employment by buying U.S. assets instead of goods, but no longer wish to own U.S. assets. Unwillingness on the part of an exporter to hold dollars or dollar-denominated assets would produce a corresponding decrease in the value of the dollar or dollar-denominated assets. Dollar-denominated assets sold at a discount would represent a further reduction in the price of goods previously purchased by the United States.* A weaker dollar would raise the price of their exports and dampen demand for them going forward.

In truth, an unwillingness to hold U.S. assets would mean the Chinese were willing to accept less employment from the United States. If that is so, they could simply buy more goods and fewer assets—hardly a bad scenario for the United States, especially now, with high unemployment. If the Chinese demanded more assets in exchange for goods—i.e., higher prices—we would buy fewer goods. If anything, we accuse them of the opposite; of unfairly holding up the value of the dollar by buying U.S. assets in order to drive U.S. consumers to buy more imported goods than they otherwise would.

Of course, in the future the Chinese appetite for U.S. assets could wane. In the near term, however, the world appears to need an endless amount of employment, especially given the tremendous gains in manufacturing productivity. The Germans and Japanese continue to export manufactured products, but in order to compete, they now have very little labor in these products—automobiles, for example. Until demand for labor-intensive

---

* For example, if we bought goods for a dollar of debt, where the debt was only worth eighty cents after the dollar declines in value.

services grows, the rest of the world is likely to face a surplus of labor.

Over the long run, Chinese domestic demand will grow, domestic wages will rise as the supply of labor tightens, and demand for U.S. employment will gradually wane. But in the interim, a seventy-five-cents-an-hour wage shows that the Chinese are desperate for employment. Unlike the United States, China now has no higher-valued alternative use for its labor. If it did, China's labor wouldn't cost seventy-five cents an hour.

Alternatively, surplus exporters might seek to buy equity instead of debt. If we needed to sell equity instead of debt to fund increased consumption or investment, we would likely just reduce risky investment. It makes no sense to sell the benefits from investing to fund increased investment. It would be more logical to reduce investment to fund increased consumption. Growing investment only has value to investors if they retain ownership of the future returns.

The U.S. economy has benefited from the risk aversion of off-shore investors. A preference for equity instead of debt would have restrained the trade deficit's beneficial effect on the U.S. economy. Rather than selling assets outright, including the rights to any growth in the value of assets from reinvestment, U.S. asset owners (households) were able to borrow against their assets and retained the upside. Without selling pressure, the unsold rights to the upside retained their market value. Under normal circumstances, eagerness to borrow would have driven down the market price of debt and increased interest rates. But with risk-averse exporters eager to buy low-risk U.S. assets in order to run trade surpluses, debt was bid up, which lowered interest rates despite the growth in borrowing. With upside rights retaining their market value, the demand for investment and consumption grew in response.

The ideal trading partner is risk averse, reflecting an economy that prefers to buy debt instead of equity. This allows households to borrow against their unrealized gains without selling their ownership and giving up their upside. It's no surprise, then, that the countries with whom we run trade deficits—Germany, Japan, China, and Southeast Asia—are just such risk-averse investors.

Risk aversion on the part of offshore investors is logical. Offshore investors face notorious disadvantages stemming from asymmetrical information. Relationships and context provide a surprising amount of information. Even though offshore companies can hire experienced local talent en masse through acquisitions, the best talent is hard to hire and retain; it largely works for itself.

Rather than compete with domestic investors to buy assets, offshore investors have logically chosen to stand at the front of the repayment line as lenders rather than at the back of the line as equity investors. Local equity investors aren't paid until offshore lenders are paid. This better aligns both investors' interests and allows offshore investors to piggyback on the knowledge of local investors.

U.S. companies, on the other hand, have preferred to make offshore equity investments rather than debt investments because they bring valuable brands like Coca-Cola and McDonalds and technologies like Intel and Google with them. Obviously, they want to retain the upside from expanding the offshore use of their intellectual property. Rich U.S. households have also invested equity offshore to better diversify their existing equity portfolios. Other countries have much smaller equity capitalizations relative to their economies. Their relatively poorer households prefer low-risk debt rather than equity.

An influx of risk-averse capital, however, is not without consequences. Offshore investors have been so risk averse that they have predominantly invested in government-guaranteed debt. The financing needs of the government drive the supply of debt, not the demands of offshore investors. As the trade deficit swelled, the growing demand for this fixed amount of low-risk government-guaranteed debt has driven down yields. It is likely that surplus exporters continued to buy this government-guaranteed debt, despite its relatively low yields, in order to maintain lower currency exchange rates to keep the price of their goods competitive. This demand crowded out other risk-averse investors and drove their capital into the riskier private sectors of the economy. Without government guarantees, risk-averse investors shortened the duration of their loans to reduce their risk. Short-term debt gives risk-averse investors the option to withdraw their capital if conditions grow unfavorable. All forms of short-term debt—money-market funds, asset-backed commercial paper, and repurchase agreements, for example—swell along with the growing trade deficit.

This leaves us caught on the horns of a dilemma. The economy will not reach its full potential if we leave risk-averse capital sitting idle. However, if we put risk-averse short-term capital to work—whether to fund increased investment or consumption—it exposes the economy to the dangerous risk of panicked withdrawals.

If we fail to put risk-averse capital to work, growth will slow and unemployment will rise. If we spend domestic production to buy offshore goods and that production returns to the United States to buy assets (i.e., debt) instead of goods, then we must take the proceeds from the sale of those assets and use them for consumption or investment. Failure to invest or consume the proceeds leaves Americans out of work.

Something similar happened to Britain in the 1920s, when the pound was the world's reserve currency. Trading partners needed British pounds as a medium of exchange. They sold goods to Britain and failed to buy either goods or assets from Britain in return. When the rest of the world's economy roared in the 1920s, Britain faced high unemployment. The same thing could happen to the United States if proceeds return to the United States to buy assets but then sit idle.

On the other hand, the use of short-term capital to fund long-term investments carries risks. You may recall the scene in *It's a Wonderful Life* in which George Bailey tells the panicked citizens of Bedford Falls that his savings and loan can't refund their deposits because the bank spent the money to build their homes. In 2008, the risk of widespread panicked withdrawals turned subprime defaults into a raging forest fire that rendered our entire financial infrastructure insolvent. One of the only ways to mitigate this risk is to leave short-term capital sitting idle available to fund withdrawals in the event of a panic. In the aftermath of the Financial Crisis, cash now sits idle and unemployment has risen.

Even worse, Reinhart and Rogoff's 800-year history of finance[7] warns that domestic economies with an abundant supply of offshore capital—where other factors, such as desperation for international employment, governs its supply rather than merely the attractiveness of domestic investment opportunities—frequently misallocate this capital to unsustainable endeavors. True to form, the United States misallocated this capital to subprime mortgages.

Lawmakers have also used the abundance of this capital to grow government spending, principally entitlements. The unpopular need to tax voters normally restricts government spending. Borrowing from citizens in lieu of taxation is scarcely any different economically. Taxpayers must lower consumption or investment to buy government debt. When politicians can raise expenditures without taxing or borrowing from citizens directly, and risk-averse offshore investors eagerly buy government-guaranteed debt, there is little left to restrain government spending.

CONCLUSIONS

With the advent of the Internet, the productivity of our scarcest resource—talent—grew, investment increased, innovation and productivity accelerated, and the price of assets grew relative to the price of production. High expectations and asset prices spurred increased investment and consumption. Without the availability of offshore capacity eager to defer consumption and own U.S. assets, U.S. households could not have sold assets to finance consumption without driving down asset prices. Had they done that, investment would have declined relative to consumption as the economy neared full utilization. Instead, an abundance of cheap overseas labor and capital lowered interest rates, increased asset prices, and reduced production costs. This allowed the growth of both investment and consumption. Low-cost offshore goods contributed to increased capacity. Production for consumption moved offshore without the reciprocal need to produce goods for export. Talented workers redeployed to innovation. Growth of the large, relatively more valuable domestic service economy absorbed idle resources—doctors, lawyers, teachers, drivers, salesclerks, and waitresses. Far from demonstrating a lack of competiveness, the trade deficit facilitated increased U.S. competitiveness and was essential to U.S. growth.

With unemployment above 9 percent in the aftermath of the Crisis, we may wonder whether employment would have been greater had we not moved manufacturing jobs offshore—but this is not the case. The economy prior to the recession would have been smaller, and unemployment would now be worse. High productivity gains in manufacturing have accounted for two-thirds of lost manufacturing employment since 2000.[8] Productivity gains have been the predominant reason for the slow growth of manufacturing employment, not imports. Labor has been redeployed to other sectors of the economy, sectors that have grown faster than manufacturing as their value has risen relative to low-cost goods manufactured offshore. Today, manufacturing is only 10 percent of U.S. employment.[9] A small amount of growth in the other sectors of the economy can offset a large decline in manufacturing. Again, the United States grew 60 percent since 1991 while Europe and Japan grew only 20 percent to 30 percent. Without this growth, unemployment would have been higher before the Financial Crisis. If anything has restrained lower-middle-class wages, it's likely an abundant supply of cheap immigrant labor.

Without this redeployment, the retreat from risk taking in the aftermath of the Financial Crisis may have boosted unemployment even higher from a smaller base of employment. Declines in manufacturing employment have been steeper in this recession than in other sectors of the economy. Nonmanagerial and non-professional jobs, excluding production workers, fell 5 percent over the course of 2008, the period when almost all post-Crisis job losses occurred. Production workers' jobs fell 12.5 percent over the same period.[10] Not only have Europe's and Japan's economies declined more than the United States' in the recession, they have declined more from smaller bases of employment and recovered more slowly.[11] In a world filled with seventy-five-cents-an-hour labor, we can no more increase prosperity by returning to manufacturing than by returning to the farm or by winding back the clock on productivity improvements.

In the long run, the only way to support domestic unskilled wages in a world awash in unskilled labor is by exiting manufacturing—at least where products lack enough proprietary intellectual property or capital intensity to render $17-an-hour labor (the median wage rate of high-school graduates with no higher education) competitive—and successfully redeploying the labor to other sectors of our economy. Then we have to drive up demand in those domestic sectors of our economy by growing prosperity by continuing to innovate successfully. The 10 percent of workers who create close to half our GDP have to create more value through increased productivity and risk taking. And we have to recruit idle talent to enlarge the ranks of the most productive workers. That group has to keep innovating successfully, which will in turn grow both domestic investment and consumption and put upward pressure on domestic wage rates. Unfortunately, a worldwide surplus of unskilled labor will drive manufactured goods offshore and manufacturing will become a smaller and smaller percent of our employment. Luckily, it's already small. Innovation is the only way to keep our economy at full utilization. And it's the only way to return to the heated level of employment and growth our economy achieved prior to the Financial Crisis.

But let's be realistic. An economy whose production skews toward investment is a more cyclical economy and more vulnerable to the ebb and flow of investor confidence. The increased use of risk-averse capital leaves the economy more vulnerable to the panicked withdrawals. Failure to employ this capital, however, shrinks the economy and slows growth.

CHAPTER FOUR

THE ROLE OF INCENTIVES

THE UNITED STATES has poured investment into innovation since the early 1990s. It opened trade borders to lower costs, freed up resources, and relaxed capacity constraints. When besieged by low-cost seventy-five-cents-an-hour unskilled offshore labor, it transitioned quickly from manufacturing to more productive endeavors. These endeavors included innovation and services that cannot be produced offshore. In contrast, Europe and Japan remained wedded to manufacturing-based economies with attendant lower levels of innovation and slower growth rates. In Germany and Japan, about 20 percent of employment remains in manufacturing versus only 10 percent in the United States.[1] Why did Europe and Japan resist change when the United States embraced it?

Few economists would dispute the fact that the radical transformation of the United States since the early 1990s, relative to Europe and Japan, stems from increased risk taking. What caused the United States to take more risks is what is relevant to the debate. Proponents of income redistribution emphasize differences in cultures. The United States, they claim, is a culture of risk takers. Some go so far as to claim that immigrants to the United States brought with them a genetic bias for risk taking and entrepreneurialism.

Opponents of income redistribution claim innovation is like

any game of chance. Lucky risk taking produces innovation. The greater the payoffs, the greater the willingness of gamblers to take risks. The greater the amount of wagering, the greater the resulting innovation. One need only look at state lotteries to see the power of this effect. As the payoffs rise, wagering increases remarkably, even though the increased jackpots in state lotteries don't increase the expected value of the gambler's payoff. Unlike investment, state lotteries are zero-sum games: more betting increases the payoff but proportionally decreases the chances of winning. Nevertheless, the opportunity to obtain extraordinary wealth is so seductive, it renders the odds irrelevant. As innovation grows more valuable relative to everyday activities, it motivates increased risk taking and investment, like the payout in any game of chance.

Europe and Japan lacked the economic incentives to take the risks necessary to transform their economies. High labor redeployment costs imposed by their well-intended but misguided pro-labor governments discouraged European and Japanese manufacturers from exiting manufacturing, laying off workers, and redeploying them to more productive endeavors. Instead, they invested in antiquated manufacturing to avoid high-cost layoffs. Pro-labor governments obstructed trade borders to slow workforce dislocations. This slowed their transition out of manufacturing and left their best thinkers mired in a declining sector of advanced economies. Meanwhile, the most talented U.S. thinkers created near-impossible-to-duplicate communities of experts around companies like Google and Facebook—companies that remain critical to the advancement of cutting-edge innovation.

In the United States, more valuable on-the-job training, lower labor redeployment costs, and lower marginal tax rates increased payouts for successful risk taking. Higher payouts, in turn, increased risk taking. The outsized gains of successful risk takers diminished the status of other talented workers, which increased their motivation to take risks. Successful risk taking accelerated growth and the accumulation of equity. With more wealth in the hands of risk takers, U.S. investors underwrote more risk. Larger, more liquid U.S. financial markets allowed investors to further parse risk and sell risks they were reluctant to bear. From this perspective, a risk taking culture is largely a by-product of incentives.

HIGH LABOR REDEPLOYMENT COSTS
SLOW GROWTH AND HURT WORKERS

Companies don't bear the full cost of human suffering caused by layoffs; workers do. Presumably, company decisions would be fairer to society if employers bore the full cost of layoffs, as they do in many other countries. The Japanese expect large companies to mitigate layoffs with lifetime employment. European governments charge companies for the cost to society of laying off workers. In my own business experience, the cost of laying off European employees is one to two times a worker's annual wages. In the United States, it's only a quarter to half their annual wages. That makes the cost of laying off European workers two to four times more expensive than laying off U.S. workers.

As with the low-cost tractor, which displaces workers with a low-cost alternative, layoffs and redeployments create value that consumers, not producers, predominantly capture. Consumers capture this value from lower-priced existing products and, ultimately, from valuable new products. Competition among producers prevents them from capturing much of the value from cost reduction. Producers pass lower costs to consumers through lower prices.

Ironically, unless companies capture the benefits of layoffs, producers will endeavor to avoid layoffs and their costs no matter the benefits to society, especially higher costs imposed by the government on layoffs. One way to avoid higher layoff costs is by hiring workers where the cost of layoffs is lower, in the United States or Asia, for instance. Higher redeployment costs slow the rate of change, reduce return on investment, and drive future investment and employment away from Europe and Japan.

Producers will seek to avoid higher labor redeployment costs

unless they can pass government-imposed costs to consumers—
the chief beneficiaries of layoffs—through higher prices. They can
only do this if their government seals trade borders; otherwise,
producers without imposed costs will capture market share with
lower prices. If economies close trade borders, they must forego
cheap offshore labor and capital.

Another reason governments seek to shield workers from layoffs
is to protect them from the risk that the newly created jobs for redeployed workers will be less valuable than their lost jobs. In that case,
redeployed workers must accept lower pay to fill the remaining positions economically. The logic behind the fear works as follows: All
jobs are ranked in order from most valuable to least valuable; the
number of workers determines the last job filled; the unfilled jobs
are less valuable than the filled jobs. If innovation removes one job
from somewhere in the queue of filled jobs, the next job available
to be filled at the end of the line is less valuable and pays less.

While this might lurk as a theoretical possibility, after decades
without a decline in the unskilled wage rate, it's hard to find convincing evidence for concern. The unskilled wage rate in the
United States appears to be flat, at worst, over large increases in
the supply of labor. In fact, incomes have grown substantially
across all demographics at a time when productivity growth has
been high for two decades and the economy has added tens of millions of Hispanic immigrants to the workforce. In reality, lower
costs increase the relative value of all jobs in the queue, including
the ones beyond the end of the queue, and innovation keeps discovering new jobs to add to the queue at all levels.

Because of these miscalculations, well-intended laws designed
to benefit workers created unintended consequences that hurt
labor far more than they helped. Imposed costs may have slowed
layoffs in Europe and Japan, but at the expense of greatly diminished employment growth. As we saw in Figure 1-4, Europe suffered higher unemployment and reduced working hours largely at
the expense of marginal workers—the young, the old, and women.
Japan achieved higher employment but only by suffering much
lower productivity and GDP per hours worked.

With lower redeployment costs, the United States aggressively implemented productivity improvements. It also used offshore manufacturing to lower costs and relax capacity constraints. In the face of seventy-five-cents-an-hour offshore labor, it redeployed its most talented workers to innovation and the rest of its workforce to the now more valuable service economy—doctors, teachers, drivers, and so forth. Non-manufacturing sectors of the U.S. economy now employ 90 percent of workers.

Meanwhile, Germany and Japan pursued export-based strategies to avoid layoffs, boost employment, and (they hoped) increase economic growth. But this left their creative thinkers stuck within the archaic context of manufacturing—a declining sector of advanced economies. Allocating brainpower to crack the insurmountable problem of competing with hardworking seventy-five-cents-an-hour labor was a poor use of their time. Nor does the solution—ultraproductive manufacturing—add much employment to their economies in the long run.

The CEO of a state-of-the-art German machine tool company complained to me that the lack of capable U.S. machine tool programmers was indicative of a failing U.S. economy. Yes, the United States has a shortage of capable machine tool programmers—because all those programmers are working on Google and Facebook!

While the United States was dominating the commercialization of the Internet, Germany was programming unprofitable machine tools now largely used by the Chinese. Imagine trying to create the next Internet breakthrough without deep access to the workforces of Facebook, Google, or Microsoft and their myriad spin-offs. The incremental nature of progress makes it difficult—impossible in some cases—for late entrants to gain the knowledge and market share needed to leapfrog existing competitors. The next generation of opportunities offered by U.S. industry increases the payouts for risk taking and investment. Meanwhile, Europe and Japan have eaten their children!

At the same time, the success of innovation has driven up demand for U.S. domestic services. It drove it up so much that we employed tens of millions of workers offshore to free up workers onshore. That wasn't enough labor to meet our growing demand. We also employed 20 million immigrants.

Ironically, the Germans and Japanese pursued exports to grow their employment and domestic demand in order to avoid high labor redeployment costs, but this slowed their growth relative to the United States and reduced employment growth. Unlike their German and Japanese counterparts, U.S. companies built low-cost factories offshore to compete internationally. They largely kept the cash flow from these international investments offshore to fund international growth and to avoid high U.S. corporate tax rates. Meanwhile, growing international profits drove up the U.S. market value of these multinational companies. Nowhere in the trade accounts are these stock market gains recognized as cross-border flows. Nevertheless, these gains increased the net worth of U.S. households. This increase provides collateral for increased borrowing from offshore lenders. Households use these loans to increase U.S. consumption and investment. Unfortunately, this more logical business strategy didn't allow Europe and Japan to avoid high labor redeployment costs.

THE DISTRIBUTION OF INCOME AFFECTS RISK TAKING

It's unlikely that high labor redeployment costs alone account for the differences between Europe, Japan, and the United States. In recent years, young European workers faced high unemployment or employment as temporary workers, so there were no redeployment costs for them. These unemployed and underemployed workers should have flocked to innovative startups, no matter the risk. Why didn't European innovators and their investors take advantage of this opportunity? Instead, innovative start-ups sprung up in the United States and workers flocked to them, even though it meant walking away from great jobs at Google and Facebook to join risky startups with almost certain failure.

Unlike diversified investors, most people get only a small

number of chances to be successful—often only one chance in a lifetime, and then only if they're lucky. While there are exceptions to every rule, careers at failed ventures and on failed projects are generally fatal to the careers of responsible employees. Young employees derailed from the "fast track" can take years to reestablish their credibility while successful peers get the most sought-after assignments and advance further still. Failed senior leaders rarely have the negotiating leverage to regain power in existing organizations. Lions around the carcass don't invite others to enjoy the spoils—they fight to keep them out. New ventures outside existing power structures rarely succeed, and the need to feed one's family quickly forces subordination to the powers that be. People who have never struggled for power and money underestimate the ferocity of these struggles. Talented workers with valuable careers face more risk than most people realize. Powerful incentives must overcome their logical aversion to risk.

Money doesn't motivate us as much as status does. It's primal. Skill doesn't win sought-after mates; relative skill does, and then only if the differentiation is large enough to be recognized—even if only among one's immediate peers. Look at the surprising number of people willing to face impossible odds in their desire to become a movie star or a professional athlete. In everyday life, people buy fancy cars, expensive suits, and homes with large entertainment spaces they rarely use in order to display their success. Men seek beautiful women—even unintelligent, unfriendly ones— for the recognizable status of having attracted a desirable mate. Academics seek recognition for their intellectual prowess. It's all the same. Money is just a means to these ends.

That's not to say that status is the only motivator, only that money and status are powerful motivators—*the* most powerful motivators—of economic risk taking, and that money is the predominant way talented people pursue status. Few people have enough talent to pursue status in alternative ways, and the economy does not offer many such opportunities.

It's not so much the rewards per se that motivate people, but the lack of status that comes from *not* having achieved them. The cost of shame is far greater than the value of success. I once made an effort to motivate a company's branch managers to improve their inventory turns. I linked a portion of their bonus to improving turns, but it had no effect. However, when I posted each manager's results at a monthly meeting of their peers and made them walk to the front of the room to account for the differences, turns soared. Recognition, both positive and negative, lit the fire for improvement. But the walk of shame generated all the change.

It is therefore no surprise that when Internet valuations boomed in the late 1990s, MBAs abandoned lucrative, previously sought-after careers at investment banks and hedge funds and flocked to risky, one-in-a-million Internet start-ups. The numbers of students majoring in computer science skyrocketed from 2 percent of male students to more than 6 percent.[2] Every talented young person seemed to have a friend who struck it rich. Not achieving the same level of success drove them crazy. Previously, few had much interest in entrepreneurial endeavors. Risk taking went through the roof because they couldn't bear the shame of falling behind.

Status is not just a powerful motivator for the lucky few who achieve it, but, more important, for the millions who fail trying. It's the thirst for recognition, the idealized myth of differentiated status—impressive homes, sleek boats, and exotic vacations, an Academy Award, a Nobel, or Pulitzer Prize—and not necessarily the reality of it that motivates people. Truly differentiated success requires devoting your life to work, forsaking your family, enduring the psychological weight of crushing responsibilities, and taking risks to achieve it. A wise man once joked, "It's lonely at the top . . . because nobody really wants to be here!"

Over time, success begets success. As the most talented Americans took risks and grew more successful, they motivated others with the necessary talent to duplicate their success. The most talented students no longer aspired to be doctors and lawyers. An increasing portion of the best of the best now attend the top business schools. Doctors have less status because success has raised the bar. Workers have responded by taking more risks. This hasn't happened in Europe and Japan.

It's easy to see why this would make a big difference to the success of one economy relative to another. The top 10 percent of income earners produce 40 percent to 50 percent of GDP and the top 1 percent about 20 percent of GDP.[3] It's not the hours worked that matter but the work they do and the risks they take—innovative entrepreneurialism over the assured high income of corporate lawyers, for example. Hours worked are merely indicative of increased responsibilities and risks talented workers have taken.

The commercialization of the Internet and email has increased the value of innovation relative to the everyday jobs common to the economy. As innovation has grown relatively more valuable, the share of pretax income produced by successful innovators has naturally risen. This growing share of income indicates increasing success by U.S. innovators relative to Europe and Japan (see Figure 4-1). It's not as though the outsized success of the top 1 percent has lowered median wages in the United States relative to those of Europe or Japan. Quite the contrary; rather than bemoaning unequal distribution of income, we should be celebrating the extraordinary success of U.S. innovation relative to the rest of the world and its beneficial effect on domestic employment.

The quest for status leaves us stranded on a never-ending "aspirational treadmill."[4] But this treadmill is the very engine that drives economic success. God didn't put talented people on earth to be happy. He put them here to take responsibility, lead, innovate, and take prudent risks.

Liberal economist and *New York Times* columnist Robert Frank misconstrues this important dynamic. Frank claims that if we could eliminate competition between individuals, "we could liberate trillions of dollars in resources each year" where "no painful sacrifices would be required."[5] He claims regulation would cure Darwinian evolution of the unnecessary burden of big antlers. Frank argues: "Larger antlers serve the reproductive interests of an individual male elk, because it helped him prevail in battles with other males for access to mates. But as this mutation spread, it started an arms race that made life more hazardous for male elk overall. And despite their utility in battle, they often become a

FIGURE 4-1: Share of Income Earned by Top 0.1% of U.S. Workers

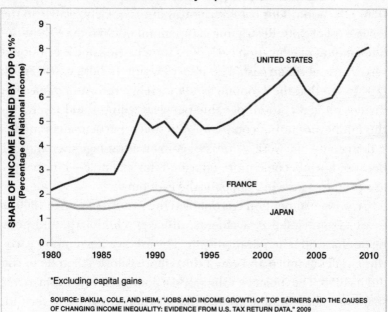

*Excluding capital gains

SOURCE: BAKIJA, COLE, AND HEIM, "JOBS AND INCOME GROWTH OF TOP EARNERS AND THE CAUSES OF CHANGING INCOME INEQUALITY: EVIDENCE FROM U.S. TAX RETURN DATA," 2009

fatal handicap when predators pursue males into dense woods." He continues, "Individual and group interests are almost always in conflict when rewards to individuals depend on relative performance, as in the antlers race. . . . If male elk could vote to scale back their antlers by half, they would have compelling reasons for doing so, because only relative antler size matters."[6] However, the protection big antlers afford and the strength their use demands allow the most athletic bulls to compete fiercely for mates. This very competition produces offspring strong enough to compete successfully with the toughest predators, so successfully that only the lame and the old fall to predators, least of all the dominant bulls. Obviously, whatever costs large antlers require of individuals are more than offset by their overall benefits to the group—the opposite of Frank's assertion.

Frank similarly claims that competition among job applicants leads them to wear unnecessarily expensive suits. He mistakenly believes this practice has cost without benefit. Again, he overlooks the fact that this same competition drives applicants to maximize their education. This has enormous value to society relative to the trivial cost of suits. Restricting competition would reduce the absolute amount of education each of us sought, the same way it would restrict the absolute cost of an interview suit. In both cases, Frank fails to see that the economy is not merely a zero-sum game that divides a fixed amount of value between winners and losers. Although never-ending competition between participants remains stalemated—one worker does not gain an advantage over another because both become more educated, for example—it nevertheless produces growing value for the economy.

Growing competition has doubled life expectancy since 1800 as deaths from violence, accidents, diseases, childbirth, and poor health have all fallen dramatically. The average person now earns three times as much and eats a third more calories than he or she did in 1955. The income of the world's poor grew twice as fast over that time. The Chinese are ten times richer, one-third as fecund, and twenty-eight years longer-lived than they were in 1955.[7] According to the World Bank, the number of people living on less than $1.25 a day has fallen from 50 percent of the world's population in 1981 to 25 percent in 2005.[8] Clearly, mankind—at least in the case of the suffering poor—has benefited greatly from the growing prosperity of the world.

Proponents of income redistribution are skeptical that payoffs motivate increased effort. They ask why work effort hasn't increased as the economy has grown richer if payoffs motivate effort. They reason that work effort must have reached some natural limit.

This argument overlooks the never-ending spiral of competition between work and leisure. As wealth and innovation improve the quality of leisure, pay must rise to motivate a similar amount of work. The same is true of the competition between consumption and investment. This competition is no different from the continual evolution of offense and defense in sports. Both must evolve to remain at a stalemate. This ever-increasing, albeit stalemated, competition propels the economy to deliver an increasing standard of living.

It's true that success often arises from differences in relative performance. I don't have to run faster than the proverbial bear— just faster than you! But it's also true that the relative difference between a peashooter and a flyswatter doesn't force Russia to capitulate in an arms race. Rather, it's the size of the difference, not just the relative size of the difference; the absolute difference, not just the percentage difference. Competition drives us to maximize the size of the difference. If for no other reason, the larger the absolute size of the difference, the less likely extraneous events will randomly determine competitive outcomes.

As a result, motivation is not strictly relative. Higher probabilities of success and payouts for success have motivational effects as well. You might recall that the most talented students and those genuinely struggling to pass work harder, on average, than everyone else. Even at Harvard Business School, the students competing for honors and the ones at risk of failing work much harder than the rest of the students, who barely work at all. Why? A small amount of effort yields a much larger likelihood of payoff for those students than for average students. For average students, more effort has almost no differentiating result. They have little to gain from working harder and little to lose from coasting. They are average, no matter their effort. They prefer leisure to hard work. The size of payoffs and the probability of payoffs matter.

In his 2004 study for the Federal Reserve, "Why Do Americans Work So Much More Than Europeans?"[9] Nobel Prize–winning economist Edward Prescott shows that earning an additional dollar of income in the 1970s gave U.S. and European workers the same amount of after-tax income. At that time, workers in the United States and Europe supplied the same number of hours. But since then, the United States has lowered its marginal taxes while Europe has raised value-added taxes on consumption. Today, a dollar of incremental income produces sixty cents of after-tax income for the average U.S. worker but only forty cents in

France—a large difference. And, as previously mentioned, the work supplied by European workers since the 1970s relative to their U.S. counterparts has declined significantly.

Unfortunately, most tax studies measure only short-term changes in taxpayer behavior from changes in tax rates. These studies consistently show that taxable income declines when governments raise tax rates, and that this decline occurs exclusively among the highest income earners.[10] But these short-term studies have been unable to determine whether taxpayers simply deferred taxable income to later tax periods or decreased their risk taking and work effort over the long term. Bradley Heim, a researcher for the U.S. Treasury, concludes, "Whatever long-run effects of tax changes are, an estimate of this elasticity is notoriously difficult to pin down, even with a data set that is close to ideal for estimating it."[11] Ironically, Heim is referring to three-year effects, not twenty-year trends! Short-term studies can't measure whether lower marginal tax rates encourage increased risk taking over longer periods of time—that is, they can't tell us if the best students will skip medical school and go to business school instead.

A recent pair of studies by the Organisation for Economic Co-operation and Development[12] finds significant evidence that higher marginal tax rates reduce productivity over the long term. The studies compare the tax structures of twenty-one countries over the last thirty-five years, including industry-by-industry comparisons between countries. The studies find "a strong reliance on income taxes* seems to be associated with significantly lower levels of GDP per capita than the use of taxes on consumption and property [which spread taxes more broadly to lower income groups]. . . . High top marginal rates of personal income tax reduce productivity growth by reducing entrepreneurial activity. . . . Industry-level evidence covering a subset of OECD countries suggests that there is a negative relationship between top marginal personal income tax rates and the long-run level of total factor productivity." Total factor productivity (TFP) is innovative know-how.

---

*   . . . over other types of taxes, such as value-added taxes or property taxes.

Many skeptics counter that if higher marginal tax rates slow growth, why did growth accelerate when the Clinton administration raised marginal tax rates. Obviously, the Internet increased growth despite higher taxes. So did the fall of the Berlin Wall. Twenty-dollars-a-barrel oil didn't hurt growth either. The fact that Clinton could raise the marginal rate only to 39 percent, when previously Democrats had been able to raise it to 70 percent and higher, may have boosted investor confidence as well. Investors may have increased investment and risk taking that was previously constrained in anticipation of higher rates.

Looking at one data point, with blinders on, is dangerous. Republicans use the same mistaken logic when they claim lower tax rates increased growth. Income might have grown anyway following the advent of the Internet. Multicountry comparisons, like those cited above, reveal the true effects of different variables. And there is no way to know what would have happened under the Clinton administration if marginal rates had remained lower. Perhaps the economy would have grown even more. We do know that the manufacturing sector immediately began cooling off after the tax increase took effect, as did the overall economy prior to 9/11, despite enormous monetary stimulus leading up to Y2K. We ought to be careful about other lessons we might draw from any single complex data point.

Less sophisticated tax arguments point to the growth of Scandinavian countries—Finland in particular, where academic test scores are among the highest in the world and knowledge-based industries thrive—as evidence that the United States can also remain competitive, even with high taxation and equality of incomes, despite widely disparate demographics. They overlook the lower growth rates in Europe versus the United States, especially among countries like Italy and Greece, where test scores are similar to those in the United States. Nor do they project into the future, where lower growth rates have an increasingly cumulative effect. They fail to acknowledge the high degree of homogeneity that exists in Scandinavian countries, where social insurance is exactly that—insurance and not redistribution of income between highly disparate contributors. They simply ignore the fact that most of these countries impose highly regressive sales and value-added taxes. Such taxes spread taxation more broadly to lower-income workers rather than to high-income risk takers and better match tax payments to the beneficiaries of government-provided insurance. And they conveniently overlook the fact that tax rates are lower for corporations and investors in order to raise investment incentives. Ironically, all of this in the interest of arguing that taxes don't matter!

In the United States, which has lowered marginal taxes on the highest earners and where the innovative U.S. economy affords the most opportunity for success, the hours worked by the most productive workers have increased. A 2005 study published by the National Bureau of Economic Research[13] shows that the portion of American men working more than fifty hours per week increased from 15 percent for the highest quintile of earners in 1970 to 27 percent in 2006. At the same time, the portion of American male workers in the lowest quintile of earners working more than fifty hours per week fell steadily from 22 percent in 1979 to 13 percent by 2006.

Why did talented Americans work more? A 2000 study published by the National Bureau of Economic Research[14] finds that a widening in the variation of pay correlates to an increase in hours worked. Progressive tax rates narrow the spread in pay. "Pay for performance" is more typical in the United States than elsewhere. According to the study, in the United States, unlike in Germany, a 10 percent increase in hours yields a 1 percent increase in future pay. That turns out to be a better payoff per hour than an hour spent earning a college degree! Simply put, talented Americans worked harder because the payoff was better. Some combination of lower taxes and higher rates of success relative to Europe and Japan motivated the most talented American workers. Again, the hours worked are indicative of the risks taken and the responsibility assumed.

The failure to recognize that getting lucky requires taking risks leads some proponents of income redistribution, like Robert

Frank, to underestimate the cost to society of taxing success more heavily. Frank rhetorically asks, "When fortune falls into your lap, should you really protest about your taxes?"[15] Lucky reward is the payoff for suffering almost certain failure. To incentivize risk taking, we must pay lucky risk takers. If we fail to pay lucky risk takers after the fact, we will get less risk taking before the fact. With less unlucky failure comes less lucky success.

Two important long-term multicountry studies by Kristin Forbes and Robert Barro find further evidence of the enduring benefits to society from the unequal distribution of income. Forbes finds "that in the short and medium term, an increase in a country's level of income inequality has a significant positive and robust relationship with subsequent economic growth."[16] Barro finds "higher inequality tends to . . . encourage growth in richer places."[17] Despite faster growth, Barro, unlike Forbes, finds no corresponding increase in investment. But it's easy to see why that might be the case. First, Barro only measures tangible investment when the growth is likely to come from intangible innovation. And second, he has no way to measure changes in the risk taken per dollar of investment. Unequal distribution of income has critical motivational effects that are especially important for growth via risky innovation.

EQUITY AFFECTS RISK TAKING

It's not enough to lower the cost of redeploying workers and motivate talented workers to take risks. Someone has to finance those risks. Microsoft, Google, and Facebook commercialize their ideas on the backs of tens of thousands of employees. Those employees can't afford to live or die solely on the unlikely success of their employers. Win or lose, they need to feed their families. They demand bond-like salaries that pay them whether investments are successful or not. Investors take the risk of funding those salaries. What motivates companies and their investors to take risk? Proponents and opponents of income redistribution are deeply divided over the answer.

Proponents of income redistribution point out that successful businesses are self-funding—even Microsoft, Google, and Facebook. They don't need capital from outside investors. From this perspective, the risk taking of managers, not investors, drives economic growth. Opponents of income redistribution counter that success is a by-product of failure and that failure is not self-funding.

Opponents also argue that managers are agents of investors who respond to investors' demands for returns, and ultimately to the need for risk taking to achieve those returns. The value investors place on risky assets reflects their demands for managers to take risks. The resulting values of these assets govern the investment decisions of investors and managers. The market values of future profits are, after all, the payoff for successful risk taking.

Opponents of income redistribution believe that leaving income and wealth in the hands of successful risk takers through lower marginal tax rates and unequal distribution of income, rather than redistribution to poor consumers, increases the willingness of investors to bear risk. This drives up the demand for assets, which increases their price. This increases the payout for risky investments that produce increases in future profits. Higher payouts lead to increased risk taking. Again, consumers and wage earners are the chief beneficiaries of increased investment.

Opponents claim low-income wage earners are far more disposed to consume than to invest. They tend to sell assets to increase consumption, which puts downward pressure on the price of future cash flows. What little the middle class saves largely funds their personal housing. Housing investment does little to increase growth, productivity, employment, and wages. Middle-class savings over and above housing largely provide risk-averse short-term savings. They demand capital preservation and the right to withdraw their savings and consume them at any time. This type of capital underwrites too little risk to grow the economy.

Proponents of income redistribution argue that managers look past fickle market values to their long-term expectations of the future and make decisions based on those expectations unaffected by today's supply and demand for assets. They believe managers will make the same investment decisions regardless of the market value of assets. It doesn't matter if a lack of demand for assets drives down their price. They are also skeptical that the supply and demand for assets affects the price of assets over and above investors' expectations about the future value of assets. They don't believe the saving rates and risk profiles of low-income earners are different than those of high-income earners. From these perspectives, investors don't matter.

Which is true?

The Distribution of Wealth Affects Risk Taking

Economic activity is proportional to risk taking. The willingness to take a risk drives both investment and consumption. Consumers take more risk by consuming rather than hoarding their incomes. They can take even more risk by investing rather than consuming. There is a significant possibility that investment, unlike consumption, will produce little if any value; investment spans a spectrum of risk. Adding inventory in response to growing demand is less risky than building additional capacity. A company that adds inventory can subsequently sell it off if demand contracts, whereas capacity additions are fixed in the long run regardless of the ebbs and flows of demand. Investments to produce innovations are riskier still and often produce no value at all. When they work, innovations often create enormous increases in value and subsequent economic activity. Capacity additions, on the other hand, are often duplicative and transfer value from one investor to another rather than increasing value overall. Adding restaurant seats, for example, may do little more than take customers from the restaurant down the street. One investor's gain is another's loss.

The willingness to take risk is largely a function of wealth. Wealth and equity are the same thing. A consumer who believes he has equity embedded in his home, for example, might be willing to spend rather than hoard a greater share of his income. Economist Robert Shiller, creator of the Case-Shiller real estate price index, coined the phrase "wealth effect" to describe this relationship. He might have called it an equity effect.

Risk taking is a function of the amount of wealth, namely equity, available to underwrite risk and the willingness to take risk per dollar of equity. Equity investors have the right to whatever profit is left over in a business after everyone else has been paid. Unlike equity investors, short-term debt holders demand capital preservation and the right to withdraw and consume their savings at any time. Because of these demands, short-term debt may fund investment but only if equity holders underwrite investment risk. Short-term debt bears too little risk to grow the economy. The amount of equity, and its tolerance for risk, grows the economy.

In the long run, the amount of equity accumulates slowly over time and its tolerance for risk remains relatively fixed. In the short run, however, perceptions of the value of equity can change rapidly, as evidenced by fluctuations in the market value of assets. Beliefs about the value of Internet investments in 2000 and housing investments in 2007 fell quickly, for example. The willingness to put equity at risk ebbs and flows in parallel with these changing beliefs. The economy contracts and falls into a recession when the willingness to take risk recedes. But aside from these short-term fluctuations, what drives risk tolerance over the long run?

Generally, richer investors are willing to make riskier investments. A 2000 study published by the National Bureau of Economic Research finds "a strong positive relationship between current income and saving rates across all income groups . . . Estimated savings rates range from 5 percent for the bottom quintile of the income distribution to more than 40 percent of income for the top 5 percent."[18]

The Federal Reserve and the Department of Labor's surveys show that the bottom 50 percent of income earners consumed more than 100 percent of their incomes leading up to the Financial Crisis. The surveys also show that assets owned by high-income households are three times larger as a multiple of their income than low-income households. Whereas low-income households predominantly invest in their homes, richer households invest half their savings in the equity of businesses—in assets that increase productivity and employment.

This difference in risk tolerance has a significant impact on the capital available to underwrite risk. The deferred consumption of middle-class consumers largely yields risk-averse debt. These investors refuse to underwrite risk. Instead, they demand government guarantees as a condition for making their savings available for investment. These guarantees include government-issued Treasuries, municipal bonds, and the debt of government-sponsored entities like Fannie Mae and Freddie Mac as well as Federal Deposit Insurance. With an abundance of risk-averse debt flowing into the United States from the trade deficit, additional risk-averse domestic debt is of marginal value to the growth of our economy. There is plenty of risk-averse capital to fund increased investment. So much so, that an abundance of investors willing to buy debt contributed to the growth of subprime mortgages and the erosion of credit standards that triggered the Financial Crisis. What's needed is more equity.

Keynes certainly recognized that the rich, and not the poor, save. He argued, "It was precisely the inequality of the distribution of wealth which made possible those vast accumulations of fixed wealth and of capital improvements which distinguished that age from all others. The immense accumulations of fixed capital which, to the great benefit of mankind, were built up during the half century before the war could never have come about in a society where wealth was divided equitably."[19]

The same is true of risk underwriting today: the wealthier the economy, the more risk it should logically bear. It's no surprise that the value of the U.S. stock market relative to GDP—the economy most willing to take risk—is twice as large as Europe's and Japan's.

Proponents of income redistribution argue that it does little good to encourage U.S. savings because cross-border flows of capital mitigate policy effects. These flows will bring capital to the United States if investment opportunities are attractive regardless of U.S. savings and tolerance for risk. And capital will easily flow out of the country to underwrite risk elsewhere if we encourage savings here. It's hard to affect policy in a leaky sieve.

Perhaps there is an opportunity for us to take advantage of the rest of the world's savings without the need to increase our own. Maybe we can redistribute and consume our income without concern for savings and the risk tolerance of our investors. Unfortunately, offshore savings have proven woefully risk-averse. The businesses powering U.S. growth, meanwhile, tend to be risky innovators in need of equity-risk underwriters. Research also shows that home bias—the extent to which investors, especially equity investors, invest their capital at home rather than across borders—is very high.[20]

In addition to an increased tolerance for risk per dollar of equity, an economy also needs more dollars of equity to tolerate risk. In the long run, what creates equity? Successful risk taking. Traditionally, economists define savings as the accumulation of deferred consumption because savings defined that way are straightforward to measure. But savers largely lend deferred consumption as short-term debt. Successful risk taking that creates innovation largely creates equity, not the accumulation of deferred consumption. Risky investments to create innovation at Google, for example, created $250 billion of equity, not the accumulation of deferred consumption. Rich investors willing to bear risk beget equity, which begets rich risk underwriters.

Equity created through innovation, however, largely exists as the market value of future cash flows—cash flows that we can't teleport back from the future to fund increased investment today. Only deferred consumption or offshore borrowing can fund investment. Investment, however, requires both funding and risk underwriting.

While future cash flows can't fund investment today, they can underwrite increased risk taking. Promising risk-averse investors rights to unrelated future cash flows—a share of American International Group's (AIG) property and casualty insurance subsidiary, for example—if they fund risky investments and suffer losses in the future will logically induce investors to fund riskier investments than would otherwise be the case. Similarly, government guarantees—the promise to cover losses with future tax increases, if necessary—encourage risk-averse offshore investment into the United States via government-guaranteed debt (such as U.S. Treasuries) that domestic investors or taxpayers must otherwise fund. An increase in risk taking accelerates the growth of the economy.

With an abundance of risk-averse offshore capital, the constraint to increased investment and risk taking has been the capacity of risk underwriters, not capital providers. Today, Wall Street uses financial innovation to decouple risk from investment capital and predominantly sells risk to risk underwriters, which is no different from an insurance broker or insurance company. Wall Street deconstructs, prices, underwrites, syndicates, trades, and makes markets for risk. Because Wall Street now performs the more abstract function of syndicating risk rather than merely raising capital, people— even people as well informed as former president Bill Clinton—have naïvely concluded that these transactions serve "no economic purpose."[21] Risk underwriting is every bit as important as funding investment, perhaps even more so in today's economy where the trade deficit leaves us awash in risk-averse short-term debt to fund investment provided someone else underwrites the risk.

It's hard to believe that the economy's growing demand for Wall Street resources serves no economic purpose. Quite the contrary; as a larger share of the U.S. economy is invested rather than consumed, and when investment is increasingly funded indirectly by risk-averse offshore saving, we should expect Wall Street's share of our economy to grow proportionately. And it has.

Asset Prices Influence Risk Taking

It's not difficult to see why American investors would be willing to underwrite more risk than their European and Japanese counterparts. First and foremost, the returns are better here than there. Labor redeployment costs are lower. Talented employees are more motivated to take risks. And the communities of experts surrounding companies like Google and Facebook make talented employees more productive than their counterparts elsewhere. Also, American investors are richer. They have more equity, and they are importers of capital rather than exporters by necessity. Larger, more liquid U.S. capital markets also allow risk to be more easily parsed into their individual components and sold to investors who fear them least—investors who charge the lowest price for bearing the risk.

The more complicated question is how investors impose their tolerance for risk on the economy. Managers, as the agents of investors, should respond to investor demands both directly—through aligned incentive schemes—and indirectly—through the market value of assets. As the market value of assets rises, managers and investors should find more incentive to invest.

It is widely assumed that the price of assets plays an unquestionable role in the motivation for investment and risk taking. When housing prices rose prior to the Financial Crisis, investors responded by pouring money into housing. High real estate market prices sucked in sophisticated commercial real estate investors, too. It's hard to believe that high valuations didn't drive increased investment and risk taking, but this conclusion is more controversial than most people realize.

In the late 1960s, Nobel Prize-winning economist James Tobin formalized the relationship between asset prices and investment. Tobin argued that investment increases when the price of assets rises above replacement cost and declines when the price falls below replacement cost. Why wouldn't investors build houses and sell them if the resulting market value was greater than the cost to build them? If Tobin is right, redistribution of income from investors to consumers, which lowers the demand for assets and therefore the price, discourages investment.

Consistent with Tobin's hypothesis, Harvard economist Robert Barro found a very strong causation between stock prices and investment in his 1989 study, "The Stock Market and Investment."[22] Changes in stock market values lead rather than lag changes in investment, and both stock prices and investment rates are substantially more volatile than the economy—all indicators consistent with causality. Without such a relationship, how would the economy regulate investment relative to consumption?

Federal Reserve Chairman Ben Bernanke also expressed support for the belief that asset prices affect behaviors that drive investment. He justified his decision to buy $600 billion of longer-term financial assets—namely, Treasuries—in the fall of 2010[23] by arguing that "higher stock prices will boost consumer wealth and help increase confidence, which can also spur spending. Increased spending will lead to higher incomes and profits that, in a virtuous circle, will further support economic expansion." Bernanke clearly believes the Fed's increased demand for financial assets will increase their price and that higher prices will motivate behavior. What's not clear is why the Fed's buying would drive up asset prices when investors recognize that it represents an artificial, one-time demand for assets, not sustainable long-term demand.

In response to Barro's study, former Clinton administration Treasury Secretary and director of the National Economic Council Larry Summers argues that economists can't distinguish between the effect of higher asset prices on investment rates and the extent to which higher prices merely reflect expectations of a brighter future. Perhaps expectations of the future alone drive asset prices and motivate managers to increase investment. Correlation, after all—even lagged correlation—does not prove causation.

The empirical difficulty of separating expectations from the demand for assets leaves room for proponents of income redistribution, like Summers, to argue that expectations alone price assets, that the demand for assets relative to the supply plays only a minor role in setting the price of assets, and that the price of assets plays an insignificant role in motivating investment. Obviously, advocates of income redistribution from wealthy investors to poor consumers would not want investor demand to contribute to higher asset prices or for higher asset prices to motivate increased investment. Redistributing income from rich investors and risk underwriters to poor consumers should logically lower the demand for assets and, therefore, the price of assets relative to the cost of producing them.

Summers is right, of course, that expectations of future performance affect asset prices. No economist would argue otherwise. That doesn't mean, however, that demand for assets doesn't also contribute to the price. Harvard economist Kenneth Rogoff, for example, described asset prices prior to the Financial Crisis as a "debt-fueled asset price explosion." He and Carmen Reinhart use 800 years of economic history to show that real increases in the supply of capital—in this case, debt from the trade deficit—systematically drive up asset prices.[24]

Despite the difficulty of separating expectations from the price of assets, numerous studies provide evidence of stock market prices affecting investment. A 2002 study of eighteen OECD countries over thirty years[25] found that stock market valuation had a significant effect on tangible investment spending. Studies of the Japanese stock market bubble in the 1980s[26] show that Japanese business investment soared when stock market prices were high and collapsed in the 1990s when prices were low while the rest of the world's investment grew. Given Japan's divergence from the rest of the world, it's hard to believe expectations alone shaped their investment behavior. A study for the International Monetary Fund[27] also found that U.S. stock market "volatility has independent effects on investment over and above that of stock market returns."

Simple comparisons of stock prices to rates of investment overlook a central issue: an economy can only use unrealized capital gains from rising stock prices to underwrite risk and not to grow investment. Only current production—including current production borrowed from offshore producers—can be invested or consumed. In a capacity-constrained economy, like the U.S. economy prior to the Financial Crisis, investment can only rise if consumption falls, and vice versa. Under those conditions, rising asset prices should drive up risk taking per dollar of investment as much as, if not more than, it increases the amount of investment. Unless consumption declines, tangible investments may moderate to free capacity for intangible investment if conditions favor a shift to riskier intangible investments, because investment opportunities compete with each other for funding and equity to underwrite risk.

A study of twenty-seven industries across fourteen OECD countries over twenty-five years[28] supports this conclusion. It found "investment in R&D rather than fixed capital formation appears to be the main route through which financial systems affect economic activity." R&D may be a better proxy for gauging risky intangible investments than tangible investments. Similarly, a 2002 study of "equity-dependent firms"[29] found that the investment decisions of these firms have increased sensitivity to stock market valuations. Equity-dependent firms tend to be small, faster growing, innovative technology-oriented firms. These types of firms have created almost all the jobs in the United States over the last twenty years. It hardly seems surprising that the United States, with a stock market value twice the size of Europe and Japan relative to GDP, underwrote more risk that produced innovation.

The correlation between stock market values and the historic ratio of savers to spenders in the U.S. population also provides evidence that supply and demand, and not just investors' expectations of underlying investment performance, drive equity values. It hardly seems coincidental that stock market values peaked in 2000 when baby boomers reached their prime saving years of thirty-five to fifty-four years old and fell in the late 1970s when thirty-five- to fifty-four-year-old savers fell as a percentage of the population.[30]

The anecdotal evidence is compelling, too. When Internet valuations rose in the late 1990s, venture capital poured into risky startups. Top MBA graduates, caught up in the frenzy, abandoned previously sought-after careers in investment banking, hedge funds, and LBO funds and flocked to risky Internet startups. Had market values not risen and provided opportunities to get rich quick, would behavior have changed so drastically? That seems doubtful, to say the least.

Ironically, the recent stock market and real estate booms and resulting investment frenzy even sucked in Larry Summers. As noted earlier, while president of Harvard, Summers initiated a massive expansion of Harvard and its campus when the university's endowment rose in value. Unlike managers who expect increased investments to grow their company's market value, Harvard's capital expansion could only have indirectly affected the value on its investment assets through a gradual increase in alumni giving from expanded enrollment. Was it Summers's long-term view of the future, independent of market valuations, that drove his decision to increase investment and risk? Or was he also reacting to the higher value of Harvard's investment assets? If he truly had insight into the future, why did Harvard's plans change so drastically as soon as market valuations fell? With less equity, clearly Harvard could no longer afford to take the risks Summers initiated when valuations were higher. It's hard to believe the market value of Harvard's investment portfolio didn't deeply affect these radical changes in its behavior, both before and after the run up in asset values.

Investors' Tolerance for Risk Motivates Managers

The agency problem—that the behavior of managers (or agents) is somewhat independent of the demands of investors—complicates the transmission of investors' demands to the economy. Proponents of income redistribution argue that managers do what's in their best interest; investors have limited control over their behavior. Investors may disagree with the decisions of managers, sell off the stock and drive down its price, or, similarly, income redistribution may lower market values and raise risk-aversion, but regardless, managers will look past fickle market prices and continue to take risks.

While there is some truth to this characterization, it's important to recognize that the vast majority of jobs in the U.S. economy since 1996* were created by small ventures like Google and Facebook that grew larger.[31] Active owners/founders are typically intimately involved in the operation of these companies. Also, these successful companies emerge from a much larger pool of churning failures. In most cases, these failures represent investments where founders and investors actively chose to invest.

Nevertheless, agents do manage a large swath of the U.S. economy. These managers have power, and their interests are not fully aligned with investors. Executives have undiversified once-in-a-lifetime careers. They face far more company-specific (situation-specific) risks than diversified investors who own many different companies with many situation-specific risks. The long-term value of executives' careers far exceeds their annual pay. As a result, managers tend to resist the risk of losing the success of their careers far more than they seek increased pay. Anyone who sits on company boards knows, for example, that CEOs and their executive teams are highly resistant to career-ending takeovers, even takeovers that deliver upwards of 30 percent increases in shareholder value. These differences put them at odds with investors. Ironically, the issue is not that managers will take risks despite low share prices, but rather that they won't take appropriate risks regardless of the price!

To overcome management's resistance to risk, investors have instituted exaggerated incentives—namely, pay-for-performance—to align the motivation of agents with the higher tolerance for risk of diversified investors. Wall Street, for example, aligned employee incentives with investors by allowing employees to accumulate equity in their firms based on their annual performance. Their ownership of this earned equity vested over time, typically five years. On one side of the balance, this compensation scheme motivates employees to take more risk than they otherwise might. Employees must take risks to earn bonuses. On the other side of the balance, the accumulation of employee-owned equity tempers

---

* The U.S. Census Bureau began collecting data on the number of net jobs created by size of firm in 1996.

imprudent risk taking by exposing employees to substantial loss from the value of their accumulated equity. The company's prerogative to fire employees for poor performance also tempers imprudent risk taking. Ironically, many proponents of income redistribution who have historically claimed incentives are wasteful because they don't motivate managers, now claim supercharged Wall Street incentives caused bankers to take inordinate amounts of risk.

Do these incentive schemes align the motivation of management with shareholder interest? A July 2009 study of financial industry CEO compensation,[32] for example, found that "on average, the value of stock and options . . . was more than ten times the value of the CEO's compensation in 2006. Consequently, changes in his bank's stock price [its long-term value] could easily wipe out all of a CEO's annual [or short-term] compensation. . . . Consequently, financial CEOs suffered extremely large wealth losses as a result of the [C]risis." Yet CEOs permitted substantial risk taking despite the enormous risks to themselves personally—both career and financial risk. Why?

It was not CEOs acting in the interest of their own good fortune who demanded increased risk taking, it was shareholders. At the time, shareholders believed markets were undervaluing risk and bid up the stock prices of financial companies that took more risk. As the market value of competitors who take more risk rises, the demands of shareholders on management teams whose stock price underperforms their peers grow more threatening. Senior executives, like former Clinton administration Treasury Secretary Robert Rubin, understood very well that there was no way a CEO and his team could retain their jobs as competitors took risks and successfully increased the relative value of their companies. That's why Rudin alledgedly admonished the Citigroup board of directors and senior executives to take more risk.

With CEO tenures declining from about eight years in the early 1990s to six years by 2005, it's hard to believe that CEOs and their teams aren't increasingly responsive to the demands of shareholders.[33] Two years may not seem like a lot, but it represents a 25 percent increase in turnover. And anyone who has worked through bankruptcy or near-bankruptcy has felt firsthand the difference between the demands of long-term equity holders and risk-averse short-term debt holders. The former invests for upside while the latter demands increased profit, no matter what the long-term consequences are.

ROE V. WADE INFLUENCES PRO-INVESTMENT POLITICS

It's possible, but unlikely, that small differences in culture alone can explain the very large difference in the performance of the United States relative to Europe and Japan following the introduction of the Internet. Admittedly, the evidence is circumstantial, but it hardly seems surprising that the United States differed significantly from Europe and Japan on the very incentives one expects would drive risk taking: lower labor redeployment costs, more valuable on-the-job training, greater pay-for-performance, lower marginal tax rates, greater value from avoiding loss of status, and equity in the hands of risk takers. Prior to the introduction of the Internet, those differences were not significant, nor did cultural differences produce faster relative growth in the United States.

But the questions remain: Why did these underlying incentives emerge in the United States and not elsewhere? Why does the United States have lower labor redeployment costs, more open trade borders, lower marginal tax rates, and, ultimately, more tolerance for unequal distribution of income?

By the random dint of history, the landmark Supreme Court case *Roe v. Wade* brought pro-investment voters to power in the United States. This faction, representing about 35 percent of the electorate, combined with enough of the now-mobilized social conservatives—principally the Christian Right, who vote Republican and represent 15 percent of the electorate—seized the majority and permanently shifted the political economic center to the right. Without a similar legal ruling in Europe and Japan, a similar shift in political power never occurred. Pro-labor anti-investment majorities continued to control those economies. Unlike in the United States, pro-labor majorities there raised labor redeployment costs and closed trade borders to slow the need for redeploying labor; supported unionism by strengthening trade barriers; failed to lower marginal tax rates as much as the United States; and discouraged unequal distribution of income and wealth. I've often wondered whether God is an ironic tax cutter who gave the United States *Roe v. Wade* to grow and strengthen its economy!

The United States differs from Europe and Japan in four ways. Europe and Japan have parliamentary democracies where parties represent their share of the vote. In the United States, it's winner takes all. This has distilled U.S. politics to a two-party system, and that makes it easier for a large minority of voters—in this case, pro-investment tax cutters—to join forces with another large minority of voters—the Christian Right—to seize power.

Roe might have had a minimal effect on U.S. politics were it not for the fact that Christian fundamentalists are a large enough portion of the country's population to affect the outcome of an election. Twenty-five percent of U.S. voters identify themselves as evangelical Christians. Prior to *Roe v. Wade,* evangelical Christian voters were split 15 percent Democrat, 10 percent Republican.* When Reagan endorsed the pro-life movement, these percentages reversed. Reagan combined the Christian Right with the pro-investment tax cutters to create a majority. Pro-investment tax cutters maintained control of the party, selecting fiscally conservative but socially moderate presidential candidates like John McCain, George W. Bush, Bob Dole, George H.W. Bush and Gerald Ford.

The fact that conservative Southern Democrats controlled political power throughout the southeastern United States amplified *Roe*'s political impact. As conservative pro-life voters defected to the Republican Party over *Roe*, it became increasingly difficult for

---

* A significant portion of Evangelicals are African Americans who are more committed to the Democratic Party's goal of income redistribution than to the pro-life agenda.

fiscally conservative Southern Democrats to win elections as Democrats in the South. Gradually, these conservative Southern Democrats joined the ranks of Republicans. The rise of southern Republicans at the expense of Democrats shifted political power to Republicans.

Most voters don't realize that *Roe* does more than legalize abortion. It legalizes controversial third-term abortions and takes away the electorate's right to vote on this controversial issue by making third- term abortions a judicial right rather than a legislative decision.* Third-term abortions are illegal throughout most of the democratic world. The legalization of third-term abortions, even if few women chose to have them, made opposition to *Roe* more tolerable to pro-choice moderates. The Court's denial of the electorate's right to vote on an issue where both sides have legitimate points of view—in fact, where the majority of voters oppose third-term abortions—further increased the tolerance for opposition to *Roe* by pro-choice moderates. Supporting the denial of the other side's right to vote—because one fears the possible outcome of that vote—is difficult for many to swallow when they acknowledge the reasonableness of the other side's position.

The stance of pro-investment Republicans adds to this tolerance of pro-choice voters toward their position. Pro-investment Republicans oppose outlawing abortions by shrewdly arguing that the decision should be legislative, not judicial. Pew Research shows that more than half the voters support *Roe*. Only a quarter supports a ban on all abortions. If put to a vote, support among voters

---

* Despite writing that states can prohibit abortions after "viability" in the third trimester, the Supreme Court eviscerated these limitations by allowing abortions "where it is necessary, in appropriate medical judgment, for the preservation of the life or health of the mother . . ." and by citing specific examples of what may be considered harmful to a woman's mental health, including the "stigma of unwed motherhood . . . the financial burden of raising a child" and the "distress . . . associated with the unwanted child." In *Doe v. Bolton*, it ruled against allowing a committee to determine whether an abortion was necessary to preserve the health of the mother and ruled that a doctor could make this decision based solely on his or her "best clinical judgment." In other words, a woman could have a third-term abortion if she could find a doctor willing to perform one. The Court has since reaffirmed that states cannot deny third-term abortions.

for first- and second-term abortions would assure legalization in all but a handful of states. If *Roe* remains as a judicial matter, it is far more likely that courts will outlaw abortions.

This marriage of convenience between odd bedfellows— pro-choice fiscal conservatives with pro-life social conservatives— brought the larger pro-investment faction in this coalition to power. Without the unique set of circumstances surrounding *Roe*, the United States likely would be in the same place politically as Europe and Japan with respect to well-intended but misguided anti-business economic policies. Instead, lawmakers cut marginal tax rates from an astonishing 70 percent prior to *Roe* to about 30 percent after *Roe*. They also left trade borders open and allowed labor redeployment costs to remain low.

If a politician shouts, "Tax the rich!" two-thirds of the U.S. electorate will raise their hands and shout, "Yes, and more!" As lawmakers threaten to raise the tax rate higher and higher on rich investors to distribute income to poor consumers, more and more voters will grow apprehensive about its effect on the economy, and lower their hands. A populist politician, whose objective is to redistribute income, seeks the highest tax rate possible on rich investors without losing 51 percent of the vote (or a few points more, perhaps, depending on the value of the margin of safety). A smaller tax increase that wins more of the vote unnecessarily leaves money on the negotiating table. Similarly, a politician aiming to lower taxes on rich investors seeks the largest tax cut that still captures 51 percent of the vote.

Nixon was the last Republican president before voters contested *Roe*. Without the 15 percent bloc of evangelical Christian voters in his back pocket, Nixon had to accept a 70 percent marginal tax rate to capture 51 percent of the vote. Even then, he only won the election because of the unpopularity of the Vietnam War. Eisenhower only won by accepting a 90 percent marginal tax rate! Clinton was the first Democratic president in office after voters contested *Roe*.* With only 85 percent of the vote available to him,

---

* Carter was elected before *Roe* was truly contested.

where 40 percent* of that vote supported tax reduction, Clinton could only support marginal tax rates as high as 39 percent and still capture 51 percent of the vote. With this 15 percent bloc of evangelical Christian voters in his pocket, Reagan was able to lower marginal rates to 28 percent and still capture the election. *Roe* lowered the marginal tax rate from at least 39 percent— perhaps even 70 percent to 90 percent—to 29 percent to 34 percent.

Most pro-investment tax cutters are pro-choice. They endorse the pro-life agenda for no other reason than to bring their minority bloc of voters to power. Because of this endorsement, Republicans lose a small number of pro-investment tax cutters to the Democrats. Opposing social conservatives is more important to this group than defeating redistribution—the raison d'être of populist liberal politics. These defectors admonish Republicans to move to the center socially in order to win their vote. But they fail to realize how much Republicans would have to raise taxes to win enough votes from the center of the electorate to compensate for the loss of the pro-life Christian Right. Capturing an additional 10 percent to 15 percent of the electorate at the center likely demands at least a ten-point increase in the marginal tax rate— probably significantly more. Ironically, the defection of these pro-investment tax cutters to the left increases the clout of social conservatives within the pro-investment coalition—exactly the opposite of their objective.

This permanent shift in the center to the pro-investment right had a significant effect on U.S. economic policy. People remember the Reagan administration using its alliance with the Christian Right to cut marginal tax rates, tame inflation, and implement deregulation of numerous industries, including trucking, telecommunications, and airlines. Less recognized is the administration's profound effect on labor polices and private-sector unions. By deregulating industries and leaving trade borders open to international competition, Reagan put enormous pressure on

---

* 40% = 35% / 85%

heavily unionized industries, like trucking, airlines, steel, and automobile manufacturing. He fired air traffic controllers and replaced them with non-unionized workers, symbolically signaling to business leaders that he expected them to take a more aggressive stance toward unions. His ally, Margaret Thatcher, did the same thing in the UK, suffering a large strike to weaken the coal miners' union.

Reagan recognized that high-priced union wages were little more than a tax that transferred money to union members from consumers. He also recognized that union contracts and work rules were a significant hindrance to productivity improvements and to the creative destruction necessary for innovation. Some readers may be too young to remember it, but in the decade prior to Reagan's taking office, the United States averaged close to 300 major strikes per year involving 1,000 or more workers per strike— a rate on par with the decades that preceded it. In the thirty years since Reagan, the United States has averaged fewer than fifty significant strikes per year, and only twenty per year in the last decade.[34]

Private-sector union membership peaked the year before Reagan was elected and has declined steadily since. Before he took office, in 1979 there were 15 million union members in the private sector—over 20 percent of the workforce. By 2007, there were only 9 million members despite a 40 percent increase in the workforce— a representation of only 8 percent of the workforce.

The defeat of private-sector unions reduced their clout within the Democratic Party. The success of the U.S. economy prior to the Financial Crisis further reduced employment concerns among voters. The Democratic Party shifted its focus to growing public-sector unions that were less concerned about open trade borders and government-mandated private-sector work rules and more concerned about growing government employment.

Democratic lawmakers and their public-union supporters recognize that consumers (voters) ultimately bear the increased cost of private-sector unions, closed trade borders, and the restriction on trade necessary to maintain them. They result in higher prices, slower growth, and less employment. Why would public-sector unions bite the hand that feeds them? Unlike private-sector unions, they have not pushed for these inefficiencies.

CONCLUSIONS

When you peel the onion on what drove U.S. economic performance, it's likely that *Roe v. Wade* brought pro-investment voters to power. They used that power to implement economic policies that incentivized risk taking. Those incentives accelerated innovation at a time when the advent of the Internet magnified their value.

Roe v. Wade gave the pro-business minority a unique opportunity to challenge proponents of income redistribution for a political majority in the United States. This shifted the political center away from income redistribution toward investment. Pro-investment Republicans used their newfound political power to cut marginal tax rates, maintain open trade borders, keep inflation low, and minimize regulation that would have increased labor redeployment costs.

Business investment in the United States grew as a share of GDP, especially risky investment to produce innovation. Unlike their counterparts in Europe and Japan, the most productive American workers began working longer hours—a strong indication that they were taking more risk and responsibility. Talented American employees flocked to risky start-ups and internal projects despite slim chances of success. Successful start-ups like Google, Facebook, Microsoft, Intel, Apple, and Cisco powered U.S. employment growth. Productivity growth accelerated from 1.2 percent per year prior to the mid-1990s to 2.0 percent per year afterwards, with almost all the gains coming from a doubling in the contribution of know-how.[35] The United States achieved theses gains despite less productive workforce demographics.

Europe and Japan had similarly educated workforces, access to the same technology, and an abundance of capital. Nevertheless, they produced a surprising lack of innovation. Their productivity remained mired in slow pre-1990s growth rates. With high labor redeployment costs, their business leaders fought to defend their existing manufacturing sectors from layoffs. They worked to grow employment by exporting manufactured products. These efforts diverted the attention of their talented employees away from developing innovative information technologies.

In the United States, information technology increased both the productivity of the most talented workers and the value of intangible investment. Lower labor redeployment costs and lower marginal tax rates magnified already high returns on investment. The increased prospects for success, and the increasing loss of status by those who failed to take the risks necessary to succeed, motivated increased risk taking.

Successful risk taking created valuable training grounds at companies like Microsoft, Google, Facebook, and elsewhere that solidified the continued success of the United States from innovations that followed incrementally. These companies not only trained armies of U.S. talent but also spurred investors and talented innovators to duplicate and expand on their success. A lack of similar successes in Europe and Japan shut them out of these emerging opportunities. Their reduced likelihood of success logically dampened the risk taking of investors and talented employees.

Open trade borders gave the United States access to a world filled with unused seventy-five-cents-an-hour labor and risk-averse savers eager to loan money to the United States. This allowed us to continue to grow investment and consumption even as the economy neared full capacity. Low-cost imports freed resources for other endeavors. Lower production costs and the increased availability of capital contributed to higher asset prices and increased risk taking.

It's possible that higher labor redeployment costs alone slowed European and Japanese growth; surely, it contributed significantly. But on its own, it does not explain why their leaders and investors failed to take risks to utilize labor in markets with considerably higher unemployment and underemployment than the United States. Here, talented workers walked away from robust employment opportunities to join risky start-ups almost certain to fail. They took risks despite better employment opportunities elsewhere in the United States. In Europe, young employees faced with high unemployment should have flocked to start-ups.

It's also possible that the United States simply had a more entrepreneurial culture, albeit one that did not produce differentiated results prior to the early 1990s. Perhaps culture played a role, but the United States offered substantially better payoffs for lucky risk takers than Europe and Japan, which should have motivated increased risk taking in the United States. Lower marginal tax rates, lower labor redeployment costs, more valuable on-the-job training relevant to successful start-ups, greater loss of status for failing to take risk successfully, and easier access to capital markets increased the payoffs here. More active shareholders skewed management incentive schemes heavily toward a pay-for-performance ethos and significantly shortened the tenure of CEOs. These differences put more equity in the hands of successful risk takers, which made them more willing and able to underwrite risk. Larger, more liquid capital markets were better able to parse and sell risk to the investors most willing to bear it. Political quirks that brought supporters of pro-business economic policy to power diminished labor's role in the opposition and facilitated increased investment. And open trade borders lowered costs, freed up resources for other, more valuable endeavors, and secured an influx of low-cost capital. It's hard to believe these powerful incentives didn't play a central role in the success of the U.S. economy and gradually shape its culture. Proponents of income redistribution may cavalierly continue to insist that lower marginal tax rates and payoffs generally do not motivate increased risk taking, but their argument would have a lot more credibility if the results of the United States were similar to those of Europe and Japan instead of dramatically better.

Whether incentives contributed to the success of the United States grows increasingly important as the economy shifts from a manufacturing-based economy to an economy more dependent on the risky investment needed to discover unproven innovations. Voters elect lawmakers who share their beliefs, and lawmakers act on their beliefs about the economy to guide policy. Robust employment prior to the Financial Crisis strengthened U.S. middle-class tolerance for lower labor redeployment costs, more open borders, and more unequal distribution of income despite the obvious pain caused by the increased rate of creative destruction. But confidence in the benefits of these hard-to-understand trade-offs is fragile, and high unemployment in the aftermath of the Financial Crisis has shaken that confidence.

Opponents are quick to challenge the status quo when given an opening—especially those who shoulder a disproportionate share of its cost. Unscrupulous leaders are quick to put forward popular solutions without regard for unintended consequences. They are quick to offer the false promise of improvement without risk in order to seduce followers who fear the risk of loss.

The poor and the lawmakers who represent them have seized on this opportunity to demand more redistribution of income without regard to the long-term consequences. They claim misguided incentives corrupted Wall Street bankers who then manipulated markets and that free markets don't work. They seek higher incomes through higher taxes on successful investors, more government spending, increasingly closed trade borders, and more restrictions on banking and trade. They justify these demands by claiming that culture, not incentives, predominantly motivates increased risk taking. In an era when the success of the United States requires businesses to pour money into risky investments in order to find unproven innovations, talented U.S. employees to risk their precious once-in-a-lifetime careers to lead these efforts, and investors to defer consumption to underwrite this risk, it's a dangerous time to experiment with unconventional and unproven economics.

PART II

WHAT WENT WRONG

CHAPTER FIVE

THE ROLE OF BANKS, CREDIT RATING AGENCIES, AND REGULATORS

IF THE ECONOMY was truly as robust as the portrait painted in the first section of this book, why did the mere threat of subprime defaults bring it to its knees? The value of subprime mortgages* was small relative to household net worth—about $3 trillion in 2007 relative to $64 trillion of household net worth. So small, in fact, that as late as the summer of 2007, Frederic Mishkin, a Federal Reserve Board governor, claimed the Fed's financial models of the economy indicated that even if housing prices fell by twenty percent, the slump would reduce GDP by only a quarter of one percent and add only a tenth of one percent to unemployment.[1]

Defaults have turned out to be surprisingly small as well. According to the Financial Crisis Inquiry Commission (FCIC), of the more than $2.5 trillion of subprime mortgages sold as mortgage-backed securities or through collateralized debt obligations (investment vehicles that bought mortgage-backed securities), "in

---

* The book uses the term "subprime" to include subprime, Alt-A, home equity loans, and other nonconventional mortgages except where further differentiated.

all, by the end of 2009, $320 billion worth of subprime and Alt-A tranches had been materially impaired. . . ." "Materially impaired" means that "losses were imminent or had already been suffered."[2] Why did the world's financial infrastructure and economy prove to be so fragile?

Most of the debate has centered on who started the fire. Did bankers* use predatory lending practices to dupe home owners into buying homes they couldn't afford? Did they use adverse selection or fraudulent credit ratings to syndicate these poor investment risks to naïve and unsuspecting investors? Or did misguided politicians spur demand for risky mortgages through the pressure they exerted on lenders to make subprime loans via the Community Development Act, the Community Reinvestment Act, and their eager funding of Fannie Mae and Freddie Mac?

No matter who is to blame for starting the fire, did greedy, incompetent, or fraudulent bankers unnecessarily put our financial institutions at risk by using regulatory arbitrage—the use of financial innovation to exploit regulatory loopholes—to avoid capital requirements? Or did they recklessly fund long-term loans with short-term funds, even though regulations allowed it? If so, did the Federal Reserve drive borrowers to fund risky investments with short-term debt by holding interest rates too low from 2002 to 2003? Did regulators fail to regulate banks properly because they were incompetent relative to a financial world that had grown increasingly complex? Were they "captured" politically by bankers who successfully lobbied lawmakers? Or, given the Bush administration's laissez-faire attitude, did they simply look the other way?

Opponents of government-subsidized housing blame well-intended but misguided lawmakers for increasing the supply of funding for risky, no-money-down subprime mortgages using government funding. They claim the government intentionally drove up the price of these mortgages to increase the supply of private-

* The book uses the term "banks" and "Wall Street" loosely to encompass both commercial banks that accept deposits and investment banks that do not. This usage of the terms aligns most closely with common usage. Where differences are relevant, the book delineates the differences.

sector funds for subprime mortgages, knowing that momentum investors would chase rising securities prices. Fannie Mae and Freddie Mac used low-cost financing—implicitly guaranteed by the government—to buy 30 percent to 40 percent of all the risky default-prone subprime mortgages. That was government intervention on a massive scale. It hardly seems coincidental that subprime mortgages were the focal point of defaults that triggered the Financial Crisis.

Proponents of government-subsidized mortgage lending claim Fannie and Freddie näively followed the lead of the private sector. They recognize that there would not have been a Financial Crisis had banks not eagerly participated in risky subprime lending. They also recognize that subprime defaults may have weakened banks but that defaults alone would not have caused anywhere near the damage that occurred. Panicked withdrawals rendered banks insolvent long before home owners defaulted. They blame fraudulent lending and securitization, regulatory arbitrage, bank leverage, and laissez-faire regulators for weakening the banks and causing their failure.

There is no doubt that if banks had funded loans with more long-term capital and less hair-triggered short-term debt, defaults would have been less likely to trigger withdrawals. If the government could have restricted the banks' use of short-term debt at a cost to the economy that was less than the costs of the recession, then policymakers were chiefly responsible for failing to prevent the Crisis. Obviously, if lawmakers failed to impose logical restrictions because such restrictions would have thwarted their political objectives, politicians would be to blame. If banks thwarted economically logical restrictions, whether imposed or not, that would have prevented the Crisis, then bankers were chiefly responsible. If policymakers rejected restrictions because the costs they imposed on the economy were greater than the benefits, then the failure to control triggers—like policies that encouraged subprime defaults—might have caused or contributed to causing the Crisis. It's also possible that no one is to blame.

With the benefit of 20/20 hindsight, it may seem obvious that the enormous cost of the Crisis exceeded the cost of restrictions. But regulators throughout the world have remained reluctant to limit the use of short-term debt aggressively enough to mitigate withdrawals. Even though history is chock-full of bank runs, policymakers have concluded, perhaps mistakenly, that the ongoing costs of restrictions are greater than the benefits of avoiding infrequent withdrawals and the stress it causes to the economy.

Misdiagnosing the cause of the Financial Crisis and fixing the wrong problem has costs without much benefit. Any restriction on risk taking—even inappropriate risk taking—produces both benefits and costs. Restrictions can't be refined enough to have only positive effects; the economy is simply too complex. All restrictions have costs—often, unintended costs. More importantly, failing to mitigate the true problem leaves the economy exposed to the likelihood of repeated failure. If the risks that caused the Crisis unnecessarily remain outstanding, investors and consumers will likely dial down their risk taking, and the economy will grow more slowly.

The next two chapters explore the different aspects of the debate. This chapter debunks commonly held myths about the causes of the Financial Crisis. The following chapter sets the record straight.

FINDINGS OF THE FINANCIAL CRISIS INQUIRY COMMISSION

The Financial Crisis Inquiry Commission (FCIC) issued its findings in January 2011.[3] It concluded that predatory lending and fraudulent syndication, combined with reckless overuse of short-term debt, were the primary causes of the Financial Crisis. "Collapsing mortgage-lending standards and the mortgage securitization pipeline lit and spread the flames of contagion and crisis," it states. "There was a systematic breakdown in . . . standards of responsibility . . . and ethics. . . . Lenders made loans that they knew borrowers could not afford. . . . Potential investors were not fully informed or were misled about the poor quality of the mortgages contained in some mortgage-related securities. . . .

These trends were not a secret. . . . No one in this pipeline of toxic mortgages had enough skin in the game. They all believed they could offload risks on a moment's notice to the next person in line. They were wrong." But, "To pin this [C]risis on mortal flaws like greed and hubris would be simplistic. . . . It was the failure to account for human weakness that is relevant to this [C]risis. . . . Dramatic failures of corporate governance and risk management at many systematically important financial institutions were a key cause of this [C]risis. . . . Compensation systems . . . too often rewarded the quick deal, the short-term gain . . . without proper consideration of long-term consequences. . . . Tone at the top does matter and, in this instance, we were let down. No one said 'no.' "

The FCIC concluded that the rating agencies were as culpable as other financial institutions in causing the Crisis, stating, "The failures of credit rating agencies were essential cogs in the wheel of financial destruction. . . . Investors relied on them, often blindly." The "forces at work" behind flawed ratings included "flawed computer models, pressure from financial firms that paid for ratings, the relentless drive for market share, the lack of resources to do the job despite record profits and the absence of meaningful public oversight." Moody's, the commission's case study in this area, "relied on flawed and outdated models to issue erroneous ratings on mortgage-related securities, failed to perform meaningful due diligence . . . and continued to rely on those models even after it became obvious that the models were wrong. . . . There was a clear failure of governance at Moody's. . . . The rating agencies were not adequately regulated by the Securities and Exchange Commission or any other regulator."

The FCIC also laid blame for the Crisis on regulators who failed to intervene: "Widespread failures in financial regulation and supervision proved devastating to the stability of the nation's financial markets. . . . More than 30 years of deregulation and reliance on self-regulation by financial institutions championed by former Federal Reserve chairman Alan Greenspan and others, supported by successive administrations and Congress, and actively pushed by the powerful financial industry at every turn, had stripped away key safeguards. . . . The Federal Reserve failed to meet its statutory obligation to establish and maintain prudent mortgage lending standards and to protect against predatory lending." The Federal Reserve and Treasury "did not have a clear grasp of the financial system they were charged with overseeing" and "did not recognize that a bursting of the bubble threatened the entire financial system. . . . The government was ill prepared for the [C]risis and its inconsistent response added to the uncertainty and panic in financial markets. . . . The Securities and Exchange Commission could have required more capital and halted risky practices at the big investment banks." Regulators had the authority to correct mistakes but "lacked the political will" to make corrections "in a political and ideological environment that constrained it. . . . Where regulators lacked authority they could have sought it."

The FCIC adds: "This was in no small measure due to the lack of transparency in key markets. . . . Leverage was often hidden—in derivative positions, in off-balance sheet entities, and through 'window dressing' of financial reports. . . . The dangers of this debt were magnified because transparency was not required or desired. . . . Over-the-counter [OTC] derivatives contributed significantly to this [C]risis. . . . Credit default swaps fueled the mortgage pipeline. . . . They amplified losses from the collapse of the housing bubble by allowing multiple bets on the same securities. . . . Without any oversight, OTC derivatives spiraled out of control. In addition, the existence of millions of derivative contracts of all types between systematically important financial institutions—unseen and unknown in this unregulated market—added to the uncertainty and escalated panic, helping to precipitate government assistance to those institutions."

Unlike other financial institutions that bought large quantities of risky mortgages, the FCIC absolves Fannie and Freddie: "The GSEs* contributed to, but were not a primary cause of, the [F]inancial

---

* Fannie Mae and Freddie Mac are known as government-sponsored enterprises, or GSEs.

[C]risis. . . . They followed, rather than led, the Wall Street firms." The commission also asserts that the Community Reinvestment Act "was not a significant factor in subprime lending," although the report ignores political pressure generally to increase home ownership and discourage the restriction of subprime lending.

Accusations of regulatory arbitrage are also decidedly absent in the FCIC report. The report says only that "AIG engaged in regulatory arbitrage by setting up a major business in this unregulated product [credit default swaps], locating much of the business in London, and selected a weak regulator, the Office of Thrift Supervision (OTS)."

Sophisticated investors other than bankers also avoided blame. Despite the fact that they knowingly bought risky subprime mortgages without down payments or documentation of income, the FCIC nevertheless claims investors "were not fully informed or were misled about the poor quality of the mortgages" by bankers and mistakenly "relied on [ratings], often blindly." The report clearly asserts that bankers as representatives of sellers and the government were responsible for protecting buyers from their mistaken valuations, no matter the buyers' level of sophistication.

The FCIC also ignores the role of elected officials. Their study is clearly not an inquisition of politicians but of unelected officials and private-sector executives.

Also noticeably missing from the report are top-down perspectives. Instead, the FCIC analysis is exclusively bottom-up. As mathematician Benoit Mandelbrot's fractal geometry shows, viewing problems from either the bottom up or the top down often leads to vastly different conclusions. He points out that, unlike the view from a satellite, from the perspective of an electron microscope the length of the British coastline is nearly infinite.

The FCIC, with its bottom-up approach, blames incentive systems, risk management processes,* and U.S. regulatory regimes

---

* Risk management systems are databases, mathematical formulas, and governance processes used by banks to analyze and manage the combined risks of the loans and other assets they hold on their balance sheets.

for failing to rein in risk taking, but it never compares and contrasts alternative systems that did and didn't work. In fact, it provides virtually no description or analysis of them whatsoever. Similarly, it blames Alan Greenspan's philosophy of "self-regulation by financial institutions" and financial lobbying for leaving the banking industry inadequately regulated, but again, it offers no specific examples of their victories over competing alternatives. The report makes no attempt to analyze the trade-offs at stake from imposing one regulatory regime versus another, and steadfastly refuses to make any recommendations, which avoids having to consider any real-world trade-offs. It similarly fails to put issues into an evolving economical, historical, or political context, as if context were wholly irrelevant. It is simply a chronological narrative of selected anecdotes and accusations, rather than an analysis of the various issues. The report is oddly extreme in this regard.

PREDATORY LENDING

Without a top-down perspective that looks at issues in their broader context, a laundry list of bottom-up complaints is liable to reach mistaken conclusions. The FCIC presents substantial anecdotal evidence of predatory lending and concludes that "an erosion of standards of responsibility and ethics exacerbated the [F]inancial [C]risis." The dissenting commissioners write that despite hearing "convincing testimony of serious mortgage fraud . . . the Commission was unable to measure the impact of fraud relative to the overall housing bubble. . . . It is likely that the housing bubble and the [C]risis would have occurred even if there had been no mortgage fraud." Without the benefit of a top-down perspective, how can we adjudicate these conflicting claims?

The complication with designing a mortgage suitable for low-income home ownership is making it both profitable for lenders but also affordable for home owners, despite the fact that lending to low-income home owners is riskier and therefore more expensive than lending to high-income home owners. Obviously, government-guaranteed repayment helps to solve this dilemma, but Fannie and Freddie didn't guarantee all subprime loans. They picked and chose which loans to buy and guarantee.

So-called 2/28 and 3/27 adjustable-rate mortgages (the numbers refer to years and sum to thirty years, as the loans amortize over thirty years)—the vast majority of subprime mortgages— satisfied the competing objectives of banks and home owners. Banks make these loans to home owners with poor credit histories who lack the financial wherewithal to fund substantial down payments or who can't fully document their income. These loans typically have low, fixed-rate interest-only payments, pejoratively called "teaser rates," in the first two or three years before the rate ratchets upward to compensate the lender adequately for the true risk of the loan. Both lender and borrower hope the borrower will make regular mortgage payments and establish a better credit rating. They also hope a rise in the market value of the house will improve the loan-to-value ratio of the loan (the amount of the loan relative to the value of the house), in effect earning the home owner the equity needed for a full down payment, which reduces credit risk through overcollateralization (the value of the home over and above the amount of the loan). If both occur, the borrower can refinance the loan on substantially better terms before the higher terms reflecting the home owner's poor creditworthiness kick in. For decades, housing prices have risen and home owners have profited from this arrangement.[4]

Initial teaser rates over the first two or three years of the loan leave lenders open to accusations of predatory lending, even though initially low rates are valuable to subprime home owners. Critics complain that naïve home owners may simply find the initial low rates, the prospect of home ownership, or the opportunity to borrow and spend their home equity irresistible no matter what it will cost them later. Apparently, no good deed goes unpunished! If banks don't offer subprime mortgages, critics accuse them of shutting low-income households out of the housing market. And if banks offer them, critics accuse them of predatory lending. You're damned if you do and damned if you don't.

Few critics recognize that even if housing prices fall, gains to households as tenants largely offset losses as home owners. Home owners, after all, are both landlords and tenants. A drop in the value of real estate lowers the rent of similar housing. If a home owner sells his house at a loss and rents (or buys) the now lower-cost house across the street, the savings from the reduced monthly payment will approximate the value of the home owner's lost equity. The reduction in the monthly payment is approximately equal to the interest the home owner would have earned if he had deposited his now-lost equity in the bank.

These offsetting gains and losses, however, can vary significantly from one home owner to another. A retiree planning to live off a portion of the equity in his home by selling and downsizing his housing, for example, would benefit from the reduced rent of only the downsized home while suffering a loss on the larger home. On the other hand, thirty-five percent of households rent (but aspire to own their homes), so lower home prices and rents benefit them. In most cases, home owners seeking to buy bigger houses as their families and incomes grow benefit from lower prices as well. The reduction in the price of the bigger home is more than their loss on the smaller one.

Some home owners who bought at the peak of the housing boom may be reluctant to sell their homes or default on their mortgages and prefer to continue making high monthly payments despite the availability of savings from lower rents. The vast majority of home owners, however, bought homes long before the peak and have only suffered gains and losses on paper. In most cases, the price of their homes is still up significantly, despite the Crisis. On average, the prices of houses today are about where they were in 2004 and are still up 40 percent from prices in 2000. And many home owners who bought at the peak may have done so with little or no money down, and so have suffered truncated losses far smaller than the savings available from lower rents. In fact, plenty of home owners bought before the peak, refinanced their homes at the peak, extracted and consumed their gains, and have now defaulted on their mortgages, capturing both increased consumption from gains at the peak and the monthly rent savings after the trough. Inevitably, critics will point only to the losers to make their case.

Sophisticated investors understand that it's prudent to minimize the amount of collateral they put at risk—in this case, the home owner's equity in the house. Down payments protect lenders from losses. Consider three home owners, each with $100,000 to buy an identical $100,000 house. The first one buys the house with his cash, $100,000 of equity; the second one uses 80 percent debt and 20 percent equity, leaving $80,000 in the bank upon which to earn a return; and the third uses 100 percent debt and leaves his $100,000 in the bank, again upon which to earn a return. If the house rises $20,000 in value, they each make the same gain of $20,000. If the house falls in price to $70,000 and the home owners decide to sell, who is worse off? The first home owner loses $30,000, the second $20,000—his banker loses $10,000—and the third loses nothing—and his banker loses $30,000. Each then pays the same reduced rent for the house across the street—a foreclosed home owned by the same set of banks. Reduced down payments shift risk and losses from borrowers to lenders.

The best measure, then, of whether home owners were victims of predatory lending or the beneficiaries of subprime mortgages is the amount of equity they were required to put at risk via their down payment. From 2005 to 2007, the percent of mortgages originated with loan-to-value ratios greater than 90 percent rose from 15 percent to 30 percent. For subprime adjustable-rate mortgages, originations exceeding 80 percent loan-to-value rose from 47 percent in 2002 to 64 percent in 2006. The share of subprime loans made to borrowers with "piggyback" loans—loans that finance down payments instead of home owners having to put their equity at risk—rose from 3 percent to 33 percent over the same period.[5] This is inconsistent with the notion that predatory lending caused the Financial Crisis. Predatory lending shifts risk from lenders to borrowers, not the other way around.

Analysis by Stan Liebowitz of the University of Texas of foreclosures[6] provides further evidence that, on average, home owners were the beneficiaries of loose credit standards—namely, low down payments that transferred risk to lenders—and not the victims of predatory lending. If they had been predominantly victims, interest rate resets would have been the primary cause of defaults, but that's not the case. Liebowitz's analysis of loan-level data covering 30 million mortgages shows that resets were responsible for only a small portion of foreclosures. "Loans with initial teaser rates had virtually no impact on foreclosures." In fact, "interest rate resets did not measurably increase foreclosures until the reset was greater than four percentage points," and "only 8% of foreclosures had an interest rate increase of that much."

Instead, he shows that "by far, the most important factor related to foreclosures is the extent to which the home owner now has or ever had positive equity in a home." He points out that "a simple statistic can help make that point: although only 12% of homes had negative equity, they comprise 47% of all foreclosures." He notes that the difficulty of identifying second mortgages makes his estimates conservative, and adds that "a home with negative equity does not imply that . . . [the home owner] cannot make mortgage payments so much as it implies that the borrower is more willing to walk away from the loan." In other words, home owners with little of their equity at stake walked away from their homes to capture the value of lower rents—exactly as the economics detailed above would predict.

A study by staff economists at the Federal Reserve Bank and several other studies reached nearly identical conclusions.[7] Like Liebowitz's, the Fed's study finds that, despite the fact that defaults skewed toward adjustable-rate mortgages, neither higher interest rates nor interest rate resets significantly increased defaults. Low interest rates and refinancing options mitigated this factor. Clearly, reduced down payments shifted the risk of subprime defaults from home owners to banks. They spurred defaults in the face of falling real estate prices, not interest rate resets.

Now, you might ask, Didn't home owners pay banks to bear this risk? The answer is decidedly no. Banks charged subprime borrowers low teaser rates, not high rates that reflected their increased risk. Also, spreads between risk-free rates, government rates, and benchmark mortgages narrowed significantly from 2003 to 2007, the years leading up to the Financial Crisis. This drop in spreads in the face of a large increase in subprime lending indicates that the supply of lendable funds was greater than the demand for funds. This imbalance increased the negotiating leverage of home owners, not lenders.

However, it's also true that, among mortgage deals as a whole, the outliers surely are odious. Arranging a mortgage is a complex transaction that, like the purchase of a car or a house, leaves plenty of room for negotiation between buyer and seller. Competition between lenders results in razor-thin profit margins; lenders, as a matter of course, don't start by offering their lowest price to borrowers. Like buying a car, a borrower may have to trade one lender off against another to negotiate the best possible terms. Lenders pay commissioned salesmen—real estate agents and mortgage brokers—to increase margins at the expense of buyers. All but the most naïve buyers understand this. Uninformed borrowers will likely pay a higher interest rate, closing costs, or prepayment penalties. There are shysters in every business, including mortgage brokers who will make matters worse for naïve buyers. Critics, of course, will point only to these examples. But, on average, home owners and not lenders were the overwhelming beneficiaries of these negotiations. From a top-down perspective, it's virtually impossible to conclude that predatory lending, and not credit standards that benefited home owners, was a major contributor to the Crisis.

FRAUDULENT SYNDICATION AND CREDIT RATINGS

The more relevant question is why bankers made risky loans with low down payments that shifted losses to lenders. The FCIC claims bankers made poor-quality loans because syndication, especially syndication through collateralized debt obligations (CDOs), allowed bankers to dupe naïve investors into buying risky loans.

Credit rating agencies that knew ratings were mistaken supposedly aided and abetted this fraud. Proponents of this argument, including the FCIC, point to the fact that banks—the sellers of rated securities—paid for ratings (an apparent conflict of interest) and that rating agencies competed against each other for the business of sellers by loosening ratings. These proponents ignore the fact that regulators and sophisticated investors must also fail to discern changes in the way securities are rated, despite the fact that changes should be obvious.

If banks were merely duping naïve customers, why were they holding over 40 percent of all mortgages and home-equity loans on their balance sheets rather than passing them on to investors?[8] The abrupt closure of securitization markets in the summer of 2007 caught perhaps a third of these mortgages in the pipeline for securitization. But banks were clearly holding mortgages on their balance sheets as investments, just as they always have—banks earn profits for making loans and bearing default risk. Under the hypothesis of fraud, it makes no sense for them to be holding mortgages. To counter this objection, proponents claim short-term incentives motivated bankers and other regulated investors to buy misrated securities to game internal incentive schemes. To bolster this claim, they ignore the fact that sophisticated unregulated investors bought a high percentage of these securities at identical prices.

Proponents of the fraudulent securitization argument begin by overlooking the fact that securitizations allowed investors, chiefly nonbank investors, to make down payments on behalf of home owners. Securitization splits cash flows from pools of mortgages into tranches, with non-AAA-rated tranches, including subordinated mezzanine and equity tranches absorbing losses before AAA-rated tranches suffer losses—no different than the function served by home owner down payments. Rating agencies gave AAA ratings to tranches protected by subordinated non-AAA-rated "first-loss" tranches equal to about 20 percent to 30 percent of the loan (or 20 percent to 30 percent of the value of the underlying home, in the case of a no-money-down loan), on par with a

20 percent home owner down payment. From this perspective, AAA ratings were not illogical.

In effect, AAA ratings designated assets safe enough for banks to hold. The buyers of AAA-rated tranches were not looking to the creditworthiness of home owners to protect their investment; they were looking to the market value of homes and the cushion (called overcollateralization) of subordinated tranches to absorb potential losses in the event of declines in market prices. Issuers typically sold these risky subordinated tranches to non-bank investors.

Proponents of the fraudulent securitization argument point to the widespread post-Crisis downgrades of AAA-rated mortgage debt as evidence of fraudulent ratings. But in the face of a 30 percent drop in real estate prices, the FCIC reports that "by the end of 2009, [only] $320 billion worth of subprime and Alt-A tranches had been materially impaired,"[9] meaning losses were imminent or incurred. The commission adds that "most of the triple-A tranches of mortgage-backed securities have avoided actual losses in cash flow through 2010 and may avoid significant realized losses going forward."[10] Non-bank investors, who bought the risky subordinated equity and mezzanine tranches that substituted for home owner down payments, suffered most of the losses.

It's disingenuous to claim the loss of AAA ratings is evidence of fraudulent or mistaken ratings. AAA ratings are based on 20 percent to 30 percent overcollateralization. Every investor knew that *if* real estate prices fell similarly, AAA-rated tranches would lose their high ratings. It's simple arithmetic. With the benefit of hindsight, AAA ratings conservative enough to endure the Financial Crisis would have required 50 percent overcollateralization to survive a 20 percent to 30 percent decline in real estate prices with enough overcollateralization to maintain their AAA rating. Even worse, critics who claim that regulators, banks, and investors statistically underestimated the risk of extreme events recognized that down payments would have to have been substantially thicker than historic market declines to truly assure minimal risk to ratings. If credit rating agencies had demanded home owners or lenders

FIGURE 5-1: Home Price Appreciation Relative to Other Developed Economies

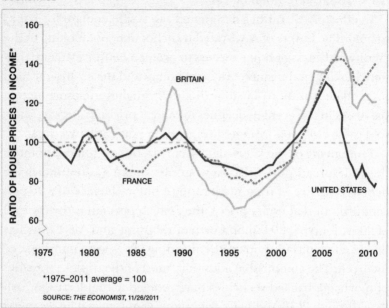

*1975–2011 average = 100

SOURCE: *THE ECONOMIST*, 11/26/2011

make 50 percent or greater equity down payments, Americans would have found mortgage financing prohibitively expensive. The world would have been very different—a place few politicians or voters would likely have tolerated. Instead, politicians demanded quite the opposite—no money down—as we will see in Chapter 6.

In effect, this line of criticism claims the rating agencies should have assessed real estate price risks more accurately than the market, despite the fact that stock markets, commodities, and real estate in other countries (Britain and France, for example, which were typical of many other countries)* rose more than U.S. residential real estate prices (see Figure 5-1).[11] And that they should have predicted a 30 percent drop in residential real estate prices,† despite U.S. real estate prices having fallen more, percentage-wise,

---

* Unlike most other countries, Germany and Japan suffered real estate declines. Japan suffered from a real estate bubble and bust in the early 1990s. Germany integrated East Germany. As surplus exporters, both exported capital.

† From 2007 to 2009

than many other advanced countries, relative to income. It rose less and declined more. Who could have predicted that?

No serious economists on either the left or the right, except perhaps those eschewing economics to demagogue the public, would argue that anyone can systematically outguess the markets, and surely not by enough of a margin to matter. The market price of assets represents the market's consensus assessment of an asset's value and the risk of the accuracy of that assessment—half assessing its value higher, and half lower. No investor can logically demand either a different or a more accurate assessment of the price than the market's.

Proponents of the fraudulent syndication argument counter by portraying mortgage investors as naïve retail investors who depended on the rating agencies and banks to analyze risk for them. But mortgage buyers, especially the buyers of risky mezzanine and equity tranches, were anything but retail customers. Historically, Wall Street has repackaged mortgages into some of the most complex financial products on the planet. Mortgages have been the purview of the largest and most sophisticated investors— banks, insurance companies, pension funds, sovereign wealth funds, and hedge funds.

Bankers, who represent sellers of mortgages—ultimately home owners—tested the price limits of buyers and discovered that, for a price, investors would eagerly buy the subordinated tranches of risky no-money-down loans from home owners with poor credit histories and undocumented income. To suggest that these buyers, even retail buyers, didn't understand what they were buying is farfetched. Declining down payments was widespread news and investors commonly referred to loans without fully documented income as "liar loans" and "NINJA" loans—no income, no job, and no assets. According to the FCIC report, "Prospectuses usually included disclaimers to the effect that not all mortgages would comply with the lending policies of the originator" and that "a substantial number or perhaps a substantial portion of the mortgage loans will represent these exceptions."[12] Once an investor agrees to buy no-money-down loans from poor credit risks who lack documented income, how much more due diligence can they logically require? None.

Irrational Exuberance

A more sophisticated version of the fraudulent syndication argument points to the fact that rating agencies rated mortgage securities more loosely than other loans, and that ratings drifted upward. There is little doubt that rating agencies bestowed low-risk AAA ratings on increasingly risky mortgage securities and that this allowed regulated financial institutions such as banks and pension funds to hold more risk than they otherwise could have. The question is whether these were fraudulent ratings that intentionally benefited rating agencies and their clients—the banks—at the expense of buyers, or if they were reflections of the market's changing, albeit mistaken, view of risk. If the latter, investors and regulators would have recognized the changes in rating standards, but would not have cared.

In part, the difference in mortgage ratings relative to other loans was an artifact of history. Prior to 2001, regulations allowed banks to hold capital adequacy reserves of 4 percent against residential mortgages, half the 8 percent required on other loans. In effect, regulators deemed mortgage assets protected by a 20 percent home owner down payment and a 3.2 percent capital adequacy reserve,* or 23.2 percent equity, safe enough for banks to hold.

After 2001, regulations established reserves based on ratings. All AAA-rated loans, whether mortgages or otherwise, required the same reserve. Banks and rating agencies worked backwards to create AAA-rated loans safe enough for banks to hold. For example, if subprime home owners made 5 percent down payments and a securitization subordinated 20 percent of its capital to the AAA-rated tranche, then 24 percent equity† protected

---

* $3.2\% = 4\% \times 80\%$

† $24\% = [5\% + [20\% \times 95\%]]$

FIGURE 5-2: Volatility of U.S. GDP

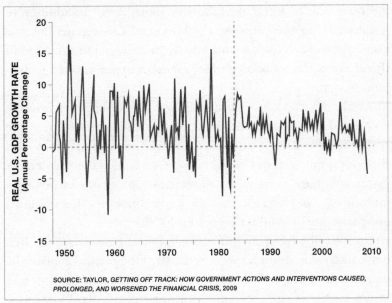

SOURCE: TAYLOR, *GETTING OFF TRACK: HOW GOVERNMENT ACTIONS AND INTERVENTIONS CAUSED, PROLONGED, AND WORSENED THE FINANCIAL CRISIS,* 2009

foreign capital flows, like the inflows that accompanied the trade deficit, have systematically increased the chances of economies misallocating resources. Economies that ran trade deficits and/or imported capital, like the United States, Ireland, and Spain, as opposed to countries that ran trade surpluses and exported capital, like Germany and Japan, tended to see unsustainable increases in the price of residential real estate relative to household incomes and a subsequent misallocation of capital to housing.

From this perspective, one might argue that had the Crisis not been caused by a meltdown in subprime mortgages, it would have been caused by something else. While there is surely a historical correlation between a rapid influx of foreign capital and the increased risk of banking crises, it's not the influx of capital per se that caused the Crisis. An influx of offshore capital increases the chances of misallocations by facilitating them; it doesn't render them a fait accompli. It is the specific uses of the capital and the economic policies that encourage those uses that cause a misallocation of resources. In this case, risk-averse offshore capital indirectly flowed into risky subprime mortgages.* In addition to understanding the causes of the Financial Crisis generally, it is also important to understand why the misallocation occurred in this sector of the economy and to take steps to prevent it from happening again.

We should also separate the value of the trade deficit and the reciprocal flow of offshore savings to the United States from the cost of misusing these funds. We took risk-averse funds and used them for unnecessarily risky purposes—we loaned them to default-prone subprime borrowers without down payments or personal guarantees, largely to increase their consumption. That was not a good investment. And it triggered the Crisis.

On the other hand, an influx of risk-bearing equity, rather than debt, likely would not have caused a banking crisis. Comparable increases and decreases in the value of equity in the 2000 Internet boom and bust, for example, did not cause a banking crisis. Rather, an influx of risk-averse capital that demanded capital preservation and on-demand liquidity, which requires bank intermediation—that is, bank-related equity to bear the risk of investing this capital—combined with overly optimistic equity providers, increased the chances of a banking crisis.

Sophisticated Buyers

The issue is not whether ratings drifted upward but whether investors failed to notice the drift and were subsequently defrauded. The FCIC makes no attempt to discern this critical difference. It's not even clear that it understands the difference. Some non-political studies, however, do shed some light on this issue.

A 2005 survey of lenders for the Bank for International Settlements (BIS)[18] found that "few respondents said that they rely solely

---

* Offshore capital bought government-guaranteed debt; the displaced investors bought short-term debt; short-term debt funded mortgages.

on external ratings, but instead use them as independent second (or third) opinions. . . . Most investors seem to be fully aware that structured finance poses different and more complex risks than ordinary credit investments. . . . When asked, several asset managers acknowledged that they were aware of the different levels of risks of structured finance versus corporate finance products with identical ratings. . . . The spread over corporate bonds with similar ratings was perceived as an attractive feature of structured finance products, despite recent spread narrowing. This spread is considered by some as a premium for complexity, which sophisticated investors seem to be eager to pick up."

The report notes that "sophisticated investors claim to have better models" than the rating agencies and that "some investors make use of the models that the rating agencies have made available to stress-test the assigned ratings with more conservative assumptions . . . Sometimes the models are also used to simulate ratings of agencies that were not involved . . . The relatively coarse filter a summary rating provides is seen, by some, as an opportunity to trade finer distinctions of risk within a given rating band." The report claims investors "appreciated . . . the transparency of rating agencies. . . . Several investors felt that the similarity in ratings was remarkable, given differences in methodology." The report concludes, "Conflicts of interest are seen to be less of a concern now than they used to be in the past. . . . In general, investors appear to be satisfied with the services provided by the rating agencies." That hardly sounds like investors overlooked miscalculated ratings.

While the report notes that some smaller investors may lack the resources to conduct these types of sophisticated analysis, we should remember that's true of all capital markets and that small investors are simply price-takers who depend on efficient markets to establish fair prices. Large, sophisticated investors, described above, are the investors who drive pricing and market efficiency.

Columbia University banking expert Charles Calomiris reaches a similar conclusion.[19] He argues that institutional investors were "well aware" that "rating agencies were rating CDOs [collateralized debt obligations] using a different scale from the normal corporate bond ratings. . . . Moody's published retrospective data on the probability of default (as of the end of 2005) for Baa [rated] CDO tranches and for Baa corporate debts. As of 2005, the Baa CDO offerings had a roughly 20 percent five-year default probability, compared to a roughly 2 percent five-year default probability for corporate Baa bonds. Despite the rhetoric rating agencies published claiming to maintain uniformity in their ratings scale, it was common knowledge before and during the subprime boom that investment grade debt issues of subprime MBS and CDO conduits were much riskier than their corporate counterparts." Again, it seems highly unlikely that investors overlooked these differences.

The notion that banks bought fraudulent ratings on specific securities in order to dupe investors is equally far-fetched. Rating agencies use proprietary models to assess risk. The rating agencies Standard & Poor's and Fitch use a "probability of default" methodology while Moody's uses an "expected loss" methodology. Sophisticated investors who set prices in the marketplace understood fully the two approaches and the nuances of difference between rating agency models. A 2009 study for the Swiss Institute of Banking and Finance[20] did find evidence that issuers of securities tended to choose rating agencies with methodologies that were favorable to the type of security they were issuing. But this is hardly revelatory to sophisticated market participants. And while their empirical evidence does find differences between methodologies and agencies, it also finds homogeneity within models and methodologies, suggesting the agencies were not bending the results of their models to meet the demands of issuers.

A study for the Bank of International Settlements[21] finds that "to the extent that investors do not fully understand the possible implications of these effects [i.e., for rating differences between agency models] . . . ratings shopping is a theoretical possibility. Evidence of this sort of strategy being applied in practice, however, is limited, suggesting that the methodological differences . . . are at least partially ironed out elsewhere in the rating process or that investors 'see through' the incentives that may arise in this context."

The report concludes, "The scope for ratings shopping should not be overstated."

Sophisticated buyers obviously knew what they were buying—recklessly risky subprime mortgages made to poor credit risks who lacked down payments or fully documented income. They recognized the risks but didn't care. In fact, the most sophisticated of these investors—hedge funds—bought the riskiest slices of securitizations—the mezzanine and equity tranches of both mortgage-backed securities and CBOs.

Overly optimistic investors eagerly provided capital in lieu of 20 percent home owner down payments, despite the risks. Investors who wanted to buy the loans were chiefly responsible for risky lending, not predatory lending, fraudulent securitization, or mistakenly optimistic but transparent credit ratings. They thought the collateral of the house would protect them from the risky standing of the home owner. Buyers who eagerly underwrote hundreds of billions of dollars of mortgage risk have only themselves to blame. We should blame them, too.

Collateralized Debt Obligations

Proponents of the argument that investors failed to recognize ratings drift point to the complexity of CDOs and demand to know how the securitization of the risky mezzanine tranches of prior mortgage securitizations can produce low-risk AAA-rated CDO securities if CDO ratings aren't fraudulent. The FCIC uses the words of James Grant (of the highly regarded *Grant's Interest Rate Observer*) to describe this as a "mysterious alchemical process." Others simply claim CDOs were used to "launder" ratings.[22]

Securitization splits the cash flow from a pool of mortgages into tranches. With increasing amounts of collateral—even subprime collateral—to pay the first-to-be-repaid tranche, the likelihood that it will be repaid grows increasingly likely—hence the AAA rating. The lower risk of the first tranche is directly proportional to the increased size and risk of the subordinated tranches, which serve as additional collateral to the first tranche. This is hardly alchemy; it's straightforward math, a simple matter of proportions. Sophisticated buyers are not confused. In fact, they are quick to arbitrage pricing differences. The FCIC notes that hedge funds commonly took offsetting positions in different tranches of the same CDO.[23] Aggressive trading to exploit price differences between tranches would have equilibrated mistaken differences.

Mezzanine tranches of securitizations were bundled into CDOs to create more AAA-rated debt by funding CDOs with additional equity and correspondingly less debt to increase the amount of collateral available to repay the CDO's debt. CDOs often also purchased credit default insurance to increase the amount of equity at risk to absorb losses. Until 2007, rising home prices also improved the loan-to-value-ratio of the CDO's collateral between the time when underlying mortgage securities were first issued and rated and when they were repackaged into CDOs.* The text of the FCIC report—whether unwittingly or otherwise—never references this fact.† Instead, it leaves the mistaken impression that the mere repackaging of debt via CDOs improved ratings, and that banks used this fraudulent alchemy to dupe investors. It makes no attempt whatsoever to explain the role of equity in credit enhancement or the extent to which investors recognized the trade-offs associated with CDOs. With hindsight, we can see that rating agencies underestimated the amount of CDO equity and collateral necessary to enhance creditworthiness fully, just as they did with the underlying mortgage-backed securities. But the ability to enhance the creditworthiness of debt by funding loans with additional equity and mezzanine debt is not, on its own, evidence of fraud.

---

* The FCIC accuses the rating agencies of willingly misrating CDOs after markets began to decline by failing to first update the ratings of underlying securities—the opposite of the situation when prices were rising. If investors had failed to recognize this error, the FCIC's accusation would be true but inconsequential relative to the magnitude of the losses underlying the Crisis.

† The FCIC report only references this fact in a graphic; it does not appear in the text of the report.

Banks logically turned to CDOs (and CDOs of CDOs—"CDO^{2}s") to raise additional mortgage-related equity to improve the credit-worthiness of underlying mortgage-backed securities as market conditions grew increasingly risky. As the demand for overcollateralized CDOs grew, the demand for the underlying securities correspondingly declined. It's simple arithmetic. The two securities are substitutes largely bought by the same investors. The FCIC ignores this link and claims that banks like Merrill Lynch duped investors using CDOs when the demand for the underlying securities declined. Because the FCIC doesn't acknowledge the role of equity and mezzanine debt, nor the substitutability of the two securities, it can't see that banks were using CDOs to raise additional at-risk capital. As the U.S. trade deficit grew, banks gradually expanded the worldwide distribution of mortgage-backed securities and raised more and more capital from non-bank investors (see Figure 5-3).

It's true that these CDOs also reduced investors' visibility and exposed investors to the unavoidable risk of adverse selection.

FIGURE 5-3: U.S. Mortgage-Backed Securities Holdings by Type of Investor

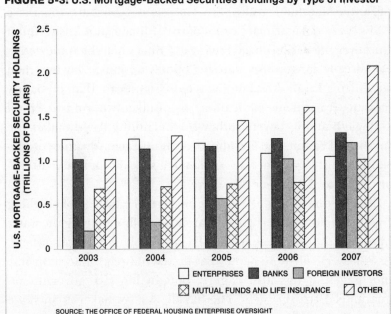

SOURCE: THE OFFICE OF FEDERAL HOUSING ENTERPRISE OVERSIGHT

These exotic securities were also more thinly traded than the underlying mortgage securities. The question is whether investors recognized these risks and therefore accepted payment to bear them. The FCIC report acknowledges, "CDOs paid better returns than did similarly-rated mortgage-backed securities."[24] Anyone who has traded mortgage-related securities recognizes the true complexities of the risks investors recognize and delineate. The assertion (without further evidence) that CDOs aided and abetted fraudulent securitization simply doesn't add up.

ULTERIOR MOTIVES FOR BLAMING BANKERS

Why then does the FCIC insist on placing the blame on bankers rather than investors? Bankers are the agents of sellers, namely, home owners. Their job is to get the best terms for sellers. Blaming bankers instead of buyers avoids several thorny issues.

First and most important, the single largest buyer of subprime mortgages was the U.S. government, through its aggressive subsidy of Fannie Mae and Freddie Mac. The report[25] concludes that these GSEs "were not a primary cause of the [F]inancial [C]risis." But if the government subsidized buying at a time when the trade deficit was already dangerously spurring blindly optimistic buying, then subsidizing Fannie and Freddie is more significant than predatory lending, fraudulent syndication, or mistakenly optimistic credit ratings. Blaming buyers rather than claiming fraud makes the funding of Fannie and Freddie more significant. Advocates of subsidized mortgages—or any government subsidy, for that matter—are eager to shift blame elsewhere.

If we blame buyers like Fannie and Freddie instead of claiming fraud, we must also recognize that successfully damming the water in one sector of the economy will cause capital to flow elsewhere. As risk-averse offshore money has flowed indirectly into subprime mortgages, it has also eagerly bought low-risk government-guaranteed Treasury debt. This has allowed lawmakers to increase expenditures without raising taxes. Access to low-cost offshore funds is inadvertently pumping up government spending by loosening the electorate's control over political initiatives. Similarly, lawmakers have promised voters and municipal labor unions retirement benefits that future taxpayers cannot afford to pay them. We must recognize policies that lead to misallocations in all forms and take steps to rationalize the incentives they distort.

Blaming buyers other than the government takes us into other deep waters. In his *New York Times* article, "How Did Economists Get It So Wrong?"[26] leading liberal economist Paul Krugman complains, "Finance economists believed that we should put the capital development of the nation in the hands of what Keynes had called a casino." He argues that "Keynes considered it a very bad idea to let such markets . . . dictate important business decisions." If not the consensus of markets—no matter how flawed they might be—then what alternative is Krugman proposing? The dictates of learned scholars who overrule investors?

Leading conservative University of Chicago economist John Cochrane counters Krugman in his September 16, 2009 paper, "How Did Paul Krugman Get It So Wrong?"[27] "Crying 'bubble' is empty unless you have an operational procedure for identifying bubbles, distinguishing them from rationally low-risk premiums." Unless you can "elaborate your theory to the point that it can quantitatively describe *how much* and *when* risk premiums, or waves of 'optimism' and 'pessimism,' can vary, you know nothing. No theory is particularly good at that right now." He goes on, "The central empirical prediction of the efficient markets hypothesis is precisely that nobody can tell where markets are going—neither benevolent government bureaucrats, nor crafty hedge-fund managers, nor ivory-tower academics." He concludes that "the case for free markets never was that markets are perfect. The case for free markets is that government control of markets, especially asset markets, has always been much worse." Accusing bankers of fraud instead of blaming overly optimistic buyers opens the door to increased regulation without engaging this central issue directly.

If there is no rational model for predicting irrational valuations, then there is not much more we can do to protect our

financial infrastructure from irrational exuberance and the resulting rise in defaults it causes except to increase capital adequacy
reserves. But we must also recognize that we are increasing reserves
to protect against aggressive government policies that promoted
and subsidized increased default-prone subprime home ownership. If a small increase in reserves provides a lot of additional
protection from bank failures, then subsidies that increase risky
home ownership may be less costly. But if banks are vulnerable to
failure despite large increases in reserves, then policies that
increase the chances of defaults are very costly.

WALL STREET INCENTIVES

To avoid these conclusions, when the FCIC blames banks as buyers
(rather than as the agents of sellers), it doesn't blame irrational
exuberance but rather poorly constructed incentive schemes that
rewarded short-term over long-term performance and failed risk
management and corporate governance systems. Ironically, liberal
economists, who advocate redistribution of income and who steadfastly claimed that incentives don't motivate managers, now insist
that they do. Again, the report does not analyze or compare these
incentive systems. Rather, it assumes they failed because banks
failed, which we will see in Chapter 6 is a very weak assumption. It
is widely recognized that panicked withdrawals leave banks vulnerable to failure under economically logical management regimes.

It's true that at some point, disincentives that instill more fear
in those with authority will obviously reduce risk taking. We can,
after all, threaten to jail people for their mistakes (although it
hasn't discouraged many criminals). Without a top-down perspective, it is impossible to know at what cost and with what probability
disincentives would have worked under varying circumstances.

Even without that perspective, the conclusion that misguided
incentives caused the Financial Crisis is inconsistent with the facts.
In Chapter 4, we saw that executives are reluctant to take risks that
jeopardize their chief asset—their once-in-a-lifetime careers. It's

hard to believe that bank CEOs would have jeopardized their careers by allocating hundreds of billions of dollars of capital to mortgages, including risky subprime mortgages and mezzanine debt, to goose their annual pay if they didn't believe these were risks worth taking. Clearly, allocations of this magnitude stemmed from top-down investment strategies formulated at the highest levels of the firms. A 2009 study of bank CEO pay[28] published by the National Bureau of Economic Research found that "on average, the value of stock and options . . . was more than eight times the value of [the CEO's annual] compensation in 2006.*. . . Changes in his bank's stock price [i.e., long-term value] could easily wipe out all of a CEO's annual [short-term] compensation . . . Consequently, financial CEOs suffered extremely large wealth losses as a result of the [C]risis." CEOs like Dick Fuld at Lehman Brothers, Stan O'Neal at Merrill Lynch, Jimmy Cayne at Bear Stearns, and others lost well over a billion dollars and the social status they each had worked a lifetime to achieve.

New Wall Street pay restrictions proposed by the FDIC on February 7, 2011, require banks to pay half the compensation of top managers in stock that can't be sold for three years. But, according to *Bloomberg Businessweek*, "many of the financial companies that ran into trouble . . . were deferring more than that before the [C]risis. . . . Lehman Brothers . . . paid more than 65 percent of each of its top executives' bonuses in restricted stock in 2007, including 89 percent for then–Chief Executive Officer Richard Fuld." None of the shares could be sold before five years. "Merrill Lynch . . . awarded its top executives more than half their compensation from 2004 to 2006 in restricted shares that vested over four years. Former CEO Stanley O'Neal received his entire $31.3 million bonus in 2004 in such restricted shares."[29] Again, actions speak louder than words. If pay were the issue, newly proposed regulation in the wake of the Financial Crisis would have modified banker pay significantly. It hasn't.

One of the only places where the FCIC provides any detail on the structure of pay is for Bear Stearns, which paid 50 percent of

---

* Average CEO tenure is only six years.

employee compensation with stock that it made employees hold for five years. (The other reference is to Citigroup's clawback scheme, although it was never invoked.) Similarly, in his book, *A Colossal Failure of Common Sense: The Inside Story of the Collapse of Lehman Brothers,*[30] Larry McDonald and others (notably in *Vanity Fair*)[31] report that close to half of the total compensation paid to senior Lehman employees was paid in stock that had to be held for five years. In his *Vanity Fair* article, "The Man Who Crushed the World,"[32] Michael Lewis reveals that his primary contact at AIG, Jack DeSantis, "watched more than half of what he'd made over the previous nine years vanish." Lewis notes, "The incentive system at A.I.G. Financial Products Group, created in the mid-1990s, wasn't the short-term-oriented racket that helped doom the Wall Street investment banks as we know it. It was the very system that U.S. Treasury Secretary Timothy Geithner, among others, had proposed as a *solution* to the problem of Wall Street pay." All three firms were at the center of the Crisis. CEOs and their executives took risks despite incentive pay that exposed them to significant downside risk. Banks weren't taking risks to game incentives; they were taking risks despite them.

Why? It's shareholders—not CEOs and employees acting in their best interests—who demanded increased risk taking. Sophisticated investors knew full well that virtually all return comes from underwriting systematic market risk, not from outperforming markets. Investors believed risk was undervalued and bid up the stock prices of financial companies that took more risks. The rising stock prices of competitors that took risk threatened the tenure of executives who failed to follow them.

Nobel laureate Edmund Phelps succinctly summarizes the case against compensation as the driving factor.[33] He argues that "we have to recognize that expectations played a role [in rising housing prices]. Speculators appear to have expected that housing prices would go sky-high, so prices climbed in anticipation. The banks, seeing that houses, offered as collateral, were worth more, responded by supplying an increasing flow of mortgage loans." From this viewpoint, speculation drove the Crisis, not Wall Street incentives. Phelps concludes: "Bubbles have long predated bonuses" and "misaligned incentives were not sufficient . . . and not necessary either" to precipitate the collapse. "The [C]risis could have happened with a 1950s financial system" just as easily as it happened in the modern-day environment. "The lesson the [C]risis teaches, though it is not yet grasped, is that there is no magic in the market: the expectations underlying asset prices cannot be 'rational' relative to some known and agreed model [of value] since there is no such model." Without a rational model of value to differentiate circumstances, incentives must either increase or decrease risk in all circumstances. Incentives can either align managers more closely with investors, or do the opposite. It's almost impossible to believe the latter could work without dangerous consequences.

Every poker player knows that some risks are worth taking, even if they turn out badly. The point of finance is to pay investors the amount necessary to motivate them to bear risk. Prices will rise and fall to equilibrate supply and demand. It's easier, after the fact, to claim that investors should not have borne the risk of subprime home owners owning rather than renting homes, or that it would have been wiser to leave short-term debt sitting idle rather than putting it to use. Before the fact, it's much harder—perhaps impossible—to draw conclusions opposite the market. Even the FCIC acknowledged that all but a handful of investors did not bet real money against the market, not even Warren Buffett.[34] Obviously, the nearly universal consensus of politicians, investors, bankers, rating agencies, and regulators was that the risks were worth bearing. Had that not been the case, prices would have changed until it was.

CAPITAL ADEQUACY REQUIREMENTS

Even if investors with sufficient knowledge eagerly bought risky, no-money-down mortgages made to poor credit risks who lacked documented incomes, this nevertheless shifted risk to banks that were large mortgage investors. This shift in risk to the banks ultimately triggered the Financial Crisis. Why didn't regulators step in and stop it? Were regulators, like others in the market, irrationally exuberant? Were regulators incompetent, as the FCIC broadly asserts, or were they "captured" by the financial services industry's lobbyists, caught under the spell of Greenspan's laissez-faire philosophy, or simply lacking in political will? Historical context clarifies the true forces that were at work.

Despite claims to the contrary, policymakers under Greenspan and in the Bush administration substantially tightened capital adequacy requirements in 2001 through changes to the Recourse Rule.[35] Prior to these changes, banking regulations required banks to hold 8 percent capital adequacy reserves against traditional loans and 4 percent against conventional residential mortgages. Banks thwarted these simple rules by splitting pools of loans into two tranches representing 10 percent and 90 percent of the loan's funding. Proceeds from a loan were used to pay the 90 percent tranche first, with the 10 percent tranche—called the "first-loss" tranche—absorbing any losses until the tranche was depleted. Obviously, the first-loss tranche contained almost all of the default risk. Prior bank regulations didn't differentiate between the tranches and allowed banks to hold the same percentage of reserves—8 percent—against each tranche. Banks held the risky but higher-yielding first-loss tranche and sold the rest of the loan to other investors. By holding 8 percent against only the 10 percent first-loss tranche, banks, in effect, held capital in reserve equal to eight-tenths of a percent of the loan (8 percent times 10 percent) against what was essentially almost all of the default risk of the loan. Despite this thin capitalization, banks remained protected by 20 percent home owner down payments that suffered losses ahead of the banks.

Changes to the 2001 Recourse Rule closed this dangerous loophole. It didn't change the overall capital adequacy requirement of 8 percent but allocated it logically to the tranches according to the level of risk (called "risk weighting" in financial parlance). It required banks to hold reserves equal to 20 percent of 8 percent against low-risk first-to-be-repaid A-rated tranches and 80 percent of 8 percent against risky, first-loss tranches. The rule also did away with the 4 percent exception for conventional mortgages, reasoning that A-rated was A-rated, no matter the type of loan.

Arguments that the 2001 changes required banks to hold only 20 percent of 8 percent against A-rated tranches and not more either unwittingly or intentionally overlook the fact that an increase in reserves held against one tranche would have come at the expense of a decrease in reserves held against other tranches unless regulators raised overall capital adequacy requirements beyond 8 percent. That radical change hasn't happened in decades. Carried out in isolation, it would have burdened U.S. banks with an insurmountable competitive disadvantage relative to foreign banks. Even in the wake of the Financial Crisis, the newly drafted Basel III Accord pushed worldwide increases in capital adequacy requirements off until 2018.

The objective of the change to the Recourse Rule was to incentivize banks to sell off the riskiest tranches to non-bank investors. This would better protect banks from default risk. In the case of a default, the bank holding AAA-rated debt would not incur losses until a drop in housing prices was large enough to eat through first the home owner's down payment and then the approximately 20 percent first-loss tranches of the loan largely sold to non-bank investors. It accomplished this objective by lowering the capital adequacy requirements on the least risky tranches and raising them enough on the most risky tranche that banks seeking to maximize their return on regulatory capital would earn a higher return by holding the least risky tranches.

A second objective of the change was to maximize the reserves held against the least risky tranche—the tranche largely held by banks. If regulations required banks to hold more than 20 percent (of 8 percent) against the least risky tranches, banks might choose to hold riskier tranches to maximize their return on regulatory capital. Less than 20 percent (of 8 percent) might allow banks to hold less reserves than what was needed to incentivize them to hold the least risky tranches. It's a simple algebraic tradeoff: 20

percent of 8 percent maximized reserves held against the least risky tranche without motivating banks to hold riskier tranches. And it worked. Banks went from holding the most risky tranches while holding almost no reserves, to holding the least risky tranches with not only a large buffer of non-AAA-rated securitized mezzanine and equity protecting them from losses, but with substantially larger capital adequacy reserves relative to the true risk of the tranches they held.

A simpleminded view that overlooks the risk associated with tranches gives the mistaken impression that banks grew increasingly leveraged, when in fact the opposite is true. Banks went from holding what appeared to be 8 percent reserves to only 2 percent reserves.* Ignoring the differences in the risk held by banks, there appears to be a fourfold increase in bank leverage.

Unfortunately, calls for increased restrictions on bank leverage, like those imposed by the Dodd-Frank Wall Street Reform and Consumer Protection Act, will cause banks to put their regulatory capital to work by shifting their holdings to riskier tranches (with larger capital requirements) unless capital adequacy reserves are raised to bring them into alignment with leverage restrictions. Again, it's a simple algebraic trade-off. If a bank is required to hold 8 percent equity (i.e., 12.5:1 leverage†) no matter the riskiness of its assets, it will hold risky assets that require 8 percent reserves, such as first-loss mezzanine debt and equity, instead of less risky assets that require 2 percent reserves.‡ Banks can't maximize returns on regulatory capital by holding low-risk tranches and leaving equity sitting idle to meet leverage limits. Making banks hold more equity has little value if regulations don't also restrict the riskiness of the assets they hold by harmonizing capital adequacy requirements with limits on leverage.

In part, that's why the Securities and Exchange Commission

---

* $\quad 8\% = [8\% \times 10\%] / 10\%; 2\% = [20\% \times 8\%] / 80\%$

† $\quad 12.5 = 1 / 8\%$

‡ $\quad$ Assets that require 2% capital adequacy reserves allow 50:1 bank leverage $(1 / 2\%)$.

(SEC) loosened leverage limits on investment banks in 2004. At the time, SEC-imposed leverage limits were tighter than capital adequacy requirements already imposed on investment banks by changes to the Recourse Rule. These leverage limits were also tighter than capital adequacy requirements that were going to be imposed on their international competitors by the Basel II Accord ratified in the same year. Critics have used the SEC's decision to loosen investment bank leverage as proof of a philosophy of deregulation. The math shows otherwise. The SEC logically allowed capital adequacy requirements, and not leverage restrictions, to be the binding constraint on investment banks. This reduced rather than increased the default risk held by investment banks. Critics fail to acknowledge that the structure of the limits placed on investment banks only allows them to increase leverage by holding comparably less-risky assets.

Some critics complain these changes to the Recourse Rule "ironically . . . increased banks' incentives to sell the residual interest in securitizations."[36] There is nothing ironic about it! The goal of the changes to the Recourse Rule was to minimize the default risk held by banks by motivating them to sell first-loss risk to non-bank investors. Similarly, critics complain that the changes increased the incentive for banks to hold "tail" risk[37]—the risk of remote events, in this case, where heavy losses have eaten through riskier first-loss tranches. Like all investors, banks earn profits for bearing risk. It's better that banks earn returns for holding low-risk assets rather than risky assets. I am reminded of a joke in which a difficult mother gives her son two ties for his birthday. The next day he wears one of them and his mother scornfully asks, "Why didn't you wear that tie I gave you?" Misleading arguments ignore tradeoffs.

Critics also often ignore the context within which regulations operate. Competition from alternatives, such as money-market funds and international banks, was forcing modernization independent of regulations. U.S. commercial banks were losing market share as money simply flowed around them (see Figure 5-4). The Fed, under the split between commercial and investment banks,

FIGURE 5-4: Banking's Share of U.S. Credit

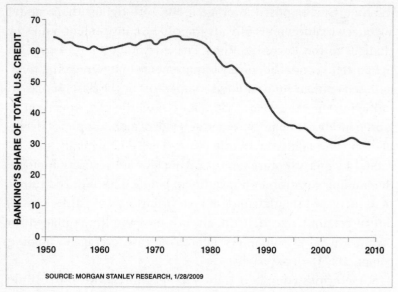

SOURCE: MORGAN STANLEY RESEARCH, 1/28/2009

was becoming the emperor without clothes, regulating a smaller and smaller portion of the financial infrastructure.

Until the Financial Crisis, international regulators were more lenient than U.S. regulators. They were late to tighten capital adequacy rules consistent with the 2001 changes to the Recourse Rule. When they did make changes, they effectively lowered the capital adequacy requirement on AAA-rated debt to 12 percent rather than the 20 percent specified in the United States. This needlessly lowered reserves necessary to induce banks to hold the least risky tranches. Their version allowed large money-center banks to determine how much regulatory capital they should hold against each tranche of repayment risk with the approval of the relevant regulatory authorities. This compromise allowed individual countries some jurisdiction over their capital adequacy standards. Because international banking plays a much larger role in European economies than it does in the U.S. economy (see Figure 5-5)—both because they seek international banking business and their publically traded capital markets are smaller relative to GDP—international regulators mistakenly lower capital adequacy requirements to compete for banking business (see Figure 5-6). U.S. regulators allowed their international counterparts to lead these changes, and then gradually allowed U.S. banks to meet the relaxed international standards rather than the tighter U.S. standards over the next three years. Had they done otherwise, U.S. banks and their regulators would have continued to lose market share.

FIGURE 5-5: U.S. Bank Assets as a Percent of GDP Relative to Other Developed Economies

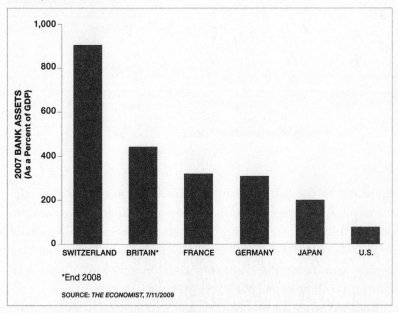

SOURCE: *THE ECONOMIST*, 7/11/2009

U.S. policymakers also reacted when Europe united under a single currency, the euro, in 1999. They expected previously fragmented European banks to consolidate and mount considerable competition to U.S. banks. In the United States (but nowhere else) the Glass-Steagall Act had separated commercial and investment banks. In 1999, legislators passed the Gramm-Leach-Bliley Act, which repealed Glass-Steagall and strengthened the competiveness of U.S. banking. The bill passed Congress with the overwhelming support of 75 percent of Democrats in the House and 84 percent of Democrats in the Senate. What little opposition

FIGURE 5-6: U.S. Bank Leverage Relative to Europe

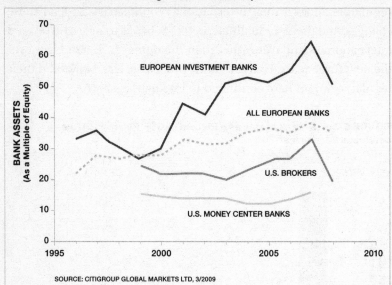

SOURCE: CITIGROUP GLOBAL MARKETS LTD, 3/2009

there was to the bill came mainly from a compromise over the strength of mortgage redlining provisions, which had nothing to do with the core issue. During that time, Credit Suisse took control of First Boston, Deutsche Bank bought Bankers Trust and Alex Brown, and Union Bank of Switzerland bought Swiss Bank, S.G. Warburg, Dillon Read, and Paine Webber.

Because of the tightening of capital adequacy rules from the 2001 Recourse Rule, banks once again became capital-intensive businesses, holding the 80 percent of loans rated AAA rather than just the 10 percent first-loss tranches (see Figure 5-7). They raised risk-bearing capital from non-bank investors to underwrite the risky subordinated tranches of securitized loans. By ignoring these layers of capital—the non-AAA-rated subordinated mezzanine and equity tranches of securitizations that bore losses ahead of capital adequacy reserves—banks superficially appeared thinly capitalized. For example, critics often claim banks imprudently financed risky no-money-down loans to poor credit risks, but they fail to acknowledge that non-bank mezzanine and equity investors

FIGURE 5-7: Shift in Riskiness of Bank Assets

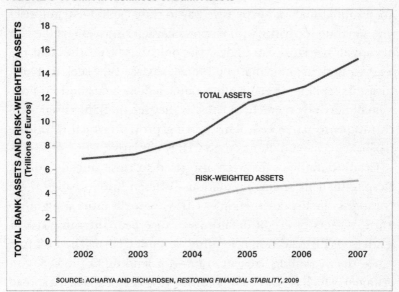

SOURCE: ACHARYA AND RICHARDSEN, *RESTORING FINANCIAL STABILITY*, 2009

principally bore the risk of home owner defaults—no different than home owner 20 percent down payments.

Under this revised and more logical regulatory regime, banks raised risk-bearing capital in three ways: through securitization described above, collateralized debt obligations (CDOs), and credit default swaps (CDSs). Traditionally, banks raised capital in "blind pools" on their balance sheets. The banks then used the funds to make loans at their discretion. They are called blind pools because at the time of their investment depositors and equity investors don't know where banks will choose to invest those funds; investors are "blind" to these decisions at the time of their investment. Small retail depositors, unable to diversify on their own, may prefer the resulting diversification from investing in blind pools, but they are increasingly becoming a smaller and smaller portion of the capital markets.

In today's more sophisticated world, large institutional investors overwhelmingly demand the ability to manage their own allocation of funds to various asset classes and risks. Blind pools prevent investors from controlling these allocations. As such, blind pools are a suboptimal and expensive way to raise capital. Parsing risks into separate securities with narrow characteristics lowers the cost of capital. Investors can underwrite only those risks they fear the least without also having to underwrite risks they seek to avoid. Investors seeking diversification can assemble a customized portfolio of narrowly segmented risks, as they see fit. Banks used securitizations to parse risk. This parsing proved critical to raising risk-bearing capital. Banks used CDOs similarly.*

Credit default swaps were also used to raise outside equity. Despite their infamous reputation—Warren Buffett called them "weapons of mass destruction"—CDSs are really quite straightforward. Writers of credit default insurance bear the same risk as lenders. With traditional lending, a lender earns the risk-free rate—the prevailing Treasury rate—for lending to the U.S. government, which is extremely creditworthy. They also earn a spread over the risk-free rate for taking the risk that borrowers who are less creditworthy than the federal government—such as businesses and home owners—might default. Banks also earn a spread for taking liquidity risk by "borrowing short and lending long." Earning spreads for underwriting default and liquidity risk is *how* and *why* banks earn profits.

Writers of credit default insurance agree to bear the default and, in some cases, the liquidity risk of lenders (chiefly banks), and earn the same return as lenders for bearing these risks. They do this, however, without funding loans. Instead, insurers stand ready to cover losses, if necessary. Insurers post collateral—akin to capital adequacy requirements—to assure buyers they have the capital to cover losses if defaults materialize. Often, the collateral is the value of their other businesses ("cross-collateralization" in financial parlance). In the event of a default, they must make the lender whole.

Some critics claim banks and AIG used CDSs to defeat capital adequacy requirements. They hypothesize that banks intentionally

---

* Structured investment vehicles (SIVs) were special-purpose CDOs also used to raise equity. The next chapter discusses SIVs in more detail.

bought bogus low-cost insurance from potentially bankrupt insurers to reduce capital adequacy requirements. But buyers have little incentive to buy insurance from risky insurance companies. If they do, they could end up buying insurance to protect themselves from events that could, should they materialize, render insurers insolvent. And regulators were quick to close this possible loophole by only allowing banks to reduce capital adequacy reserves if they bought insurance from A-rated companies.

The notion that CDSs allowed AIG and their clients to avoid capital adequacy requirements is mistaken. AIG held plenty of collateral relative to adequacy requirements. According to the Congressional Oversight Committee's 2010 study of AIG,[38] AIG underwrote a total of $527 billion of credit default risk at its peak in 2007. That may sound like a lot, but it's smaller than many of the loan portfolios of other money-center banks. Had AIG been a bank underwriting $527 billion of AAA-rated debt, it would have been required to retain $5.1 billion to $8.4 billion of equity reserves against its portfolio's default risk.* At the time, AIG was worth $250 billion. It had more than enough collateral to satisfy regulators. AIG lacked what all banks lacked in the Crisis—idle cash to fund withdrawals and meet collateral requirements.

With a better understanding of credit default swaps and their value for raising equity by better utilizing underutilized illiquid equity to underwrite risk, it's clear why Federal Reserve Chairman Alan Greenspan, Treasury Secretary Robert Rubin, and Deputy Secretary Larry Summers were all keen to encourage their growth. CDSs were a valuable means through which banks could offload risk to outside equity investors, and they were valuable to the economy generally, as demonstrated by their extraordinary growth. Because of this value, banks likely allowed CDSs to go forward in lieu of the long lead-time needed to determine logical regulations— regulations Dodd-Frank hasn't yet produced.

---

* $4.2B to $7.0B = $527B default risk × 8% reserve requirement x 12% (Basel II) to 20% (U.S. regulations prior to Basel II) risk weighting for AAA-rated debt. Even if the debt was not AAA-rated, the reserve requirement would have been only $42B = $527B x 8%.

CONCLUSIONS

The popularly accepted causes of the Financial Crisis blame predatory lending and fraudulent syndication, abetted by conflicted
credit ratings and short-term incentives. The FCIC contributes to
these beliefs, but the bottom-up anecdotes it offers as evidence don't
square with top-down logic. Critics accuse bankers of predatory
lending despite low down payments that shifted risk to lenders.
They claim bankers fraudulently syndicated loans despite it being
common knowledge that banks were making and syndicating risky,
no-down-payment loans to subprime credit risks who lacked fully
documented income. Sophisticated investors, including banks and
the government, eagerly bought these loans. The FCIC presents
little if any evidence that investors failed to recognize these risks
(including changes to ratings) or that investors were not compensated for taking these risks. In fact, the FCIC unwittingly presents
evidence that they *were* compensated. Proponents of these arguments point to CDOs improving credit ratings without acknowledging the addition of equity. They claim bankers gamed incentive
systems despite schemes that typically subjected bankers to significant long-term risks—risks whose consequences they suffered.

It is disingenuous to claim that a laissez-faire philosophy or regulatory capture held regulators under their spells. Regulators
made far-reaching improvements to capital adequacy requirements, the most important component of bank regulations. Banks
responded by selling risky, securitized mortgage-backed mezzanine debt and equity to non-bank investors. They found eager
investors willing to fully underwrite the risk of home owner
defaults. With capital equal to 20 percent or more of home values
buffering banks from defaults, credit rating agencies deemed the
other 80 percent of the loan—the AAA-rated tranche—suitable
for banks to hold. Bankers and regulators believed this layer of
non-bank capital adequately protected banks from defaults. For
the most part, they were right.

More likely, bankers, investors, credit rating agencies, and regulators all suffered from the same mistaken optimism as the markets. In fact, 800 years of financial history show that mistaken optimism is common in the face of growing offshore capital. No surprise—this was exactly the situation faced by the United States with its growing trade deficit.

The willingness of non-bank investors to underwrite real estate risk on behalf of home owners increased the likelihood of home owner defaults. When home prices fell, home owners without equity were prone to defaults. Bankers and regulators failed to recognize that home owner defaults would trigger a run on the banks despite buffers of first-loss capital large enough to protect the banks from default-related losses.

The problem with blaming the Crisis on the irrational exuberance of buyers instead of on dishonest behavior is that misplaced exuberance is unidentifiable. There is no way to protect our financial infrastructure other than by holding more capital in reserve to underwrite risk or by restricting risky lending directly. That makes the goal of increased subprime home ownership through reduced down payments and low-cost capital a nonstarter. Advocates of subprime mortgages don't want that answer, especially the ones who support the efforts of Fannie Mae and Freddie Mac to increase subprime home ownership. Unfortunately, wishful thinking is the scourge of critical thinking.

CHAPTER SIX

THE ROLE OF SHORT-TERM DEBT AND GOVERNMENT POLICY

WITH THE RATIONALIZATION of capital adequacy requirements from changes to the Recourse Rule in 2001, banks sought
non-bank investors to underwrite first-loss mortgage risk. They
found eager investors. So eager, in fact, that they underwrote
default-prone no-money-down subprime mortgages, in effect putting up the home buyers' 20 percent down payments. Bankers and
regulators expected this capital to buffer banks from default-
related losses. And it did. The FCIC estimates that subordinated
tranches of mortgage securitizations will suffer $320 billion of
default-related losses, and that most of the AAA-rated tranches
are likely to avoid losses.[1] What bankers and regulators failed to
see was that home owner defaults would trigger a run on banks
despite capital buffers large enough to absorb losses.

Three factors largely caused this bank run. First, long-standing
government policy, which allowed banks to fund loans with short-
term debt not explicitly guaranteed by the U.S. government, was
foundational. Retail deposits, explicitly guaranteed by the government, did not withdraw. Withdrawals occurred in institutional
money markets protected only by implicit government guarantees.
Had the banks been required to keep this capital idle—available
to fund withdrawals in the event of a panic—there would not have

been a financial crisis. Second, a large buildup of short-term debt enlarged the magnitude of withdrawals. And finally, a large and unexpected 30 percent drop in real estate prices triggered withdrawals. Institutions withdrew deposits from banks to protect their funds. Without explicit guarantees from the government, they had little reason to act differently.

Three additional factors increased the likelihood of panic. First, securitization facilitated the growth of default-prone no-money-down mortgages by allowing subordinated investors to make down payments on behalf of home owners. Default-prone no-money-down (and low-money-down*) mortgages increased the likelihood and magnitude of home owner defaults. The threat of defaults triggered panicked withdrawals despite buffers large enough to absorb losses. Had 20 percent home owner down payments reduced the likelihood and magnitude of home owner defaults, it's possible that depositors would not have panicked. With a 30 percent drop in real estate prices, they may well have panicked and withdrawn regardless. At the very least, it seems likely that no-money-down subprime mortgages increased the likelihood of panic. Second, government policies, which encouraged subprime lending, increased the magnitude of defaults and the likelihood of panic as well. Finally, misunderstandings about the magnitude of credit default swaps and their impact on banks in the event of withdrawals also contributed to the size and likelihood of panic.

INHERENT MISMATCH BETWEEN SHORT-TERM DEPOSITS AND LONG-TERM LOANS

Every economy has savers who are extremely reluctant to put their savings at risk, no matter the available return. They will gladly stuff their mattresses with money and accept no return for on-demand liquidity and capital preservation. They are willing to

---

* The book uses the terms "no-money-down" and "low-money-down" interchangeably.

deposit their savings in a bank or money-market fund, provided the government or bank guarantees the value of their deposits and allows them to withdraw their funds whenever they choose. The spread between short-term rates on these low-risk deposits and long-term rates on capital that bears risk is not wide enough to persuade them to bear the risk of providing long-term instead of short-term capital. Regardless of possible gain, risk-averse savers will almost never put their capital to risk.

Leaving short-term capital sitting idle causes high unemployment. Consider a simple corn economy. We can eat the corn, plant the corn, or hoard it. Hoarding the corn produces a smaller, slower-growing economy with higher unemployment. Risk taking drives economic activity. Consumers take risk by consuming an increasing share of the corn rather than hoarding it. Investors take risk by investing to expand production, lower costs, or create new products rather than consuming or hoarding. In the aftermath of the Financial Crisis, unemployment rose and growth slowed as fearful consumers and investors let the corn sit idle. Keynes described this as the "paradox of thrift"—increased saving slows growth if savers are unwilling to put their savings at risk. Lending and borrowing hoarded output, rather than letting it sit idle, increases the size of the economy, its growth rate, and employment.

Banks are the primary vehicle through which short-term savings are recycled back into investment and consumption. Loans are inherently long-term. Households that borrow money to increase consumption need years to earn enough income to repay loans. Similarly, a factory financed by loans needs years to produce enough output to pay them back. Some critics blame banks for borrowing short and lending long, but that's the purpose of banking. Long-term investors willing to put their capital at risk don't need banks.

The economic gains from borrowing short and lending long come at the risk of widespread panicked withdrawals. These withdrawals can render the economy's entire financial infrastructure insolvent. When short-term depositors rush to banks to withdraw their funds, they discover there is no money in the vault. The banks have loaned it out. To fund withdrawals, banks must sell assets—the loans in their portfolios. In the event of a run on a single mismanaged bank, the bank can sell its loans to other banks. But when a shock to the economy threatens all banks—as a 30 percent drop in real estate prices did in the Financial Crisis—it can send depositors running to banks en masse. With all banks selling loans to fund withdrawals, and no one buying them, the market value of loans sinks to fire-sale prices. Low prices make it impossible for banks to sell enough loans to fund withdrawals. This renders banks insolvent.

The outcome of this positive feedback loop is obviously highly unstable. Panics can occur for no reason other than the fear of panic itself. Depositors have no way to judge the likelihood that other depositors will panic and withdraw; they are necessarily hair-triggered in their demand for withdrawals. Fear of panic can quickly ramp withdrawals up to almost a hundred percent.

Policymakers are well aware of this risk. Withdrawals en masse have rendered banks insolvent throughout history. Policymakers have chosen to bear the risk that funds will be withdrawn in panic, because there is no reason to suffer permanent recession by leaving short-term deposits sitting idle to avoid the risk that funds will be temporarily withdrawn and sit idle—causing a temporary recession! The widespread failure of banks from temporary withdrawals is not a failure of free markets. It's a consequence of a logical policy decision.

To solve this damned-if-you-do-damned-if-you-don't dilemma, regulators rely on a two-tier safety net to reduce the risk of panicked withdrawals. They require lenders to hold capital buffers large enough to fund unexpected defaults. Banks required home buyers to make 20 percent down payments, for example, to protect them from losses in the event of a similarly sized fall in real estate prices. This holds investors, including lenders, accountable for the risk they can control—the risk that asset owners cannot repay lenders—and reduces the likelihood of losses from defaults triggering withdrawals. Rising defaults relative to these buffers increase the likelihood of defaults triggering withdrawals.

Banks also hold capital adequacy reserves to protect depositors from losses. It's hard, perhaps impossible, for banks to raise equity when panicked investors are withdrawing funds. Potential investors rightly worry that banks might withhold information about their financial condition to improve their ability to raise equity, especially in times when they need equity most. Large buffers reassure depositors that banks can withstand unexpected losses without needing to raise additional equity or sell assets.

Because withdrawals can ramp up to nearly 100 percent in times of panic, buffers large enough to fund unexpected defaults reduce the likelihood of triggering bank runs, but cannot entirely reduce the risk of withdrawals once they are triggered. Runs will occur repeatedly, if given enough time, no matter the size of the capital buffer available to cover losses. But holding idle buffers of long-term capital large enough to fund panicked withdrawals, and not just defaults, defeats the goal of putting short-term capital to work. Banks can't hold short-term capital idle to fund withdrawals in the event of a panic because it, too, would simply panic and withdraw like the rest of the short-term capital. Why would banks idle precious long-term capital that's willing to underwrite risk in order to put short-term capital to work? They would just put the long-term capital to work and leave the short-term capital sitting idle instead. But that, of course, defeats the goal of putting the short-term capital to work!

In the Financial Crisis, a 30 percent drop in real estate prices triggered panicked withdrawals. Withdrawals reached $1.5 trillion,[2] five times estimated lender losses of $320 billion,[3] which non-bank lenders largely suffered. Withdrawals reached this level despite $15 trillion to $20 trillion of explicit government guarantees.[4] Had government guarantees, or capital buffers alone, been smaller, withdrawals would have been much larger. Obviously, the cost of idling trillions of dollars of precious long-term capital—enough to guarantee withdrawals, should they occur—would be extraordinarily high, higher than the cost of idling risk-averse short-term debt.

To solve this dilemma, policymakers have chosen to supplement buffers with implicit and explicit government guarantees of liquidity rather than leaving short-term debt sitting idle. In the event of a panic, central banks, like the Federal Reserve, serve as the "lender of last resort." They fund withdrawals if they occur. The willingness of the government to guarantee the funding of withdrawals largely mitigates the need for withdrawals. In the aftermath of the Great Depression, for example, in 1934 the government created the Federal Deposit Insurance Corporation (FDIC) to insure all retail deposits. The government bore the risk but charged banks and depositors for the cost of the insurance. With the value of their deposits explicitly guaranteed by the financial strength of the government, depositors had no reason to panic and withdraw their funds, even if others panicked or if banks suffered inordinately large defaults. There wasn't a panicked run on U.S. banks in the ensuing seventy-nine years since 1929 until the Financial Crisis.

The government is the only entity large enough to provide credible guarantees without idling massive amounts of equity. When the government provides the guarantee, in effect the entire U.S. economy provides it. As the chief beneficiary of avoided recessions, why wouldn't the government, on behalf of the economy, provide these guarantees?

Remarkably, the Financial Crisis shows that the value of government guarantees is enormous and that the cost of those guarantees is cheap because the government doesn't have to set aside massive equity reserves to make its guarantees credible. Despite the $15 trillion to $20 trillion of government guarantees extended during the Crisis—including $1.5 trillion loaned by the Fed to fund withdrawals, $425 billion invested into the banks and AIG to shore up their capital reserves, and $1.5 trillion purchases of mortgages by the Fed and Treasury to prop up security prices—the Treasury expects the government to earn a profit. It only expects the bailout of the auto companies, Fannie Mae, Freddie Mac, and distressed home owners—losses related to defaults, not withdrawals—to produce significant losses.[5] The cost of providing bank guarantees is low because panic is only temporary. The government buys assets when investors panic and sells them at a profit when the panic subsides and prices bounce back.

The short-term costs, however, don't include the long-term cost of "moral hazard,"—where risk takers gain on the upside while avoiding an equivalent share of the costs on the downside. Economists (ironically, including proponents of income redistribution, who claim higher payoffs for risk-taking from things like lower marginal tax rates and higher asset prices don't significantly increase risk-taking) believe this causes risk takers to take more risk than they otherwise would. Fannie Mae and Freddie Mac had access to low-cost government-guaranteed funds, and look what happened: they bought risky subprime mortgages to maximize their profits. In the same way, deliberately underpriced government-subsidized flood insurance and after-the-fact government-financed remediation encourages home owners to build along unsafe shorelines like those bordering New Orleans. In the case of banking, policymakers believe the distortions caused by moral hazards may increase the likelihood of defaults that trigger panics.

The problem with offering insurance is pricing it properly. One price does not fit all. If the users of guaranteed funds gain on the upside and avoid losses on the downside, a uniform price will encourage the riskiest use of guaranteed funds. To reduce the risk of moral hazard, insurers like the government must charge the insured for the true cost of guarantees. It must base the cost of guarantees on the riskiness of their use. If Fannie Mae buys risky subprime mortgages, the cost of their insurance must rise to reflect this increased risk. To behave rationally, the inhabitants of New Orleans must pay a fair price to live there—a price that includes the rescue and clean-up costs we pay on their behalf. The true risks banks take are notoriously difficult to determine. Because the government is the only entity large enough to offer insurance credibly, there is also no market price for insurance.

To hold moral hazard in check, regulators have chosen to solve the complex problem of pricing insurance by offering implicit rather than explicit guarantees and by charging for those guarantees with implicit threats rather than explicit prices. This gives regulators the power to inflict insurance charges on banks after the fact for fulfilling implicit guarantees. During the Crisis, to reduce the threat of moral hazard the government effectively rank-ordered the banks based on the riskiness of their business practices and let them go under one by one, until they came to Citigroup. They allowed the Crisis to wipe out the equity of banks such as Lehman Brothers, Bear Stearns, AIG, Washington Mutual, and Wachovia, banks that took more risk than others. They required the remaining banks to raise equity when their share prices were low, which diluted the ownership of their existing shareholders. Two years after the Crisis, Citigroup's shares, for example, were down 95 percent while the rest of the stock market was down about 10 percent to 20 percent. The Treasury let Fannie Mae and Freddie Mac go bankrupt and wipe out their shareholders' equity as well.

As a matter of policy, the government logically chose to allow banks to lend short-term deposits in order to maximize employment and growth rather than leaving them sitting idle and available to fund withdrawals. It chose to use implicit guarantees rather than explicit guarantees to mitigate the risk of a run on the banks. Implicit guarantees failed in the face of a 30 percent drop in real estate prices despite capital buffers large enough to absorb losses.

They failed for three reasons. First, it's possible they never worked, but an event severe enough to matter never tested them. Second, implicit guarantees proved politically unreliable when tested. Republicans, mistakenly guided by their belief in the free market, initially voted against the Troubled Asset Relief Program (TARP) until the stock market crashed in response and their chance to win the presidential election fell precipitously. Although TARP was a small part of the overall bailout, it represented the bailout symbolically. Democrats, driven by their distrust for business, insisted the government only buy bank assets at market prices. But investors can always buy and sell assets at market prices; they don't need the government for that. Banks were insolvent at market prices and could not fund withdrawals. Selling assets to the government at fire-sale prices doesn't solve the problem of funding withdrawals. Even in the aftermath of the Financial Crisis, many Republicans and Democrats still oppose bailouts. Why would a risk-averse investor accept the implicit guarantee of unreliable lawmakers? Third, a large buildup of short-term deposits leading up to the Crisis increased the likelihood and magnitude of a potential panic. Some subset of depositors will panic and withdraw, guarantees notwithstanding. If the buildup is large, even a modest panic might be large enough to render banks insolvent, no matter the size of the guarantees.

In the years leading up to the Crisis, risk-averse surplus exporters like China gobbled up the limited amount of government-guaranteed Treasuries and GSE debt with their surplus dollars. With the amount of government-guaranteed debt limited, this pushed risk-averse dollar-denominated savings—both onshore and off—that otherwise would have purchased government-guaranteed debt into unguaranteed sectors of the economy. To compensate for the increased risk, investors shortened the duration of their lending. Retaining the right to flee at the first sign of trouble reduces an investor's risk.

At the same time, increasingly profitable companies like Microsoft and Google retained large hoards of cash, which they invested short-term. The government has never demanded or offered to let banks buy government insurance for corporate and institutional deposits the way the government requires banks to buy FDIC insurance for retail deposits. Households also moved savings from insured bank deposits to uninsured institutional money-market funds. Because of these shifts, the amount of implicitly guaranteed short-term debt grew significantly. The rapid growth in money-market funds is one manifestation of these changes (see Figure 6-1).

Today, regional banks still look like the banks of old. Retail deposits, much of which the FDIC explicitly guarantees, supply 80 percent of their capital. The availability of these funds is limited, however, and as a result, regional banks remain small and local. Retail deposits fund only a small portion of the capital of large

FIGURE 6-1: Growth of U.S. Money Market Funds

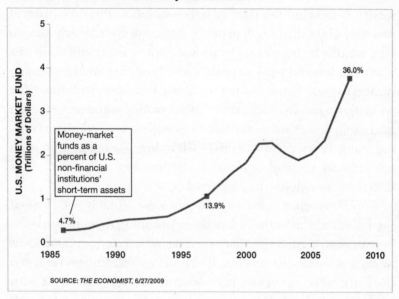

SOURCE: *THE ECONOMIST*, 6/27/2009

money-center banks. Almost all their capital comes from uninsured institutional funds. The growing size of institutional money-market funds allowed money-center financial institutions to grow large. Money-center banks are the vehicles that invest implicitly insured short-term funds. Ultimately, these debt holders panicked and ran.

Unguaranteed short-term debt flowed into commercial and investment banks in nontraditional ways, most significantly through the repo (repurchase) market. Through a repurchase agreement, banks and broker-dealers sell collateral—the financial assets of depositors, including the bank's own assets—to lenders with an agreement to buy back the collateral at a predetermined price—to repurchase it.

Because the lender owns the security, this is a very safe way for lenders to loan funds. Without explicit government guarantees, repos become a primary source of short-term risk-averse funding. At an estimated $7 trillion to $11 trillion, the repo market has become "one of the largest financial markets" and a significant source of bank financing.[6]

Just like traditional depositors, the owners of the deposited securities demand the right to sell or withdraw their securities at any time (literally, "on demand"). Broker-dealers largely accommodate this by borrowing against securities overnight. Like any other on-demand bank deposit, these funds are used by broker-dealers to make loans. During the Crisis, customers withdrew their securities—just like depositors. Without deposited securities to borrow against, banks were forced to sell assets to continue funding loans. When securities prices fell to fire-sale levels, repo lenders refused to lend against the remaining securities.[7] This effectively shut down the repo market.

Similar to repos, some securities holders, notably AIG, loaned their securities directly (rather than depositing them in banks) to borrow short-term funds. They used the proceeds from these loans to make illiquid investments. When prices fell, lenders returned the borrowers' securities and demanded their funds. As with banks, the demands for withdrawals forced security lenders to sell assets to fund their investments.

Some pundits[8] claim that mark-to-market accounting rules, which required banks to mark down the value of some assets to market prices, exacerbated the Crisis by spooking markets with low prices. The real problem with panicked withdrawals and the illiquidity of fire-sale-priced assets is hardly a simple matter of accounting. It doesn't matter where the values of securities are marked. A repo lender can estimate the market value no matter the accounting marks. What matters is whether the repo market will continue to lend against the collateral of the security. They would not.

Banks also used structured investment vehicles (SIVs) and conduits to raise short-term debt from commercial money markets. Like banks, SIVs borrowed short and loaned long. With their heavy reliance on short-term debt, lenders were quick to withdraw funding from these entities as the Crisis unfolded. SIVs became the harbinger of panicked withdrawals and a lightning rod for bank critics[9] despite their small size relative to repos and the fact that the government regulated them extensively. U.S. SIVs and conduit assets peaked at $400 billion to $500 billion in the fall of 2007,[10] and were relatively small compared to other forms of short-term lending. After the Enron scandal in 2001, all bank regulatory agencies reviewed and reissued their SIV regulations.

NO-MONEY-DOWN MORTGAGES

With short-term funds piling up, banks searched for ways to deploy them. With businesses growing increasingly self-funded, and with their direct access to long-term debt and equity markets, banks turned to mortgages. The eagerness of long-term investors to buy subordinated mezzanine and equity tranches made it easy to fund no-money-down subprime mortgages. An abundance of short-term debt funded their growth. The newly created availability of no-money-down subprime mortgages spurred households to borrow against their real estate. Why wouldn't a poor credit risk borrow money if he had little or no equity at stake? Rising real estate prices made home owners even more eager to borrow and savers to lend. Subprime mortgage lending mushroomed.

Having no home owner skin in the game increased the magnitude and likelihood of home owner defaults. As home prices fell, mezzanine and equity investors grew fearful of losses. Securitization markets abruptly closed in August of 2007 and never reopened. This left banks unable to securitize and sell accumulated mortgages to long-term investors. Without access to long-term capital, lenders' reliance on short-term financing increased. Unlike long-term capital, short-term debt matures quickly and borrowers continually need to refinance these loans. This required lenders who borrowed short and loaned long to roll over their short-term financing continually to remain solvent. As securitized mortgage markets remained closed, short-term lenders gradually lost confidence in the banks' ability to refinance their short-term loans.

It's possible that depositors would have panicked in the face of a 30 percent drop in real estate prices even if home owners had made traditional 20 percent down payments. From a depositor's perspective, it makes little difference whether home owner down payments or the mezzanine and equity tranches of securitizations protect their deposits from losses. But it's also likely that the increased threat of home owner defaults from no-money-down mortgages increased the likelihood of a bank run. The threat of defaults, after all, triggered panicked withdrawals despite capital buffers large enough to absorb losses. Fearful short-term investors overestimated the magnitude of defaults.

Non-bank investors may be willing to make down payments on behalf of home owners. God bless them and the home owners who benefit from their risky investment. But it would not be unreasonable to ban banks from funding the AAA-rated tranches of these default-prone mortgages with hair-triggered short-term debt.

U.S. SUBPRIME HOUSING POLICY

If no-money-down loans increased the likelihood and size of the panic—and surely they did—then the government's housing policy, which encouraged or even demanded such loans, did as well. Nowhere else in the world were subprime mortgages and defaults significant. In the United States, subprime, Alt-A, and home-equity loans grew to half the market. The trade deficit, the global reach of U.S. mortgage securitizations, and the United States' nonrecourse mortgage lending laws contributed to their growth. Unlike in other countries, in the United States mortgage lenders can foreclose only on a home owner's house, but not on his other possessions, to pay back their loans. Because U.S. laws protect home owners from "full recourse," they are likely to borrow more against the value of their homes and default if the value of their homes falls below the value of their mortgage. But given the magnitude of U.S. subprime mortgage lending relative to the rest of the world, it's hard to believe the government's campaign to increase subprime home ownership didn't play a major role in that difference. The government pursued an aggressive strategy to grow subprime lending. They cheered the growth of low down payment loans rather than taking steps to restrict it.

The government used legislation to pressure lenders to reduce down payments and credit standards. Its willingness—even demand—for Fannie and Freddie to buy subprime mortgages with low-cost government-guaranteed funds raised prices for these risky securitizations. Rising prices increased private-sector demand for these securities as momentum investors chased a rising market. The increased availability of funding encouraged subprime lending. Despite a large rise in subprime mortgage lending, credit standards and rates fell. This indicates an abundance of lendable funds relative to demand, which lowered borrowing costs, which pulled up demand. The federal government supplied a large portion of that abundance through Fannie Mae and Freddie Mac.

The Federal Reserve Bank of Boston planted the seeds for subprime mortgages in 1992. It produced a famous study[11] that successfully accused the banking industry of widespread discrimination against low-income and minority home buyers by using down payments, FICO scores, and documented sources of income to restrict minorities' access to mortgages. Together with its guidebook for lending,[12] the Fed threatened lenders by reminding them of their legal obligation to remedy discrimination and demanded they consider lower down payments, lower FICO scores, and undocumented sources of income as fairer ways to finance low-income home buyers.

In response to these accusations, in 1992 Congress stiffened the Housing and Community Development Act to give low- and middle-income home buyers better access to GSE* funding. The act established goals for GSE loans made to buyers with incomes below the median income. It set the initial goal at 30 percent of all GSE loans. The goal rose to 56 percent by 2008. These are tough goals to meet when you consider that a third of families, predominantly the lowest-income earners, don't own homes.

---

* As noted earlier, Fannie Mae and Freddie Mac are government-sponsored enterprises (GSEs). The two comprise the bulk of GSE assets. The book uses the term GSE to refer to both of them.

The Clinton administration also tightened regulations under the Community Reinvestment Act (CRA) in 1995 to require all financial institutions to measure and report progress against public goals for increased mortgage lending to minorities. Proponents hoped that public reporting would motivate banks to increase minority lending but scoffed at the fact that the law's compliance was only voluntary. At the same time, in 1994 the Department of Housing and Urban Development established a best practices initiative with the Mortgage Bankers Association to find ways to provide low-income borrowers better access to financing through reduced underwriting standards.

It's hard to argue that these and other steps to increase subprime home ownership were not successful: loans with minimal down payments grew steadily thereafter in the United States but not elsewhere (see Figure 6-2).

In 1995, the Clinton administration released its National Home ownership Strategy[13] with its objective to "lift America's home ownership rate to an all-time high by the end of the century." It

FIGURE 6-2: Percent of U.S. Homes Purchased with Low Down Payments

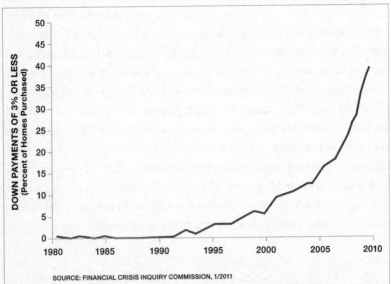

SOURCE: FINANCIAL CRISIS INQUIRY COMMISSION, 1/2011

recommended that "lending institutions, secondary market investors [principally Fannie Mae and Freddie Mac, the dominant lenders in the secondary market], and [others] . . . should work
collaboratively to reduce homebuyer down payment requirements." It also called for the increased use of "flexible underwriting criteria," which could be achieved with "liberalized affordable
housing underwriting criteria established by . . . Fannie Mae and
Freddie Mac," using "financing strategies, fueled by the creativity
and resources of the private and public sectors to help."

The logic behind Clinton's home-ownership strategy was simple: the government would use Fannie and Freddie to "prime" the
mortgage market by creating an artificial demand for risky subprime mortgages with greatly reduced down payments and credit
standards. By creating a growing demand for risky subprime mortgages, momentum investors would chase rising market prices. This
in turn would amplify the available private-sector funding for
subprime mortgages. The resulting feedback loop would become
self-reinforcing, to the benefit of subprime borrowers. Only the
government is large enough to create momentum investing in a
market as large as the mortgage market.

Assets are hard to price and notoriously prone to momentum
investing. Unlike the price of goods and services, where competition reaches a natural floor at cost, subjective assessments of the
probabilities and cost of risk drive competition for assets. The cost
of risk is often unknown until it materializes. As such, competition
between investors may never reach a natural limit. Economist
Robert Shiller noted that his housing price model for the *Wall
Street Journal* relied upon "momentum before anything else."[14] He
claimed: "When prices go up, they tend to go up for years. That's
history." Ultimately, momentum investing drove up the price of
real estate worldwide as investors underestimated the riskiness
of these assets. This same underestimation of real estate risk drove
up the price of risky mortgages.

The Clinton administration also made a change not well understood at the time that weakened the Treasury's authority to

approve the GSEs' debt issuances. According to former assistant secretary of the Treasury Emil Henry, "This hands-off approach represented an abdication of Treasury's essential oversight powers . . . and [the] strategic drift of the GSEs began soon thereafter."[15] The GSEs used their newfound authority to ramp up borrowing, which they used to fund a $1.6 trillion investment in mortgages for their own accounts (see Figure 6-3). The primary purpose for this investment was to earn profits from the difference in the GSEs' low-cost government-guaranteed financing and the higher rate earned on mortgages. Make no mistake; this was government-financed intervention into mortgage markets on a massive scale.

FIGURE 6-3: U.S. Mortgages Owned by Fannie Mae and Freddie Mac

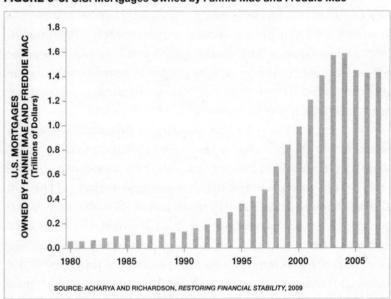

SOURCE: ACHARYA AND RICHARDSON, *RESTORING FINANCIAL STABILITY*, 2009

At the same time, the growing trade deficit flooded the world with dollars. The Asian Financial Crisis curtailed Asian investment and reduced offshore competition for dollar-denominated borrowing. The balanced federal budget reduced government-guaranteed debt. As a result, risk-averse offshore lenders flocked to GSE debt, which was implicitly guaranteed by the federal government. The portfolio of government-guaranteed mortgages mushroomed.

The GSEs were aggressive buyers and guarantors of default-prone subprime and Alt-A loans. On September 13, 2010, the Federal Housing Finance Agency (FHFA)—the regulator of Fannie and Freddie—released information on mortgages bought or guaranteed and securitized by Fannie and Freddie or securitized by Wall Street since 2001.[16] These are the mortgages sold to investors whose threatened default triggered the Financial Crisis. They represent about half of all mortgages originated over this period. Other mortgages are made and held by banks and are never securitized and re-sold to investors.

This data shows that between 2001 and 2007,* Fannie and Freddie bought about two-thirds of the non-conforming loans† and almost half of all the low-quality loans with FICO credit scores less than 660 and identified down payments of less than 20 percent‡ in these pools. They bought close to 60 percent of the toxic loans with FICO scores less than 620 and down payments of less than 10 percent. The data also shows that the GSEs used unconventional definitions of subprime and Alt-A loans to disguise the extent of their purchase from regulators and the markets, and that the GSEs were steady buyers of subprime from beginning to end. In 2006, for example, at the peak of the market, they bought two-thirds of *all* the loans with down payments of less than 10 percent, a third of all the loans with FICO scores less than 620, and 45 percent of all the loans with FICO scores less than 620 and down payments of less than 10 percent. Even if you halve these shares by assuming all loans held by banks were subprime (despite the fact that critics contend banks held the most creditworthy loans and

---

* To avoid distorting the statistics, I disregarded 2008, when securitization markets were closed, because Fannie and Freddie accounted for 100% of the mortgages originated but not held by banks.

† Conventional mortgages have traditionally had FICO scores of 720. Subprime begins somewhere below 640–660.

‡ It's not always possible to identify loans with down payments financed by third-party sources.

sold or syndicated the rest), this still represents government intervention on a massive scale.

Some ardent defenders of Fannie and Freddie, including the FCIC, pooh-pooh the significance of these statistics by arguing that the subprime loans purchased and guaranteed by the GSEs suffered lower defaults and delinquencies than loans syndicated by banks. That's true, but both pools of loans have suffered inordinately large delinquencies and foreclosures—ten times those of conventional loans. The fact that Fannie and Freddie were able to pick and choose the highest-quality toxic loans is irrelevant. Their enormous share of subprime purchases could only have distorted market pricing.

The government's intervention into mortgage markets via Fannie and Freddie was two-pronged. It not only pumped up the demand for default-prone subprime mortgages through both their own buying and the momentum-investing of the private sector, but it also diminished banks' access to the conventional mortgage. The GSEs used low-cost government-guaranteed financing to dominate the conventional mortgage market. If any loans should have been financed with hair-triggered short-term debt, it's these low-risk mortgages. Instead, the GSEs pushed banks out of the conventional mortgage market and into subprime mortgages as the supply of short-term funding grew. Banks were under pressure from their shareholders to maintain, even grow, their market shares by finding ways to put these funds to work. With Fannie and Freddie having crowded out the market for conventional mortgages, and with businesses growing increasingly self-funding, subprime lending represented a growing opportunity. Banks rushed to capitalize on it.

Politicians and policymakers fought a pitched battle for control of Fannie and Freddie precisely because their purchases mattered. In the late 1990s, Federal Reserve Chairman Alan Greenspan, Treasury Secretary Robert Rubin, and Deputy Secretary Larry Summers all objected to the growing magnitude of the GSEs' mortgage portfolio. The Bush administration's 2005 budget, released in February 2004, noted, "Even a small mistake by a GSE could have consequences throughout the economy." The budget called for a new GSE regulator housed in the Treasury Department rather than their current regulator at the Department of Housing and Urban Development, a department that had no experience regulating financial institutions like Fannie and Freddie.

A July 2009 report from the Congressional Committee on Oversight and Government Reform[17] provides details of the fight to control the policies governing Fannie and Freddie. According to the report, in 2003, prosecutors found Freddie Mac guilty of "underreporting earnings on derivatives and bonds that had dramatically increased in value due to falling interest rates between 2000 and 2003 by $5 billion." In 2004, prosecutors found Fannie Mae guilty of "deviating from generally accepted accounting principles in order to conceal losses, reduce volatility in reported earnings, present investors with an artificial picture of steadily growing profits, and to meet financial performance targets that triggered the payment of large bonuses." This ultimately led Fannie to "revise its earnings downward by $6.3 billion." The GSEs "manipulated the companies' earnings with improper accounting practices in order to hide volatility from their investors and the government."

The report concludes, "The accounting scandals caused outrage on Capitol Hill and prompted Members of Congress and the Bush administration, including Federal Reserve Chairman Alan Greenspan, to seek reform legislation that would have limited the GSEs' risky mortgage portfolios . . . Fannie Mae and Freddie Mac sought protection from their strongest political protectors, the advocates of high-risk affordable lending. The GSEs essentially doubled down on risky low down payment lending to shore up support on Capitol Hill and fend off attempted regulation. . . ." But the report notes that the GSEs "succeeded in thwarting Congressional and Bush administration attempts at reform." It notes that in 2004, Republican senators Chuck Hagel, John Sununu, Elizabeth Dole, and John McCain co-sponsored a bill that they hoped would rein in GSE lending, yet the bill emerged from the committee with an amendment that "stripped the provision which would have allowed a new regulator to limit the GSEs' leverage. This led the Bush administration to withdraw its support from the weakened legislation, which ultimately failed to pass the full Senate." Without equity at risk, the GSEs had no incentive to rein in their risky investment practices. Subsequent attempts in 2005 by the House and Senate Republicans to reform continued GSE investment also failed to pass.

The report continues, "In return for political protection from oversight and reform, however, Fannie Mae and Freddie Mac were forced to placate their congressional protectors with an ever-increasing commitment to high-risk lending. That Fannie and Freddie felt such political pressure is made clear in an email exchange [between senior executives] at Freddie Mac regarding the company's decision to not place an upper limit on the number of defaulting affordable loans the company was underwriting. Freddie Mac's senior vice president in charge of its affordable housing mission admitted that the higher default rates typical of lower-quality affordable mortgages could do serious 'harm to households and neighborhoods.' This grim reality notwithstanding, [the executive concluded] 'tipping the scale in favor of no cap on defaults at this time was the pragmatic consideration . . . [because failing to do so] would be interpreted by external critics as additional proof that we are not really committed to affordable lending.'"*

In 2006, the Bush administration struck an agreement with Freddie and Fannie to limit the size of their investment portfolios. Nevertheless, Fannie Mae still bought $180 billion of mortgages a year for its own portfolio, about 25 percent of their $725 billion holdings.[18] As home owners repaid or refinanced old mortgages, Fannie and Freddie used the proceeds to buy newer, riskier subprime mortgages. According to the congressional report, the GSEs disguised this shift in strategy by using unconventional definitions

---

* For references to additional emails, see Charles W. Calomiris, "The Mortgage Crisis: Some Insider Views," *The Wall Street Journal,* October 27, 2011.

of subprime and Alt-A mortgages, definitions "which purposely and significantly understated their commitment to subprime loans."[19] Would Fannie and Freddie have acted this aggressively without substantial support from Congress?

A study by two professors at the University of Chicago[20] shows the effect subprime lending had on poor households. It found that a burgeoning supply of funds for low-down-payment subprime mortgages encouraged poor households to borrow aggressively against the rising value of their homes and consume the proceeds. These home owners acted as if they had won the lottery and binged on consumption. With little equity in their homes, many defaulted when home prices fell.

The study shows that from 2002 to 2005, "credit growth was more than twice as high" in low-income than high-income neighborhoods. "Even [low-income] zip codes with negative absolute income growth . . . experience[d] higher mortgage credit growth than [high-income] neighborhoods with *positive absolute* income growth . . . in almost every metropolitan area of the United States." Over the period, the price of low-income housing rose more than high-income housing, even "in 17 of the 26 negative income growth subprime zip codes." The authors estimate that 40 percent of the home price growth is attributable to the increased availability of subprime lending.

Rising home prices affected the behavior of poor home owners far more than that of wealthy home owners. The study estimates that, overall, existing home owners borrowed $1.45 trillion against the rising value of their properties, 60 percent of the overall increase in debt of home owners over that period. Their household data shows that the proceeds were not "used to buy new houses, buy investment properties, or pay down costly consumer debt," but rather "was used for real outlays." Because of this debt-fueled consumption, "the default rate for low credit quality home owners increased by more than twelve percentage points from 2005 to 2008" in geographies where home prices rose significantly. Defaults increased by "less than 4%" in geographies where home prices rose less. The study estimates that, overall, 45 percent of the new defaults stem from the borrowings of existing home owners.

A clear picture of subprime economics emerges from this analysis. A poor home owner, with a home that has appreciated, extracted his equity and used it for consumption—to buy a new car, take a vacation, or send his kids to school. When his house declined in value, he defaulted and rented the identical foreclosed house across the street for a substantially smaller monthly payment. Since U.S. laws required him to put only the house up as collateral, he doesn't have to pay back the cost of the car, educations, and vacations. His cost is having to live with someone else's choice of cabinets and carpet, and a blemish on his credit record, but that's a small price to pay for the benefit of no longer having to pay the high monthly payments he agreed to pay in order to consume the things he did. Instead, he now also saves or consumes the difference between his formerly high and now lower monthly payments. This represents a massive transfer of wealth from lenders to defaulting home owners. Were it not for the deep recession and resulting unemployment it caused, a cynical politician might view this as a clever way to transfer wealth from rich investors and taxpayers to poor home owners.

While it's true that had banks not participated in subprime mortgage lending there would not have been a run on the banks, when lawmakers should have been restricting banks from holding default-prone loans they charged forward with their objective to grow subprime home ownership by reducing down payments. They were clueless about the growing risk posed by these loans. They pressured banks and the GSEs to increase subprime mortgage lending with legislation and ratcheted up their legal demands over time. They allowed Fannie and Freddie to use implicit government guarantees to guarantee or buy at least a third of all default-prone subprime mortgages. In the face of growing political opposition, they fought fiercely to maintain Fannie and Freddie's purchases. These purchases added substantially to the supply of funds chasing subprime mortgages. It drove up the prices of risky mortgage securities, which sucked in momentum investors. The burgeoning supply of funds contributed to the erosion of credit standards and the growth of no-money-down mortgages. Politicians celebrated the growth of privately financed subprime mortgages rather than acting to restrict it. Surely, their successful efforts to grow subprime lending contributed to the likelihood and size of a bank run.

CREDIT DEFAULT SWAPS

Because the Financial Crisis stemmed in large part from a temporary lack of liquidity—a lack of asset buyers—caused by panicked withdrawals and not by permanent insolvency from defaults, forward-looking equity markets stabilized in the weeks following the Lehman bankruptcy in early September 2008. The Dow stabilized at 11,000—about where it was several years later—despite political setbacks with passing TARP and extraordinary tumult in the financial sector (see Figure 6-4). This turmoil included: the bankruptcies of Fannie Mae, Freddie Mac, and AIG; the "breaking of the buck" at the Reserve Primary Fund; the acquisition and mergers of Merrill Lynch, Washington Mutual, and Wachovia; the nationalization of the British bank Bradford & Bingley and the major banks of Iceland; and the conversion of Goldman Sachs and Morgan Stanley into bank holding companies to gain access to emergency federal funding.

In the wake of this turmoil, investors grew increasingly concerned about credit default swaps (CDSs) and the magnitude of their impact on banks also contributed to the risk and size of panic. Some investors mistakenly believed credit default swaps would amplify lender losses. CDSs also made it more difficult, impossible perhaps, for investors to determine which banks were exposed to these misunderstood risks. This amplified uncertainty and added to the panic.

Remarks made by Securities and Exchange Commission Chairman Christopher Cox on October 8, 2008, typified these concerns.

FIGURE 6-4: Dow Jones Average Following the Lehman Brothers Bankruptcy

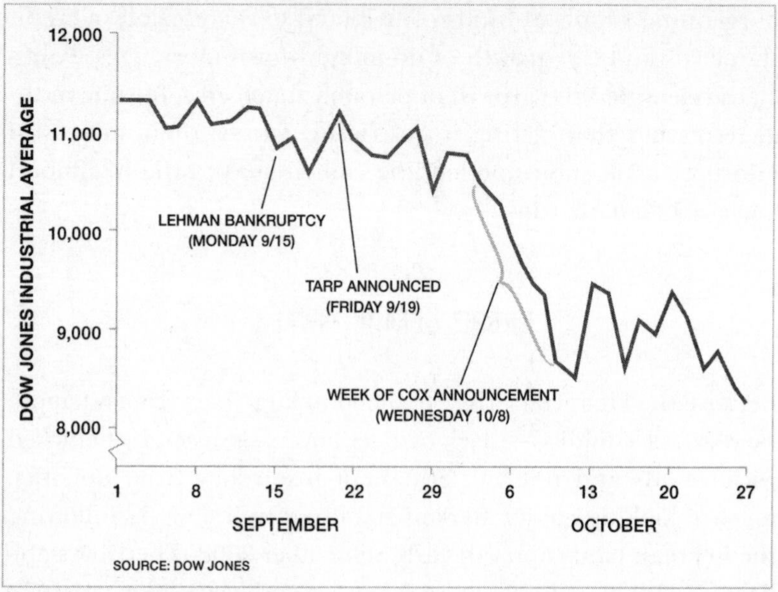

Instead of reassuring markets, Cox declared,[21] "The regulatory black hole for credit default swaps is one of the most significant issues we are confronting in the current credit crisis, and it requires immediate legislative action." He added, "It is a market that is completely lacking in transparency, and virtually unregulated." He noted that because of their large nominal exposure, "when entire asset classes fall in value, the exponentially larger losses on credit default swaps can work to amplify the risk to the financial system." He concluded that "the over-the-counter credit default swaps market has drawn the world's major financial institutions and others into a tangled web of interconnections where the failure of any one institution might jeopardize the entire financial system. This is an unacceptable situation for a free market economy."

As these fears came to the forefront, the Dow fell from 11,000 the week before Cox's remarks to 8,451 shortly after. The Chicago Board Options Exchange Volatility Index (VIX) shot up from an already high 45 to 75 over the same period (see Figure 6-5).

FIGURE 6-5: VIX Following the Lehman Brothers Bankruptcy

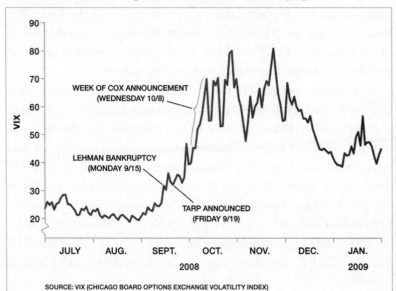

SOURCE: VIX (CHICAGO BOARD OPTIONS EXCHANGE VOLATILITY INDEX)

From there, it was off to the races. Panicked withdrawals didn't subside until the Fed guaranteed virtually all short-term debt. In total, the government issued $15 trillion to $20 trillion of guarantees. At its peak in the last quarter of 2008 and the first quarter of 2009, the Fed stepped up and bought about $1.5 trillion of short-term paper from investors who demanded withdrawals despite government guarantees.

The Fed used a variety of programs to extend these guarantees and loans. It used the Term Securities Lending Facility created prior to the Bear Stearns bankruptcy to let banks exchange illiquid collateral for liquid Treasuries so that they would have high-quality liquid collateral for repo loans. It allowed banks to use risky bank collateral at the discount window to obtain Federal Reserve loans. It extended the discount window to investment banks via the Primary Dealer Credit Facility, and allowed the Term Auction Facility, originally created in December 2007, to replace borrowing at the discount window. Eventually it used the Commercial Paper Funding Facility and the Term Asset–backed Securities Loan Facility to buy short-term paper. The FDIC's Temporary Liquidity Guarantee Program largely replaced the former. It also used the Fed's Foreign Exchange Swap Lines to extend dollar-denominated credit to other central banks.[22] Without these guarantees and funding, withdrawals would have rendered banks insolvent.

In addition to the Federal Reserve's guarantees and its purchases of short-term debt, the U.S. Treasury and Federal Reserve also replenished depleted bank reserves by investing hundreds of billions of dollars so that depositors would regain confidence and return their funding. The Treasury used TARP to invest $245 billion into the banks that were already the beneficiaries of trillions of dollars of loans and guarantees. The government used another $125 billion of TARP money to bail out General Motors and Chrysler and to help distressed home owners stay in their homes. The Fed and TARP, together, invested an additional $182 billion into AIG.

On top of all this, the Fed bought $1.25 trillion of mortgages.[23] The Treasury bought $225 million of mortgages. And to date, the government has invested $154 billion in Fannie Mae and Freddie Mac, where it expects to suffer substantial losses.[24]

With 20/20 hindsight, it's clear that Cox's comments greatly overstated the risk from CDSs, but at the time, it didn't matter. One of the market's most important regulators was adding to the market's fears about credit default swaps. Had Cox reassured markets with the truth about CDSs and AIG, the reaction might have been different.

In truth, the problems faced by AIG, the firm at the center of credit default swaps, were no different from those at other large money-center banks. Investors can use CDSs to transfer liquidity risk in addition to default risk. Credit default insurance insurers must often post an increasing amount of collateral with buyers as the market value of the underlying security falls—typically, 100 percent of the difference between the market value and the principal amount. This transfers liquidity risk to the insurer. In the event of a run on the banks, where banks are scrambling to sell assets to fund withdrawals and assets fall to fire-sale prices, the insurer must fund the difference in price, at least until prices rise again. As a result, the insurer is indirectly funding withdrawals.

What AIG, an insurer, lacked was liquidity. AIG bore the same liquidity risks as banks and suffered the same consequences. As panicked withdrawals forced sales that drove down asset prices, CDS agreements forced AIG to post increasing amounts of collateral. In effect, this required AIG to sell illiquid assets—namely, its unrelated property and casualty insurance business—to fund withdrawals. Like banks, it couldn't sell its illiquid assets fast enough to meet these demands. An inability to meet capital calls ultimately rendered AIG insolvent. The Fed extended AIG liquidity by loaning it money and buying its equity, just as it did with virtually every other money-center bank. The Fed was simply much tougher on AIG than it was on the other banks, demanding virtually all of its equity in return for agreeing to loan AIG money to fund what were, in effect, temporary withdrawals.

Some critics of the bank bailouts complained that AIG passed its borrowed government funds to banks, like Goldman Sachs, to meet their calls for collateral. They complain that the government could have negotiated lower calls. That's probably true. But what difference does it make if the government loans banks money directly to fund withdrawals or indirectly by loaning it to AIG? Either way, the government must ultimately fund the withdrawals.

At the time of the Crisis, short-term depositors did not understand why AIG collapsed. They feared credit default swaps amplified default risk and propagated that risk through the financial infrastructure in undisclosed and unanticipated ways. Short-term depositors scrambled to get out of the way.

Contrary to popular belief, CDSs do not increase or multiply risk; they merely transfer it from one investor to another.* Building a building, for example, creates risk; it may turn out not to be

* The FCIC also mistakenly claims that CDSs allow investors, in effect, to buy insurance on their neighbor's house—which is illegal—and then burn it down to collect the insurance. The reason it's not illegal with CDSs is that no investor (other than the federal government) has enough financial clout to "burn down houses" by shorting mortgages.

needed and the money spent on it would therefore be wasted. Side bets on whether the building will be needed are zero-sum; they merely transfer money from one gambler to another. Unlike the resources consumed to create an unneeded building, transfers don't create or destroy economic resources.

It's true that the secondary effect from large transfers of ownership of assets from one entity to another can destabilize the economy—if one bank transfers a huge sum of money to another and then goes bankrupt, for example—but CDSs did not destabilize banks. A 2007 Federal Reserve study[25] concluded, "Banks overall used credit derivatives to shed credit risk. Of the banks that took on credit risk with credit derivatives, exposures taken on with credit derivatives were only 2-6 percent of exposures from traditional lending. Large banks tended to be net buyers of credit protection." In other words, credit default swaps reduced rather than amplified banks' credit exposure. Banks largely used credit default swaps to reduce their credit exposure.

It is no surprise that banks were tepid buyers and sellers of credit risk using CDSs. Again, banks are in the business of earning profits for bearing credit risk. They bear that risk by making loans, not by selling credit default insurance. They reduce their exposure by selling loans to syndicated or off-balance-sheet investors. Once they have made a decision to hold or sell a loan, unless they change their minds, why would they buy what they already chose to sell, or vice versa?

The chief reason banks buy or sell risk via CDSs is that in many instances they can sell it more easily than through the cumbersome process of loan syndication, in which a bank finds investors to fund portions of a loan. Goldman Sachs did exactly that. It changed its mind about subprime credit risk and unwound its mortgage exposure as the market turned south—exactly what the taxpayers would have wanted it to do. (It may have also used CDSs to conceal its sale from investors.)

The overall transfer of risk via CDS markets is also significantly smaller than it appears. Despite large notional values of outstanding CDSs, studies have shown that approximately 90 percent of that value offsets and hedges existing positions.[26] In the case of the Lehman bankruptcy, for example, of the $72 billion of notional CDSs written on Lehman cleared by the Depository Trust & Clearing Corporation (DTCC), only $5.2 billion of cash actually changed hands once offsetting contracts were compressed.[27] The Fed study cautions, "Notional amounts are often not a good measure of the credit risk that is actually transferred in a particular transaction."

Some economists[28] claim a lack of transparency magnified the panic and that credit default swaps and collateralized debt obligation contributed greatly to opacity. Without transparency, investors cannot assess which banks will fail, so they are easily spooked and quick to withdraw their funds from all banks. With more information, presumably investors can see which banks can withstand defaults.

It's likely, however, that no amount of disclosure would have mitigated panicked withdrawals. Access to bank-specific underlying mortgages would not have provided investors with enough information to assess risks. Prior to the Crisis, investors underestimated the magnitude of real estate price declines and the cascading effect of unpredictable panicked withdrawals. Increased visibility into mortgage securities would have provided only a small portion of the information needed to determine the magnitude of these risks, if they were determinable at all. Investors and depositors would have needed a crystal ball, not data, to peer into the future and judge the price of real estate—which ultimately drove the size of defaults—to see that defaults would be smaller than expected, and predict the size of the bank run. With these factors impossible to gauge, investors logically scrambled to withdraw.

To make matters worse, modern banks loan money to one another against collateral passed between banks. If credit defaults or panicked withdrawals threaten one bank, its protracted bankruptcy proceedings may impair other banks' access to funds and collateral. When that happens, or even threatens to happen, the flow of loans and collateral through the entire network of banks can freeze like gridlocked traffic—and in the Crisis, it did. The cascading effect of a frozen financial infrastructure slows the economy, which weakens borrowers and increases defaults. In order for increased visibility to mitigate withdrawals, it must show which banks can withstand defaults, panicked withdrawals, frozen liquidity, and a rapidly deteriorating economy. It is almost certain that few, if any, banks could. In that case, visibility increases rather than decreases panic.

And even if a few banks could have withstood these extreme conditions, it costs short-term investors almost nothing to withdraw, whereas they suffer great risk if they remain invested. You stay put and analyze while I safely withdraw! With cascading effects impossible to gauge, investors logically scramble to withdraw from all banks ahead of other depositors, no matter the level of visibility.

More sophisticated arguments claim CDSs add counterparty risk, where credit insurers like AIG may default. Fear of counterparty defaults spurs panic. This is true but not unique to CDSs. In his dissent to the FCIC's report on the Crisis,[29] commissioner Peter Wallison said, "Blaming CDS for the [F]inancial [C]risis . . . is like blaming lending generally." CDSs may add nontraditional lenders like AIG to the interconnected network of banks, but it's likely that counterparty risk within the network will freeze flows between nodes with or without CDSs, exactly as it did.

The Dodd-Frank Wall Street Reform and Consumer Protection Act requires the collection of information to increase visibility, including so-called living wills, to unwind CDS positions more easily in the event of defaults. While it takes steps to separate CDSs into independent clearinghouses to reduce interconnectedness between banks, in truth it took these steps because the failure of Bear Stearns and Lehman, who served as clearinghouses for CDSs, jeopardized the functioning of CDS markets.

Separating CDSs from banks doesn't reduce the financial risk of entities that are too big and interconnected to fail. Independent clearinghouses are themselves too big and interconnected to fail and every bit as prone to failure as the handful of banks that previously cleared these trades. Both banks and clearinghouses face the same problem—systematically collecting increasing amounts of collateral from the illiquid guarantors of CDSs after assets fall rapidly to fire-sale prices.

Nor does Dodd-Frank impose designated capital requirements on clearinghouses. It recognizes that without judgment it is difficult, even impossible, to write regulations that avoid posting unnecessarily duplicative collateral for hedged positions in a market where 90 percent of the positions are hedged. It leaves margin requirements undesignated, just as regulations previously left them undesignated for the banks and other buyers of CDSs. Independent clearinghouses shift the risks associated with CDSs from banks, which previously served as clearinghouses, to independent clearinghouses, but this doesn't mitigate the risk of default.

CONCLUSIONS

Defaults didn't render banks insolvent, withdrawals did. When withdrawals forced banks to sell assets, assets sank to fire-sale prices, which made it impossible for banks to sell enough assets to fund withdrawals. This rendered banks insolvent.

The government's logical policy decision to allow risk-averse short-term savings to fund investment and consumption rather than leaving these savings sitting idle and available to fund withdrawals, comes at the risk of a run on the banks. Given enough time, a large enough fall in the price of assets, a mistaken overestimation of the likelihood of defaults, or even an irrational fear of withdrawals will eventually trigger panicked withdrawals. Leading up to the Financial Crisis, the growth of risk-averse short-term savings increased the potential magnitude of withdrawals. The trade deficit chiefly fueled this growth, albeit indirectly.

It's no surprise that a 30 percent drop in real estate prices sent risk-averse short-term savers scrambling to the banks to withdraw their deposits in order to protect them. Given 20 percent home owner down payments and similarly sized subordinated debt and equity tranches that substituted for down payments, policymakers never designed capital buffers to withstand a drop that large. The government chose to depend on implicit rather than explicit guarantees to hold short-term deposits in place in the case of an event large enough to threaten capital buffers and trigger withdrawals. Surprisingly, these implicit guarantees failed to hold risk-averse deposits in place prior to the Financial Crisis.

With the benefit of 20/20 hindsight, it's easy to claim bankers and policymakers should have seen that real estate prices were unusually high and that the risk of a fall in prices was great. There is widespread consensus among economists on both sides of the political divide, however, that asset prices are not predictable. It's possible that the abundance of short-term debt and the large-scale use of government funds to buy subprime mortgages contributed to rising real estate prices. But domestic residential real estate prices rose less than in many other countries and less than the price of other assets.

Identifying the causes of probabilistic events, like a run on the banks, is by its nature uncertain. A 30 percent drop in real estate prices may well have triggered a run on its own. And it may have triggered a run whether government guarantees were implicit or explicit. During the Crisis, withdrawals totaled $1.5 trillion despite $15 trillion to $20 trillion of explicit guarantees.

However, it's likely that the threat of defaults from no-money-down subprime loans triggered withdrawals despite capital buffers large enough to absorb losses. Low-down-payment subprime mortgages led to widespread home owner defaults. Fearful depositors overestimated the size of these defaults and had no incentive to "wait and see" if their estimates were accurate or not. Economists expect exactly this behavior. Short-term depositors are necessarily hair-triggered and investors systematically overreact. The stock market is much more volatile than the economy, for example. Had the magnitude of defaults been smaller, the threat and overestimation would surely have been smaller as well.

Given that volatile behavior, policymakers should never have allowed banks to fund the AAA-rated tranches of default-prone subprime loans with hair-triggered short-term debt. In reality, however, lawmakers aggressively encouraged, even demanded, that banks fund these loans and cheered their success when subprime home ownership grew. With the supply of funds increasing, politicians allowed the GSEs to raise low-cost government-guaranteed funds to buy $1.6 trillion of mortgages. An increase in the supply of funds available to buy subprime mortgages reduced down payments and increased mortgage security prices. Rising security prices spurred momentum investing. Surely these policy decisions added to the risk of panic.

Misunderstandings about the size of credit default swaps and their effect on banks added further to the risk of panic. The failure of AIG confused investors and increased uncertainty. Government officials unnecessarily fanned these flames at the apex of the Crisis rather than working to calm investors' concerns. Their failure to do so could have been the straw that broke the camel's back.

PART III

WHAT COMES NEXT

PREVENTING ANOTHER BANK RUN

THE FINANCIAL CRISIS leaves the United States with three unresolved issues: How does America protect its economy from another crisis? How does it reduce unemployment and revive growth? And how does it balance the federal budget—by raising taxes or cutting costs? The next three chapters take each in turn.

In the aftermath of the Crisis, voters and lawmakers have insisted that regulators reduce the likelihood of another crisis. They claim taxpayers provided guarantees that made bankers and their investors rich and saved them from ruin. They demand compensation for these guarantees and a reduction in imprudent risk taking.

Two schools of thought have emerged to address these demands. The prevailing school seeks to reduce government guarantees by pushing the risk of insolvency back onto the banks. If we allow banks to fail, presumably they will moderate the risk taking that caused the Crisis. This philosophy underlies the demand to reduce the size of banks that are "too big to fail." A related line of thinking simply imposes increased regulation on banks to reduce risk taking and increase capital buffers available to absorb losses. An ancillary line of logic seeks to reduce the amount of risk-averse short-term capital available to lend by balancing international trade. It's likely the United States can only accomplish this by restricting free trade.

A combination of these three efforts will rein in risk taking, but the country is likely to accomplish this at a cost that outweighs the benefits. The United States took risks necessary to reach full employment prior to the Crisis, and it did so without taking the risk of withdrawals into consideration. Lenders and borrowers assumed government guarantees would hold short-term deposits in place, just as they had for seventy-nine years. If the risk of damage from withdrawals remains outstanding, the economy must dial down risk taking to compensate for this now-recognized risk. If investors hold equity idle to reduce the risk of withdrawals, they can't use it to underwrite the risk of other endeavors. The use of equity to underwrite risk is zero-sum. In either case, the economy will contract, growth will slow, and unemployment will rise— exactly as has happened. The cost of permanently slower growth and higher unemployment is far greater than the temporary damage caused by infrequent withdrawals.

Restricting imports cuts the United States off from cheap labor and capital. Prior to the Crisis, lower-cost offshore goods increased the relative value of domestic goods and services, which was in no way different than any other innovation that reduces cost. This accelerated growth and provided the additional resources needed to produce that growth. The offshore demand for assets rather than goods for consumption allowed the United States to shift its production to investment. Investment in innovation proved to be far more valuable than production for consumption, especially the production we sourced offshore.

To achieve full employment, the United States must use its equity to underwrite the risk of using risk-averse short-term off-shore savings to fund consumption or investment rather than leaving these risk-averse funds sitting idle. It was easy to persuade home owners with poor credit ratings and without home owner equity at risk to borrow and consume these funds. It might be harder to find alternative uses. None are obvious. It will surely take time to find them; but the economy has always found alternatives. The harder task had always been persuading long-term investors to underwrite the risk of using these funds by putting up down payments on behalf of home owners through their willingness to fund the non-AAA-rated subordinated tranches of mortgage securitizations. Rising prices for homes and subprime mortgage securities made that task easier. But rising prices were hardly unique to housing. Housing was one of the worst-performing assets, after all.

A better alternative for putting these funds to work while avoiding another crisis is strengthening government guarantees of liquidity to reduce the risk of withdrawals while taking steps to reduce the risk of moral hazard that accompany guarantees. Rather than shrinking growth and employment, this alternative would accelerate it. This is especially important now. With unemployment high, the United States must transition from an unsustainable use of short-term debt that funded subprime consumption to more sustainable uses of this capital. However, rather than taking the risks necessary to find these new alternatives, the country has dialed down risk taking in the aftermath of the Crisis by leaving short-term savings sitting idle to compensate for the now-recognized risk of damage from withdrawals.

The government can make such guarantees at a lower cost than the private sector can. Because of its size, it needn't hold equity idle to make its guarantees credible. Because withdrawals are only temporary, the government can expect to turn a profit if banks manage the risk of defaults properly, as it did on the guarantees it made during the Crisis and the withdrawals it funded. This makes government guarantees much cheaper than the alternatives, as long as it can manage moral hazard effectively.

The government can do several things to manage moral hazard effectively. It can charge banks an appropriate price for government insurance based on the risks individual banks take. It can use public markets to price its insurance more accurately. It can increase visibility into the risks banks take to give markets better information to price insurance. And it can require banks to hold thicker capital adequacy reserves to hold banks responsible for the risk they can and must manage—default risk. Will this work perfectly? No. But it's not as if the current system of implicit threats held moral hazard in check before the Financial Crisis; quite the opposite.

UNDERWRITING LIQUIDITY RISK

Many critics of the previous bank regulatory regime recommend putting banks at greater risk of bankruptcy in order to rein in risk taking. Proponents of this approach assume that if banks are smaller and less connected, regulators will be able to permit bankruptcies with minimal system-wide consequences, and that this increased risk of bankruptcy will rein in the risk taking that caused the Financial Crisis. This is the philosophy behind the Dodd-Frank Act, passed by Congress in 2010. It hamstrings the Fed's ability to act as "the lender of last resort" and explicitly limits its role. It uses "living wills" to speed the sale and refinancing of banks in the event of insolvency to avoid protracted bankruptcy proceedings that hinder the expediency of bank liquidations. Unfortunately, this approach is dangerously misguided. It's an accident waiting to happen.

Reducing the size and interconnectedness of banks will do little, if anything, to reduce the threat of panicked withdrawals. In a crisis, bank failures do not occur in isolation. Withdrawals will render a fragmented banking industry insolvent just as easily as they will a consolidated one—just as they rendered the fragmented savings and loan industry insolvent in the early 1990s. The same thing happened to the fragmented U.S. banking system in 1929 and many times before. A 30 percent drop in real estate prices will spark widespread withdrawals that drive assets to fire-sale prices and render all banks insolvent, no matter their concentration.

Busting up big banks will only reduce our economy's competitiveness. A fragmented banking industry may have worked when the economy was highly regionalized, but today the world continues to progress to a more integrated whole, with or without us. The world now shares everything from natural resources to multinational corporations, capital markets, the media, communication infrastructures, the environment, and law enforcement. London has already overtaken New York as the world's center of finance. To strengthen our leadership in the world, we need financial institutions that can successfully serve, lead, finance, and compete in this increasingly integrated and growing market. And these institutions—especially successful banks at the center of it all—will necessarily be too big and too interconnected to fail.

Nor can banks hold equity reserves large enough to mitigate bank runs. In the current Crisis, withdrawals exceed $1.5 trillion despite explicit government guarantees of $15 trillion to $20 trillion. Had guarantees been smaller, withdrawals would have been much larger. To have credibility, a private fund would have to approximate the nearly unlimited guarantees of the federal government. And even those oversized guarantees could only contain drawdowns to $1.5 trillion. It's unlikely that banks could gather any where near that much capital. The world only has about $50 trillion of publicly traded stock market equity.

Who would pay the enormous costs of holding equity reserves large enough to mitigate withdrawals? Home owners and wage earners, of course. Investors would necessarily have to divert valuable equity from other uses. They would demand similar returns from borrowers. This would increase the cost of borrowing, and as the cost rose, borrowing would decline. If the price of homes fell to offset the increased cost of borrowing, the lifetime consumption and investment of existing home owners would have to shrink to offset their decline in wealth. Either way, home owners would pay.

Regardless of who bears the cost directly—existing or new home owners—the diversion of equity from underwriting risk elsewhere would reduce risk taking and shrink the economy. Ultimately, society pays the price. Remember, consumers, not investors, capture the vast majority of the value created by investment. It's easy to demand that banks hold enough equity to mitigate liquidity risk, but consider the consequences—higher interest rates and rents, larger down payments and lower home prices, less investment elsewhere, slower growth, and higher unemployment.

Ironically, new regulations intended to protect middle-class taxpayers from the cost of funding government bailouts by shifting liquidity risk to lenders ultimately shift the cost to middle-class

home owners and wage earners. With stronger government guarantees instead of weakened ones, rich taxpayers, who pay two-
thirds of the taxes, not taxpayers in general, bear the true cost of
government guarantees. They are the households likely to bear a
disproportionate share of the increased taxes if guarantees fail to
turn a profit. It's true that if rich taxpayers suffer losses as a result
of strong government guarantees, the reduced capacity to tax
them is shared by all households who could have taxed them for
other purposes; but in the case of the Financial Crisis, rich taxpayers who provided the guarantees were lucky enough to have
avoided losses. Nevertheless, they will still be taxed disproportionately to raise government spending in order to reduce unemployment caused by the Crisis. The rich made the guarantees, bore the
risks, and luckily avoided the losses, but they will still be taxed
eventually anyway to pay for the stimulus. The rest of taxpayers
had their cake and ate it, too.

If we do choose to divert equity to underwrite liquidity risk, a
better source of capital than equity that underwrites business risk
would be home owner down payments. It's clear from the recent
history of household savings that households reduced savings and
increased consumption as down payments declined and home
prices rose. Increasing home owner down payments would raise
equity largely at the expense of consumption rather than merely
diverting equity from other productive uses.

Thicker down payments would also reduce home owner defaults.
Defaults triggered withdrawals despite capital buffers large
enough to absorb losses. It's clear now that preventing defaults
may be as important as holding enough equity to absorb losses.

Well-intended but misguided political policies did exactly the
opposite leading up to the Crisis. Lawmakers sought to reduce the
cost of home ownership by encouraging reduced down payments,
even though this increased the risk of defaults and subsequent
withdrawals. Ironically, even if the availability of reduced down payments drives up home prices, higher home prices make prospective home owners more grateful for the availability of low down
payments! Lawmakers have similarly allowed Fannie Mae and

Freddie Mac to use free government guarantees to fund default-prone subprime mortgages to curry favor with prospective home owners, again even if higher home prices neutralize the benefits. Lawmakers have placed restrictions on recourse to home owners to transfer some of the risk of default to lenders, even though it increases the risk of withdrawals. In the aftermath of the Crisis, they have hindered the ability of banks to foreclose on defaulted home owners. This too encourages withdrawals going forward.

Policymakers know full well that Dodd-Frank's increased threats of bankruptcy are impotent. They recognize that banks will never hold reserves large enough to mitigate the risk of panicked withdrawals of unguaranteed short-term debt. It's uneconomical. Nor are threats to hold banks accountable for withdrawals credible. The cost of allowing them to fail is astronomic, while the cost of saving them is cheap. The mere threat of withdrawals sent the economy into a tailspin.

The worst moment for the economy to confiscate profits from misadvised risk taking is precisely when panicked withdrawals are melting down our financial infrastructure. It's like punishing your son for driving recklessly just after the car wreck has severely wounded him, instead of rushing him to the hospital and teaching him his lesson later. By the time panicked withdrawals begin, administering the long-term cure of fully charging for the risks banks have taken—much less the medieval cure of letting them bleed to death for the sake of free-market principles and the future management of moral hazard—is far too late, and inordinately expensive. It substantially lengthens the economy's recovery.

And if you depend on your injured son's job for income—say, to pay your pension, as we depend on the economy—then punishing him later is suboptimal, too. After the fact, it only makes sense to minimize the damage and speed the recovery. The only reason to punish him later is to reduce the long-term risk of moral hazard. Ironically, administering the punishment at the scene of the accident—wiping out the equity of banks like Lehman, Bear Stearns, and Countrywide during the Financial Crisis—only accelerated the withdrawals and consolidated the banks further in the wake of the Crisis, which permanently reduced competition, widened bank profit margins, and consolidated the financial industry into an even smaller number of banks that were already too big to fail. The next time, are lawmakers really going to bite off their noses to spite the banks and teach them a lesson? Given these economics, it is illogical, even irresponsible, not to save the banks once they begin to fail from panicked withdrawals.

Policymakers know they will never use living wills to break apart banks and sell off the pieces during a run on the banks, like the one in the Financial Crisis. That's why Dodd-Frank wisely allows a two-thirds vote of the newly created Financial Stability Oversight Council to unwind Dodd-Frank and allows the Fed near-unlimited ability to act in a crisis. In the midst of Armageddon, Bernanke, Paulson, and Geithner acted with swiftness and confidence that they could never repeat today, and still the economy suffered extraordinary fallout. Many critics of the bailout claim withdrawals soared because the Fed allowed Lehman Brothers to fail. Imagine the damage to the economy if we tried to reorganize all of the banks in the middle of a crisis! Regulators couldn't possibly use living wills to reorganize the finances of banks faster than the Fed's actions in the Crisis, especially the first time they use them! Nor would they even dare try.

Dodd-Frank's real threat to the banks comes not from its threat of allowing them to go bankrupt, but from the increased latitude of unreliable politicians to hinder the Fed's ability to act swiftly and boldly by politicizing its response. The Fed's ability to act in the aftermath of the Crisis has already become greatly politicized. Dodd-Frank facilitates political interference. This increases the potential damage to investors and the economy from withdrawals. Lenders and borrowers will logically idle more capital to protect themselves from the heightened and now-recognized risk of damage from withdrawals. Risk taking will contract proportionally, growth will slow, and unemployment will rise.

Policymakers are willing to use the compromises reached in Dodd-Frank to placate naïve voters on the left and the right who are angry about the Crisis and mistakenly place the blame on bankers. From the perspective of policymakers, the increased risk of damage caused by Dodd-Frank strengthens the current system of implicit guarantees and threats. The Crisis has weakened the government's implicit threats by making the need, willingness, and logic for government intervention in a crisis more obvious (even if it intervenes with less certainty and expediency, which allows more damage than would otherwise be the case). Despite the Fed wiping out the shareholders of many large banks to reduce moral hazard, the Crisis reveals that these threats are, in fact, quite limited. The costs of withdrawals and insolvency are enormous and the cost of avoidance is near zero. As a result, government will logically go to extraordinary lengths to stop withdrawals once they occur and minimize damage in their aftermath. Weakened threats increase the risk of moral hazard. Increasing the risk of damage from withdrawals by hampering the Fed's ability to act in a crisis serves as an offset, albeit a dangerous one.

Lawmakers are eager to leave implicit government guarantees unpriced to increase economic growth and home ownership. When lenders underprice risk, increased risk taking grows the economy. Even now, in the aftermath of the Crisis, the Fed has priced the risky use of short-term debt almost to zero to accelerate growth. They dare banks to use these cheap but risky underpriced hair-triggered funds. It's as if no one has learned their lesson! It's no wonder loose monetary policy no longer increases growth.

When the government subsidizes risk taking, borrowers benefit. Prior to the Crisis, the chief beneficiaries were home owners. They were able to buy homes with little or no down payment. They benefited from rising house prices without also suffering equivalent losses if prices declined. And they were able to buy a two- or three-year option on house prices at below-market—"teaser"—interest rates. We can see the effect of these favorable economics in home ownership rates. Hispanic home ownership increased by 47 percent between 2000 and 2007, for example, at a time when the national home ownership rate rose by 8 percent.[1] Had the price of debt included the full cost of the liquidity risk, which the government guaranteed, this would not have been possible. Dodd-Frank leaves open the possibility of continuing to allow default-prone subprime lending. It goes to great lengths to restrict predatory lending but does nothing to ban default-prone low-money-down subprime mortgages or restrict their funding with hair-triggered short-term debt.

Speculators also benefit from the government's continued failure to charge banks for the government's need to bear liquidity risk. Banks increased proprietary trading to take advantage of underpriced short-term funds. Raising the price of guarantees would drain speculators of unearned profits that inadvertently encourage speculation.

The current policy might be a political necessity, but it's an unfortunate economic policy. A policy that balances the increased risk of moral hazard with the increased threat of damage in the event of a bank run misses seeing the forest for the trees. Even if such a balance were achieved, continuing to pursue a policy that fails to mitigate the risk of panicked withdrawals drives investors to dial down risk elsewhere to compensate for the now-recognized risk of damage from withdrawals. Prior to the Crisis, lenders weren't worried about the risk of withdrawals. But now that they have seen what can happen, the economy will never return to the same level of risk taking and employment without accumulating more equity to underwrite the now-recognized risk. You can bet the partners of Goldman Sachs will no longer risk borrowing short and lending long, at least not to the extent they did before. Nor will borrowers borrow short and invest long. Instead, risk-averse short-term debt will sit idle, as it has done.

Regardless of the dangers of using short-term debt, the economy has savings that require on-demand liquidity and capital preservation. With a chronic shortage of equity to underwrite risk, we must find ways to accommodate the demands of these savers in order to recirculate their earnings as investment or consumption to increase employment and growth. The alternative of living with a smaller, slower-growing economy and higher unemployment—whether by leaving these funds sitting idle or by putting them to work and having investors dial down risk elsewhere to compensate for the now-recognized risk of panicked withdrawals—is hardly appealing. Given the value of the resulting higher growth, and the surprisingly low cost of explicit guarantees, it's illogical not to deploy these funds and suffer the consequences every seventy-nine years, even if we can't find a feasible way to mitigate these risks.

INCREASING THE CREDIBILITY OF GOVERNMENT GUARANTEES

The economy will have a difficult, perhaps impossible, time reaching full employment without putting risk-averse short-term funds to work. Truly mitigating the risk of withdrawals will help increase risk taking and employment.

Mandatory government-backed liquidity insurance, like the kind required of banks that fund loans with retail deposits, is one alternative that does this. In the case of the Federal Deposit Insurance Corporation (FDIC), which guarantees retail deposits, banks buy insurance by paying a fee based on their deposits. Only explicit government guarantees are credible enough to truly mitigate the risk of panicked withdrawals without also reducing risk taking substantially. The Crisis reveals the cost of this government-backed insurance, excluding the cost of moral hazard, to be nearly zero.

Under the regulatory regime in place before and after the Crisis, banks pay no insurance fees for using short-term institutional deposits to fund loans, despite the government providing implicit liquidity guarantees made explicit in the Crisis. This suboptimizes investment and risk taking. Mispriced risk improperly allocates risk and return to borrowers, chiefly, but also, to a lesser extent, to depositors and bank equity holders. Sustainability demands that investors earn profits for only the risks they underwrite.

Regulations that leave liquidity risk mispriced require that risk be restricted in other ways: by outlawing proprietary trading, restricting credit default swaps, regulating credit rating agencies, or prescribing banker pay, for example. The risk of unintended consequences from these ad hoc regulations is significant. Restricting bankers' pay relative to private-sector alternatives, for example, drains banks of talent needed to manage complex risks on behalf of the economy. It allows unrestricted competitors such as hedge funds to recruit talent more easily to compete against them. If we priced risk properly, we wouldn't care what risks banks and other investors took.

The proper pricing of risk frees banks to underwrite risk in the most optimal ways rather than hamstringing them with well-intentioned regulations riddled with unintended consequences. Theoretically, banks would gain little from regulatory arbitrage, lack of transparency, growing too big to fail, or using capital structures that demand protracted bankruptcy to lower the cost of capital. Properly priced mandatory government-backed insurance would mitigate the risk of bank runs and rationalize the use of risk-averse short-term debt without failing to put it to use.

The problem with government guarantees is pricing them properly. Again, one-size pricing does not fit all; it merely encourages the most risky use of guaranteed funds. The price of insurance must reflect the riskiness of its use. Clearly, regulators—whether out of complicity, incompetence, an inability to assess overwhelming complexities, or irrational exuberance—were unable to recognize and mitigate risk prior to the Crisis. How could we possibly depend on them to price insurance properly?

One alternative for pricing insurance is to sell a portion of each bank's coverage to the public. The amount of private capital at risk would only need to be large enough to provide an accurate price. Financial institutions that are too small to provide efficient security prices could be required to borrow short-term debt from banks that can. Investors who underwrite credit default insurance would have to buy liquidity insurance, obtain appropriately sized standby lines of credit from banks with insurance, or write contracts that underwrite default risk but not liquidity risk.

Despite their uncanny accuracy, criticism of public markets' ability to price risk nevertheless abounds. Most important, the asymmetry of information between inside managers and outside investors is significant. Investors are often the last to know. Investors are hair-triggered; as a result, they overreact to information. But then, so do regulators. Worse, regulators are prone to favoritism and working backwards to justify conclusions. Markets may be unreliable, but they are the most reliable alternative we have. Lest we forget, today liquidity guarantees remain unpriced.

Regulators could establish rules to increase visibility into the risks banks take in order to improve the accuracy of the market's pricing of each bank's coverage. They could perform audits and stress tests to find and bring forward relevant information. They could require experts—banks—to buy the securities insuring other banks. They could also use traditional forms of regulation, such as capital adequacy rules and restrictions on the ownership of default-prone loans, to lessen dependence on the accuracy of insurance prices.*

Another problem with market-based solutions such as insurance is that they amplify market cycles. Insurance prices tend to be low in good times and high in bad times, whereas regulations would dampen optimism (with high prices) and shore up pessimism (with low prices). Any insurance charge, however, would dampen cyclicality more than the current policy of no charge. Other traditional forms of regulation would also dampen cyclicality.

There is ample economic justification for offering insurance at a price different from the market's reference price. The more risk that is borne privately, the more marginal investors will charge to bear it. Since they will not bear all of it, the marginal price of what they do bear will be lower than the true price. Also, private insurers will price risk knowing that unlimited government guarantees reduce the chances of panicked withdrawals. This, too, will lower

---

* In a thoughtful version of government guarantees proposed by Roberto Caballero, the former head of MIT's economics department, and Pablo Kurlat in their paper "The 'Surprising' Origin and Nature of Financial Crises: A Macro Policy Proposal," which was presented to the Federal Reserve at its Jackson Hole Conference, the incentives for moral hazard are also curbed by restricting insurance payouts to a trigger event declared by the Federal Reserve, namely a financial crisis.

the market price. The value of reference prices, however, is to gauge the riskiness of one bank's use of funds relative to another's so that insurers can charge the banks that take more risk a higher price for insurance. The accuracy of the additional price charged for the additional risk is what properly manages risk.

Government insurers can add that difference to a base price that meets varying policy objectives. If the government charges banks the public's full cost of liquidity insurance, it will be no different than pushing the cost onto the public by pushing the full risk onto the banks. Borrowers, principally home owners, will bear the high costs. Home ownership and employment would likely decline.

Regulators could also adjust base insurance prices counter-cyclically relative to the market's reference prices the same way the Fed currently manipulates short-term interest rates. Delinking the average price of insurance from monetary policy would increase policy options available to policymakers. Ultimately, regulators must price insurance by trading the cost of lower growth in the short run against the increased risk of mistaken and unsustainable allocations of capital in the long run—just as they do now.

In addition to controlling risk more accurately, charging for insurance gives regulators the mandate to save banks when the inevitable financial crisis comes. The only reason the government inflicts damage in a crisis is to reduce the future risk of moral hazard. But inflicting damage in a crisis only makes the crisis and its aftermath worse. Instead, properly priced insurance reduces moral hazard before risk taking occurs instead of long afterward.

Insurance limits the rights of regulators to punish banks in a crisis. It allows regulators to respond confidently and with less interference by politicians misguidedly second-guessing and limiting regulators' decisions. Confidence that the government will act boldly will hold short-term deposits in place more strongly prior to an event—such as a 30 percent drop in real estate prices—that might otherwise cause withdrawals.

It will also reduce the dampening effect on risk taking in the aftermath of such an event. Under this regime, properly priced insurance premiums control moral hazard rather than conditional guarantees and threats enforced by the government after the fact. This prevents lawmakers and regulators from reassessing the trade-off between growth and moral hazard until after they avert the crisis. Failure to rein in risk taking properly would necessitate adjusting the price of premiums going forward. Increasing insurance premiums to control risk is a more logical and less damaging response to mistaken risk taking than the bankruptcies and consolidations demanded by regulators and voters in the Financial Crisis.

Would insurance that doesn't shift all the costs of using short-term debt to the private sector mitigate moral hazard entirely? No—by design. But we should recognize that the government already guarantees close to a third of all private-sector debt.[2] And bailouts without insurance charges, like the ones in the Crisis, add further to moral hazards. Combined with other regulations, like a small increase in capital adequacy requirements contemplated by the impending Basel III Accord and restrictions on the ownership of default-prone subprime lending, insurance would go a long way toward holding banks more responsible for the risk they can control—default risk that precipitates panicked withdrawals.

ADDITIONAL PROPOSALS FOR REDUCING THE RISK OF WITHDRAWALS

The government's policy of implicit guarantees failed to hold withdrawals in check. Its policy of implicit threats failed to discourage banks from taking risks that triggered withdrawals. The still-outstanding but now-recognized risk of withdrawals leaves short-term debt sitting idle, unused. This has slowed growth and increased unemployment to historically high levels. Despite the fact that the United States already explicitly guarantees retail deposits, explicitly or implicitly guarantees a third of all U.S. debt, and explicitly guaranteed virtually all short-term debt in the

Financial Crisis, expanding explicit government insurance remains a radical policy change. A change of this magnitude will surely produce unintended consequences. As such, lesser alternatives are worth considering.

The least invasive alternative educates, rather than misleads, voters about the causes of the Financial Crisis and the role the government must play in a bank run. For the sake of political gain, politicians on the left and the right have intentionally misled voters. The left scapegoats bankers, some on the right blame government, and others believe the government simply must allow banks to fail for the sake of free markets and the protection of taxpayers. The result is a majority of voters who don't understand the importance of putting short-term debt to use, the role of banks, the inevitability of financial crises, and the importance of government guarantees, whether implicit or explicit. In the current climate of misguided beliefs, no politician can successfully propose logical improvements. Effective political leadership would take an active role in rectifying these misunderstandings, political affiliations notwithstanding. Armed with the proper understanding, a majority of voters might support a more muscular and confident role for the government in a bank run. If a majority of voters supported such a role, it would strengthen implicit guarantees and reduce the likelihood of a bank run. Instead, partisan politics leaves us with the opposite condition.

Enhancing the credibility of government guarantees may reduce the risk of withdrawals, but it also increases the risk of moral hazard. Beefed-up capital adequacy reserves would hold banks more accountable for the risk they can control—default risk. This better separation between default risk and liquidity guarantees would reduce the risk of moral hazard. Even if having more equity at stake didn't rein in imprudent risk taking, more capital to absorb defaults would still reduce the likelihood of defaults triggering a bank run.

Bolstering the banks' ability to foreclose on home owners who fail to pay their mortgages, rather than providing home owners with legal avenues to delay foreclosures while they continue to live in their homes without paying their mortgages, would also reduce the need for panicked withdrawals in the future. The ability to foreclose would assure depositors that banks could sell real property in order to repay the depositors' loans to the bank. Well-intentioned but misguided politicians have thwarted foreclosures to help "underwater" home owners (home owners whose homes are worth less than their mortgages), but hindrances to foreclosures threaten the liquidity of depositors. When depositors are threatened, wage earners pay the price with high unemployment.

Allowing mortgages with personal recourse beyond only the collateral of the house would similarly deflect default risk away from banks and their depositors. Again, political expediency has produced the opposite result.

A fourth approach restricts the use of hair-triggered short-term debt to fund the AAA-rated tranches of default-prone low-down-payment loans. Underneath all the technicalities, during the Crisis the threat of subprime mortgage defaults triggered a run on the banks despite capital buffers large enough to absorb losses. Let's start by killing the snake.

Lawmakers eager to increase subprime home ownership are determined to avoid an answer as simple as restricting the funding of default-prone subprime mortgages. They seek a solution that allows the shifting of risk from home owners who can't afford to bear the risk to others who can. If non-bank investors are willing to bear real estate risk on behalf of risky subprime home owners by putting up the home owner's down payment and not charging for the risk, why shouldn't the regulatory regime allow it? The obvious answer is that it should allow it, provided doing so doesn't increase the likelihood of home owner defaults triggering bank runs.

Not allowing banks to fund the AAA-rated tranches of default-prone loans with hair-triggered short-term debt would do that. This restriction, however, would significantly reduce funding for subprime mortgages. Advocates of subprime home ownership seek to avoid this outcome no matter the consequences to the economy.

In order to hold open the possibility of banks continuing to fund default-prone subprime mortgages, we are intentionally increasing the risk of damage to banks and our economy in the event of a panic to reduce the risk of moral hazard. This imposes a heavy cost on society. As noted, it slows the recovery and increases unemployment. We can probably reduce the risk of withdrawals more cheaply through straightforward means: by eliminating policies that encourage default-prone lending and by restricting the funding of these loans. Perhaps we are wagging the dog by its tail.

Rather than demanding an end to default-prone subprime lending funded with hair-triggered short-term debt, bank critics have, ironically, demanded an end to proprietary trading, which they view as unnecessarily risky, but which was inconsequential to the cause of the Crisis. In a world where banks underwrite and trade risk, what constitutes proprietary trading? When a bank takes credit-default risk by making a loan, is it taking proprietary risk? It is, without a doubt. But loaning money is what banks do. When a bank like Goldman Sachs seeks to unwind that risk by shorting mortgages prior to the downturn, is that proprietary trading? Yes. So is borrowing short and lending long. With banks now primarily underwriting, pricing, and trading risk rather than merely funding loans, restrictions on proprietary trading unnecessarily imperil banks and distort capital markets to restrict banks to only the long side of the trade. Restricting banks to long-only positions substantially increases withdrawals in the event of a panic.

Banks made short-term loans to financial speculators in order to match the duration of their loans to the duration of their funds. Ironically, critics who criticized banks for borrowing short and lending long have also criticized banks for making short-term loans to speculators. You're damned if you do and damned if you don't!

Logical regulations must recognize that the role of banks has changed substantially over the years from merely raising funds to pricing, syndicating, underwriting, and making markets for risk today. It's reckless to demand that all banks take only one side of the trade—the long side. It would be nearly as reckless to restrict them all to only the short side of the trade. Sophisticated finance recognizes that restrictions that limit short-selling lead to the over-pricing of financial assets, a higher likelihood of losses for investors who hold securities until maturity, and increased speculation as a result.[3]

These measures won't fully mitigate the risk of panicked withdrawals. With the continuing build-up of unguaranteed short-term debt, the risk of withdrawals will remain significant, and may gradually manifest itself in different and unanticipated ways. But these changes would go a long way toward reducing the source of the current risk and help put short-term debt back to work.

At some point, it's debatable whether it is cost-effective to make regulations so risk-averse that they can withstand every unanticipated catastrophe or policy decision, no matter how unlikely. Sometimes it's cheaper to clean up the mess after infrequent events. We can easily eliminate the cause of the last Crisis—subprime defaults—even if that doesn't fully mitigate the evolutionary buildup of risk elsewhere.

It might also be the case that the damage caused by withdrawals is overestimated. Perhaps a different course of action would have reduced damage to the economy. Saving Lehman Brothers* and AIG, for example, and executing the bailout with even more confidence and less misguided political interference would probably have reduced the resulting damage, which, nevertheless, would have been large. Acknowledging the importance of government guarantees and strengthening rather than weakening them would also have increased rather than lessened confidence in the aftermath of the Crisis. Similarly, it's hard to know how much Dodd-Frank, proposed health care reform, and President Obama's hostile attitude toward business and investment, which was initially backed by a filibuster-proof Democratic Congress, slowed the recovery; but surely it was significant.

---

* The dissenting opinion to "The Financial Crisis Inquiry Report" makes a strong case that the Fed had no legal authority to save Lehman Brothers until TARP was passed following Lehman's failure.

CONCLUSIONS

Prior to the Financial Crisis, innovation grew productivity, spurred growth, increased optimism, and raised asset prices. The trade deficit accelerated growth by relieving capacity constraints and lowering costs. But with the trade deficit comes risk-averse savings. If we let this capital sit idle, as we have in the aftermath of the Financial Crisis, instead of using it to fund investment or consumption, growth will slow and unemployment will remain high.

When policymakers rationalized capital adequacy requirements, banks went in search of investors to fund the subordinated first-loss tranches of securitized loans. With the economy roaring, banks found eager long-term investors; so eager, in fact, that they underwrote the risk of home owner down payments, even the down payments of subprime home owners. Bankers, regulators, investors, and credit rating agencies expected capital buffers as large as traditional down payments to protect banks from fluctuating real estate prices. With these sizable buffers in place, bankers used an abundance of short-term debt to fund the AAA-rated tranches of this default-prone debt. With no equity at stake, home owners borrowed against the rising values of their homes to fund increased consumption. When home prices fell and home owners threatened default, long-term capital closed to subprime lending and banks grew increasingly dependent on short-term funding. As real estate prices fell and financial stress mounted, short-term depositors eventually lost their confidence, panicked, and withdrew their funding long before home owners defaulted in significant numbers. As banks scrambled to sell assets to fund withdrawals, assets fell to fire-sale prices. Unable to fund withdrawals, banks were rendered insolvent.

In the face of a 30 percent drop in real estate prices, implicit threats failed to rein in risk taking enough to avoid withdrawals. Angry voters now demand politicians hold banks accountable. They demand a reduction in risk taking, whether it's economical or not.

Policymakers recognize banks can't hold enough equity to stem withdrawals. They recognize that fragmenting the banking system won't stem withdrawals either. Instead, they have allowed political opposition to bailouts to increase the risk of damage in the event of a panic. Presumably, increasing the risk of damage from withdrawals will reduce risk taking and moral hazard. Dodd-Frank, by facilitating political opposition to the Fed's actions in a crisis, hampers its ability to act, which increases this risk.

But risk taking has contracted significantly to offset the now-recognized risk of damage from panicked withdrawals. Banks have grown reluctant to borrow short-term funds to make long-term loans. Businesses have dialed back discretionary costs and investment. Consumers have grown reluctant to borrow and spend in the face of an uncertain economy. Cash has piled up on the sidelines, unused. Political opposition to bailouts only exacerbates this threat.

If the risk of panicked withdrawals remains outstanding, investors and consumers will continue to dial down risk taking. Until we find a way to put short-term debt back to work, the recovery will remain slow and unemployment will remain high. Reducing rather than heightening this risk would speed the recovery. Failing to fix the true problem leaves our economy exposed to the dangers of another withdrawal.

Solutions that superficially demand banks fund loans with more equity and less short-term debt fail to recognize that risk-averse savings are highly price-inelastic and will not bear risk at any price. Near-zero returns on short-term debt have not motivated risk-averse investors to supply more longer-term debt and bear more risk. Holding more equity idle to offset the risk of withdrawals adds to the very problem we must solve in order to grow employment. We must figure out how to put all our savings to work—our risk-averse short capital and our risk-bearing long-term capital.

Simply diverting equity from underwriting risk elsewhere is zero-sum and will not increase employment. Merely shifting equity from one sector to another will increase risk taking in one sector—in this case, banking—at the expense of another. Unless we implement economic policies to accelerate the accumulation of equity—presumably, lower marginal taxes on successful risk taking—the shortage of equity relative to an abundance of short-term debt will continue and unemployment will remain high.

The only way to increase prosperity is to reduce the risk of withdrawals without also idling equity needed to underwrite risk taking elsewhere. Fortunately, the Crisis shows that the cost of government guarantees large enough to mitigate the risk of withdrawals is near zero if regulation properly manages the risk of moral hazard. No other option provides these valuable economics.

But to work, guarantees must be credible. Credibility demands both the capacity to fund withdrawals, which the government has demonstrated, and the reassurance that lawmakers will use this capacity effectively to minimize damage caused by withdrawals. Even if the government's response in the Crisis demonstrates its willingness to fund withdrawals, it doesn't demonstrate its willingness to do it in a way that minimizes the damage; quite the opposite. Despite the Federal Reserve and Treasury's heroic response in the Crisis, the behavior of lawmakers and demagogues since has proven appallingly unreliable.

Given the undependable behavior of lawmakers, investors and consumers might now demand the reliability of explicit government-backed insurance rather than implicit guarantees to put hair-triggered short-term debt to work and return the economy to full employment. Priced properly, government-mandated insurance would facilitate rationalized risk taking and reduce the risk of moral hazard. Selling a portion of this insurance to the public is the best way to price insurance based on the riskiness of its use. Regulations that increase transparency of the risk banks take would improve the accuracy of this price. Marginally increased capital adequacy reserves, which better separate default risk from liquidity risk, and properly priced insurance would reduce the risk of moral hazards further.

Expanding insurance, however, would be a far-reaching policy change, and a change of that magnitude would surely suffer from unintended consequences. Lesser changes could move us in the right direction. Educating voters about the importance of government guarantees in a panic would reduce the threat of unreliable politicians increasing damage in a crisis. Increasing capital adequacy reserves would hold banks more accountable for the risk they can control—default risk that triggers panicked withdrawals. Bolstering the banks' ability to foreclose on delinquent home owners would also reduce the damage to banks from defaults. Allowing banks to short credit-default risk would obviously reduce default risk substantially. Full disclosure of short positions would reduce possible conflicts of interest. Demanding that banks hold only long positions unnecessarily magnifies the risk of withdrawals. Dodd-Frank makes none of these improvements.

Restricting banks from funding the AAA-rated tranches of default-prone subprime loans with hair-triggered short-term debt directly addresses the cause of the Financial Crisis, although not of financial crises more broadly. Unfortunately, proponents of subprime home ownership are determined to do the opposite by successfully deflecting blame for the Crisis to secondary issues. They blame predatory lending when competition between investors shifted risk from home owners to lenders. They blame credit rating agencies for underestimating default risk despite capital buffers the size of conventional 20 percent down payments. They blame incentives that paid 50 percent of banker pay in long-term compensation, but make no practical recommendations to change it. They blame laissez-faire regulators despite far-reaching improvements to capital adequacy requirements and their own inability to recognize the risk. They blame credit default swaps, which is no different than blaming the practice of lending. They blame lack of visibility for unnecessarily triggering panic when no amount of data would have allowed investors to predict the size of real estate price declines, withdrawals, or the reliability of government guarantees—the primary drivers of the panic. They cheered the growth of subprime lending rather than taking steps to restrict it. Despite their own utter cluelessness, they claim bankers and bank regulators should have known better!

Instead of passing straightforward rules that reduce the

magnitude of defaults and the risk of damage from withdrawals, they have passed thousands of pages of regulations that do everything but. That makes matters worse. It not only makes unnecessary changes that carry unintended consequences, it also fails to solve the true problems that led to the Crisis and recession. Lenders and borrowers have dialed back risk taking to compensate for now-recognized risk of damage from withdrawals. That risk remains outstanding. Increasing the threat of damage from withdrawals by politicizing opposition to bailouts and facilitating that opposition in a panic reduces the reliability of government guarantees and adds to the compensatory reduction in risk taking. The vast array of new regulations slows the recovery further as banks cautiously learn to cope with a new regulatory regime. The net result is an increase in the risk of damage from another panic, which slows the recovery and increases unemployment substantially.

CHAPTER EIGHT

REDUCING UNEMPLOYMENT

ANGRY VOTERS NOW demand the government hold banks accountable for the Crisis. They insist that policymakers increase rather than lessen the risk to banks from withdrawals. This has left the risk of damage from withdrawals outstanding and has led the economy to hold savings idle to offset this now-recognized risk. Increased hoarding, fear of borrowing and the resulting failure to use now-idle risk-averse short-term savings for investment or consumption have substantially increased unemployment.

With the risk of defaults triggering a bank run despite capital buffers large enough to absorb losses, it is unlikely we can continue to use short-term saving to fund subprime consumption. Instead, the economy needs to use the long-term capital previously used to bear real estate risk to underwrite the risk of running a myriad of experiments to find sustainable alternative uses for short-term savings. It is difficult, impossible perhaps, to predict what those usages will be. Historically, rich home owners have been reluctant to borrow against their primary residences. And successful innovators like Google and Microsoft have generated enormous cash flow with little need to borrow.

In the interim, the government is the most obvious candidate to use the short-term debt. If the government issues long-term bonds to lock in low long-term rates, it merely crowds current and future long-term borrowers out of the market for scarcer long-term capital. Meanwhile, that leaves a surplus of risk-averse short-term savings sitting idle. It makes little sense to lure long-term capital away from the private sector with government guarantees. The private sector creates economic growth and employment and is logically reluctant to borrow short and invest long. It would be better if the government left that capital to the private sector to fund innovation that creates new jobs. It's more logical to use government guarantees to put risk-averse savings to work that would otherwise sit idle. This is part of the logic behind the Fed's Operation Twist, which issues short-term debt to buy in long-term debt. It's true, short-term rates could rise, and that would increase the government's interest costs, but one way or the other, taxpayers already bear this risk, whether through the risk of higher interest rates, government guarantees, or unemployment.

In the long run, if we leave the risk of damage from withdrawals hanging over the economy, it will slow rather than accelerate the already difficult structural transition of finding new ways to put short-term money to use. Again, the willingness to take risk is largely a function of wealth. Risk taking is a function of the amount of equity available to underwrite risk and the willingness to take risk per dollar of equity. Investors and consumers have dialed back their appetite for investment and consumption to compensate for the risk of damage from withdrawals. Unless we reduce the risk by strengthening government guarantees of liquidity, or grow the amount of equity to underwrite risk, the economy must transition to a lower level of risk taking by leaving long- and short-term capital sitting idle. This can occur either by legislating increases in reserves large enough to stem withdrawals or by private investors and consumers dialing back risk taking on their own, to compensate. Either way, risk taking will decline and unemployment will rise for a given amount of equity. The amount of wealth willing and able to underwrite risk is zero-sum. Simply diverting equity from underwriting risk in one sector rather than another will only increase risk taking in one sector at the expense of a reduction in another. It will not increase employment overall.

Of course, the economy can increase employment by dialing down wages proportionally. Equity, after all, underwrites the risk associated with a certain level of expenditures. But who wants to increase employment that way? Unless the economy accumulates much more equity to underwrite more risk taking, or takes more risk per dollar of equity, the economy is unlikely to return to its prior level of employment and wages.

Returning to the amount of equity per employee that yielded robust employment prior to the Financial Crisis—even more, now that the risk of damage from withdrawals is recognized—will not be easy. Take another look at Figure 1-9, "U.S. stock market capitalization relative to GDP." Equity per dollar of GDP reached unprecedented highs prior to the Crisis. Fortunately, the Internet is still nascent. Search, for example, is still primitive but extremely valuable. The runway of Internet-related opportunities is still enormous, especially for the United States. But creating and accumulating more equity will take a long time, especially if we dial back risk taking. Risky innovations like Google and Facebook create equity. The accumulation of deferred consumption largely creates more risk-averse short-term capital. We already have more than enough of that. Increasing taxes on successful risk takers will slow the accumulation of equity and discourage risk taking. The recovery will surely be faster if we increase the amount of productive risk taking per dollar of equity rather than waiting for the equity to grow sufficiently.

Unfortunately, misconceptions on both the left and the right make it difficult for lawmakers to take the steps necessary to reduce the risk of damage from withdrawals. Liberals and conservatives alike demand that lawmakers hold banks more accountable for withdrawals. In turn, capital sits idle rather than underwriting risky new endeavors. Unless we reduce the risk of damage from withdrawals and gradually undertake the difficult and risky task of finding alternative and sustainable uses for risk-averse short-term debt, the recovery will remain anemic. If we can't or won't take steps to reduce the risk of damage from withdrawals, what else can the government do to reduce unemployment?

FISCAL AND MONETARY STIMULUS

Every shock to the economy diminishes equity and reduces confidence. In this case, a 30 percent drop in real estate prices wiped out $6 trillion to $7 trillion of home owner equity and a comparable amount of equity in other assets, such as stocks and bonds.[1] Consumers and investors scramble to contract risk taking to compensate for an economy with less equity and more perceived risk, and to rebuild equity. Fearful consumers reduce consumption to pay off debt. Businesses cut discretionary costs and investment to reduce risk and to rebuild equity. Consumption declines without a corresponding increase in investment, and the economy contracts. As noted earlier, this is Keynes's paradox of thrift.

The natural dynamics of recession worsen the contraction. In the short run, the growth in risk-averse short-term savings overwhelms the capacity of equity to underwrite the risk of investing it. At the same time, banks weakened by losses dial back lending. Risk-averse savings and the output they represent sit idle.

Even without lenders' losses, the relative growth of weakened borrowers requires increased caution on the part of lenders. Why would investors eagerly borrow money and increase risk in uncertain times? With few, if any, ways to improve their ability to distinguish safe borrowers from risky ones, lenders have no choice but to raise credit standards.* The higher they raise standards, the more the high cost of borrowing skews loan applicants toward riskier borrowers. At high rates, only the most desperate borrowers are still eager to borrow. Credit naturally contracts, leaving output sitting idle. Without a reliable source of credit to smooth the ran-

---

* If a bank's screening process is 90% accurate and 90% of the loan applications are creditworthy borrowers in normal times, 1.2% of the approved loans will turn out to be bad investments (= [10% bad opportunities × 10% inaccuracy] / [[90% good opportunities × 90% accuracy] + [10% bad opportunities × 10% inaccuracy]]). In risky times, if 80% of applications represents creditworthy borrowers, 2.7% of the approved loans will turn out to be bad loans ([20% bad opportunities × 10% inaccuracy] / [[80% good opportunities × 90% accuracy] + [20% bad opportunities × 10% inaccuracy]]).

dom setbacks from risk taking, investors and consumers ratchet down their risk taking further.

This reduced demand puts downward pressure on prices. Declining prices (principally wages) increase the value of holding idle output relative to the value of underwriting risk. Idle output held as cash grows more valuable as prices decline. As the likelihood of lower prices increases, investors dial back risk taking and hold cash that may increase in value. This exacerbates the contraction in risk taking.

Left alone, this contraction will gradually subside. Unemployment will gradually drive down wages. Lower wages will increase the demand for labor. Reluctant capital will naturally earn returns higher than the growth of labor. Equity will grow relative to labor, less whatever portion of income and wealth the government taxes and redistributes to increase consumption. As the growth of equity underwrites more risk, employment will grow. Investment in innovation will eventually stumble upon new ideas that increase demand and redeploy idle labor. Any temporary loss of confidence will gradually recede.

Even if the reduction in risk taking is temporary, it can still do permanent damage to the economy. The value of unemployed labor is lost forever. Unless the economy converts it into output, it has no shelf life; we either use it or lose it. Unemployment inflicts suffering on families, too.

Even skilled workers who find employment elsewhere lose productivity. A productive executive learns how to navigate the unique relationships, politics, and bureaucracy of his or her organization. Starting anew destroys a significant portion of this situation-specific knowledge.

A contraction of risk taking and credit also terminates some investment projects before they are completed. Restarting these projects can be expensive, even impossible if key workers have since moved on.

Reduced output reduces the contribution that covers fixed costs and creates losses that drain equity reserves, which underwrite risk. Losses, debt covenant defaults, and bankruptcies transfer the ownership of future cash flows from risk taking equity holders to risk-averse debt holders. All of these factors slow growth going forward.

Policymakers may use fiscal stimulus in the hopes of offsetting a temporary decline in risk taking and to dampen the risk of a naturally cascading decline. If successful, this avoids permanent damage to the economy that a temporary decline unnecessarily causes. Even if we leave the economy's long-term structural problems unaddressed—in this case, the now-recognized risk of damage from withdrawals—we should still consider ways to reduce unnecessary damage.

Theoretically, the government could do this by taking risks that investors and consumers are reluctant to take on their own. The government can borrow idle cash balances and invest or consume them. Lenders face no increased risk lending to the government (as they do with other borrowers) during a recession. Investors flock to U.S. government debt for this reason.

The government could use this borrowed money, for example, to build infrastructure projects today that it had planned to build in the future. Future reduction in infrastructure spending would pay back borrowings without tax increases. You don't have to believe in Keynesian spending multipliers to see why this could work. Successfully redeploying idle labor would help to keep the rest of the economy afloat until it recovered naturally.

Similarly, the government could borrow idle cash balances and buy goods such as cars today, when demand lulls, stockpile them, and then sell them later to pay back the loans when pent-up demand resurges. They might even make a profit buying low when demand lulls and selling high when it surges. At worst, the countercyclical buying and selling ought only to stabilize prices.

If consumers and investors recognize that the government's countercyclical buying and selling can smooth demand, they might not overreact, lose confidence, and temporarily rein in risk taking because of a shock to the economy. In that case, buying any idle labor that creates the same value it would have created were it employed should produce a similar result.

The government could also borrow idle cash and buy risky financial securities from private investors. This transfers risk to the government. For a given level of investor appetite for risk, transferring risk to the government should motivate investors to expand investment. The government could pay off the debt later by selling the securities.

If layoffs have depleted the availability of savings, the government could even print money and buy securities when the appetite for risk and the price of securities are low, and sell the securities and gather the surplus cash when the appetite for risk and prices are higher. With slack demand in the economy, it's unlikely the additional cash in circulation would threaten increased inflation. Again, countercyclical buying and selling should stabilize security prices. Excess cash might even loosen credit and increase risk taking.

If that works, cutting taxes and borrowing or printing money to fund government expenditures in the interim might work as well. Presumably, a taxpayer with more cash will either spend or invest it. Taxpayers might even make more economically logical spending decisions than politicians, who can raise taxes later to pay off the debt or collect the surplus currency.

Keynes argued that government expenditures employ workers who consume and invest. In turn, the worker's expenditures employ more workers, and so forth. When the economy has slack capacity, this increased consumption yields a multiplier effect. He believed the multiplier effect was so powerful that when consumers and investors hoard output and the economy's demand for production capacity slackens, the government could hire workers to dig holes and then refill them. Better that than leaving workers sitting idle. A multiplier greater than two would allow the government to waste a dollar digging useless holes and still produce more than a dollar of value from the value of the follow-on demand the expenditure created. A two-times multiplier is substantially higher than in normal times, when the economy nears full capacity, expenditures sum to 100 percent of GDP, and the multiplier must necessarily average one time.

In his bestselling textbook, *Macroeconomics*,[2] leading Keynesian economist Greg Mankiw uses simplified Keynesian logic to estimate the multiplier at 2.5 times—a dollar spent by the government creates $2.50 of GDP—with a 60 percent marginal propensity to consume.* The calculation assumes that only increased consumption has a multiplier effect. It assumes incremental savings are hoarded rather than invested in a slack economy. In a slack economy with excess capacity, why would investors make investments to grow production capacities? Presumably, they would wait for demand to grow, and hoard their output in the meantime. In that case, the key to recovery is increasing consumption.

Today, investment that produces innovation, not investment to increase production for consumption, grows the U.S. economy. Investment in innovation may or may not sit idle, waiting for an increase in consumption. In a recession, investors might continue to hunt for innovation even if there is slack capacity, just as a miner would continue to search for gold before he ran out of money. Stimulating investment for innovation reduces hoarding and increases employment, just like stimulating consumption. In the short run, a dollar spent for innovation is no different from a dollar spent for consumption. Both should have a similar multiplier effect.

In a recession, the decline in investments to produce innovation may be greater than it appears. College graduates have remained in short supply, even in the recession. Rather than lay off college-educated workers, who are hard to recruit, companies have laid off workers who are the least costly to replace. These workers tend to be unskilled, unreliable and possibly overpaid. Talented workers may similarly cut household support staff to reduce risky expenditures in a recession. These cuts reduce investment by pushing support work onto innovators. In that case, investment in innovations shifts to support work. The economy appears to gain productivity in the short run, just as it has, by sacrificing investment that

---

* $2.5 = 1 / [1 - 0.6] = 1 / [1 - \text{marginal propensity to consume}] = 1 + \text{MPC} + \text{MPC}^2 + \text{MPC}^3 + \ldots$

produces growth in the long run. With innovators producing a large share of GDP relative to support workers, a small shift can have a big impact on the growth of the economy. A small reduction in spending for support workers can have a big impact on low-wage unemployment as well. Increasing investment in innovation will put support workers back to work.

If consumption and investment in innovation have multiplier effects, then the multiplier effect from effective fiscal stimulus should be even greater than Mankiw's estimate. The marginal propensity to consume or invest in innovation would be greater than the marginal propensity to consume alone. A 20 percent marginal propensity to hoard (versus 40 percent in the original calculation), for example, yields a five-times multiplier. But to sell the Obama administration's $800 billion stimulus spending package, Christina Romer, chairman of the administration's Council of Economic Advisors, only used a 1.5-times multiplier. Obviously, an economist recommending stimulus spending would argue for the highest multiplier they could sell to other lawmakers without looking silly. Why, then, the reluctance to use a higher multiplier?

There is a big difference between increases in government expenditures when lulls in risk taking are temporary and not permanent reactions to structural changes to the economy and when taxpayers expect lawmakers to offset increases with real cuts to baseline spending in the future. A rational taxpayer, anticipating higher taxes in the future from any increase in spending today, should dial back consumption today. That would offset any increase in government expenditures today and reduce its multiplier effect.

History has proven that lawmakers do not offset increases in government expenditures with future reductions. Future spending cuts are never certain. Quite the opposite; they are virtually nonexistent. Even worse, history suggests that lawmakers are most likely to follow increases in spending with more increases. Since passing its "one-time" stimulus plan, the Obama administration has increased projected spending $4.4 trillion over the next ten years—close to a $0.5 trillion per year increase in run-rate spending.[3] A wise taxpayer might even recognize that not only must lawmakers raise taxes tomorrow to pay for today's increased expenditures, but that these expenditures increase the likelihood of future expenditures and taxes as well. In that case, he should logically cut his consumption today even further.

In the case of using tax cuts rather than increased spending to stimulate economic activity, the taxpayer might similarly hoard the incremental cash he received from the tax cut in order to pay the tax bill when it comes due. If so, he might do the same in other circumstances. If the government borrows to make risky investments, he might recognize that taxpayers are the true bearers of this risk and compensate by dialing down his risk taking. If the government artificially pushes up the price of risky securities by buying in risky times, an investor might hold the cash he receives from the sale and wait to buy securities when government selling artificially pushes the prices down. Economists call this behavior "rational expectations," a concept that won economist Robert Lucas the Nobel Prize. Consumers, savers, and investors adjust their behavior today to fit their rational expectations of the future.

According to the theory of rational expectations, the reaction of consumers and investors to monetary stimulus should be much the same as their reaction to fiscal stimulus: they should dial back consumption and investment to offset its effect. Unexpected price inflation largely transfers wealth from lenders to borrowers and from the private sector to government. If prices rise, a borrower can pay back a borrowed dollar with a dollar that now buys only seventy-five cents of consumption. The lender forwent a dollar of consumption to make a loan, but can only buy seventy-five cents of consumption when the loan is repaid. Similarly, the borrower enjoyed a dollar of consumption, but now must forgo only seventy-five cents of consumption to pay back the loan. Inflation reduces the value of debt, which increases the wealth of borrowers at the expense of lenders. While borrowers may consume their windfall, rational lenders should reduce their expenditures proportionally. One gains at the other's expense, but gains and losses offset one another.

Similarly, because the government can print dollars and spend them, monetary inflation allows the government to spend without increasing taxes. Ultimately, someone in the private sector must pay for increased government expenditures. Rational taxpayers should respond no differently than they would to fiscal stimulus spending, which they will eventually pay—by dialing back investment and consumption.

Because the United States borrows from the rest of the world, unexpected inflation transfers money from offshore economies back to the United States, but the transfer is relatively small. Long-term interest rates should also adjust upward quickly to compensate for expected rises in inflation. The rise in rates may offset the lenders' loss of wealth. In fact, long-term rates could remain high well into the future if lenders lose confidence in the government's commitment to maintaining the value of the currency. When the Fed inflated the money supply in the late 1970s, it took more than two decades for interest rates to reach new lows. In that case, the interest rate increase may cost more than the value of any gains from inflation.

Proponents of inflation claim that it also helps to lower wages. According to the laws of supply and demand, at some lower wage level, employers will hire unemployed workers. Presumably, the unwillingness of employers and employees to cut wages is a partial cause of increased unemployment. Employers may be unwilling to take the risk of cutting wages. Wage cuts can increase the risk of unionization or of employees quitting to find work elsewhere and can lower workforce morale as well. Unexpected inflation may allow employers to cut wages without confronting employees directly. If monetary inflation causes the price of goods to rise more than the price of wages, it cuts wages, albeit obscurely. But price changes tend to be gradual, disproportionately distributed across the economy, and highly uncertain. The adverse reaction of consumers and investors to this increased uncertainty may more than offset any hoped-for benefit from wage reductions.

Increases in the money supply may also sit idle during recessions when consumers and investors are reluctant to borrow money and lenders are reluctant to lend. Unless the money is spent, and production capacities tighten, prices are unlikely to rise. In that case, a little bit of price inflation may require a lot of monetary inflation. The cost of uncertainty from a large increase in the money supply may be enormous and long-lasting relative to a small amount of near-term price inflation. Again, the adverse reaction of consumers and investors to this uncertainty might be far greater than any benefit.

Proponents of inflation also argue that it widens the spread between long-term and short-term interest rates. Long-term rates may rise to reflect expectations of future price inflation while short-term rates remain low from a glut of money available to lend in the interim. A wider spread between long and short rates may motivate risk-averse savers to stop hoarding and take more long-term risk. But if risk-averse savers are reluctant to take risk at almost any price—as surely many of them are—then a lot of highly uncertain monetary inflation may be needed to produce a little more risk taking. Again, the adverse reaction to the increased risk may be substantially greater than the benefits. Many countries tried inflationary monetary policies to stimulate their economies in the 1970s for all these reasons, and have long since concluded that the costs outweigh the benefits.

It's a fact that consumers and investors are not strictly rational, and the economy is too complex for rational calculations. Nor do the economic gears all turn simultaneously, like clockwork. They turn with leads and lags like rubber bands connecting pulleys with differential rates of change that can and do cause the economy to ebb and flow. Proponents of fiscal stimulus believe there are ways to take advantage of these differentials to stimulate growth—at least during a recession that stems from a temporary lack of confidence rather than one that requires structural changes, like the current one, in which we have permanently dialed back risk taking to compensate for the now-recognized risk of damage from withdrawals.

Opponents of fiscal stimulus question whether government spending truly increases overall risk taking and economic activity or if it simply reallocates them from one sector of the economy to another. They question whether the effects of fiscal or monetary policy are predicable enough to be useful or if government intervention merely increases risk. In the latter case, consumers and investors should rationally dial down risk taking even more than they would otherwise. At the very least, rational expectations should significantly offset the beneficial but temporary effects of fiscal and monetary stimulus.

The economy is a tangled web of overlapping feedback loops. Changes to the economy transmit their effect through this complex web differently under different circumstances and conditions. The complexity of these relationships makes it nearly impossible to look at the channels of transmission individually and accurately sum their overall effect. Politicians tend to put their nose close to the paper, point only to the places where employment has increased, ignore offsetting declines elsewhere, and claim success even though employment hasn't increased overall.

Even worse, actions that appear to accelerate growth may do so by setting the economy back. Some pundits, for example, have recommended burning down surplus houses to stimulate construction. It's like take a longer route to avoid traffic. The car might be moving faster, but that doesn't mean we will arrive at our destination sooner. To avoid these distorted perspectives, we must look empirically at the overall growth of the economy to distinguish the true effects from fiscal and monetary stimulus.

Empirical evidence suggests that multipliers are lower than the one used in Romer's sales pitch, perhaps one times or less. Harvard economist Robert Barro[4] uses historical wartime spending data dating back to 1914 to estimate the U.S. spending multiplier at 0.6 to 0.7 at an average unemployment rate of 5.6 percent. His estimate of the multiplier increases about 0.1 percentage points for each percentage point increase in the unemployment rate. That suggests that, unless unemployment reaches 12 percent, the dial-downs in the private sector are greater than the value of increased government expenditures. That's not very encouraging.

A 2009 study published by the National Bureau of Economic Research analyzes forty-five countries dating back to 1960 to reach similar, albeit more detailed, conclusions. The study estimates fiscal multipliers average 1.04 times government expenditures in high-income countries and only 0.8 in developing economies. Fiscal stimulus produces multipliers of 1.5 times in countries with fixed exchange rates, but -0.3 times in countries with flexible exchange rates. The multiplier averages 1.6 times in closed economies and -0.1 times in economies with open trade borders. Fiscal stimulus in countries with high levels of externally held debt produces multipliers that are initially more positive, but then are reduced to zero by negative multiplicative effects that follow soon after. The study concludes, "We have found that, in economies open to trade and operating under flexible exchange rates, a fiscal expansion leads to no significant output gains."[5]

What does that mean for the United States, with its high income, relatively large local economy, flexible exchange rates, and relatively high foreign-held debt? The study estimates the post-1980 U.S. multiplier—a period when exchange rates have floated—at 0.4 times government expenditures. Again, that's not very encouraging. This, however, includes a multiplier of 1.8 times for investment spending and slightly less than zero for increased government consumption. All of the multiplier effect comes from stimulating investment, not consumption.

That's not surprising, especially in an investment-oriented economy like that of the United States. If we borrow money to increase consumption, taxes must rise in the future to pay back the debt. Rational expectations should dampen consumption and investment today in anticipation of higher taxes tomorrow. Even worse, offshore manufacturers capture a substantial portion of the production for our consumption. Increasing consumption stimulates their economy instead of ours. If we borrow to make successful investments in innovation instead, the return on investment should allow us to pay back the debt without the need to raise tax rates.

It's no wonder, then, that lawmakers market fiscal spending

as investments in things like green energy and education, despite true investment being only a small portion of the actual expenditures. According to the Congressional Budget Office, lawmakers budgeted about $100 billion of the $800 billion 2009 stimulus spending for investment.[6]

Theoretically, the government could make investments in innovation that accelerate the economy's transition from a misallocation of capital to subprime consumption to more sustainable endeavors, especially at a time when the private sector is reluctant to make risky investments of any kind. But lawmakers make lousy investors. The economy operates in an environment where success is highly uncertain and in large part randomly distributed. The private sector succeeds by funding many small investments—experiments that Darwinian survival of the fittest ruthlessly rankorders and prunes. With scarce resources, new ideas must outperform existing alternatives—alternatives that are many times more valuable to consumers than their cost. Only a handful of new ideas survive this strenuously competitive process.

The political investment process is entirely the opposite. With absurd levels of confidence, politicians undertake massive endeavors without much, if any, experimentation—a trillion-dollar stimulus program, new health insurance programs for 20 million citizens, 2,000-page reforms of the finance and health care industries, and simultaneous wars in Iraq and Afghanistan, for example. Their false sense of confidence seems to know no bounds.

Nor do political undertakings compete against real-world alternatives. There is typically no reliable way to define success or failure. Political power, not economic logic, rules the day. Special interests fight to shape political choices. They fund politicians and their campaigns rather than letting economic Darwinism shape outcomes, as it does in the private sector. In fact, the political process is a way to garner allocations that Darwinian survival doesn't allow. Obviously, this process for allocating resources is highly inefficient.

Even when the government chooses investments as expertly as private investors, it still distorts capital allocations. What private investor in his right mind would choose to fund the competitors? With a competitor as advantaged and as powerful as the federal government, the game is effectively over before it begins! In a process that requires thousands of failed experiments, government intervention narrows rather than widens the funding for experimentation.

Because of their national perspective, federal policies are also ill-equipped to meet the need for local experimentation. Building a road in Wisconsin won't avoid bankruptcy costs in Florida, where real estate losses and unemployment are high. Nor will it move unemployed Florida workers into new and sustainable endeavors, as would successful local private-sector investments. Similarly, federal lawmakers can't target tax cuts to the regions that need cuts most. Instead, they must spread federal tax cuts evenly across the nation. Even if lawmakers *were* skillful investors, it would be all but impossible for them to target investment where it is needed.

Also, investment projects hastily launched by the government for the sake of short-term economic stimulation are likely to be much less valuable than real investments. Real investments take substantially longer to identify, plan, and undertake. Even President Obama now admits, "There are no shovel-ready projects."[7] Only the private sector has shovel-ready projects.

What then is the true likelihood of success from government-directed investment? The subprime mortgage fiasco demonstrates just how bad politically directed investment decisions can be. The Iraq War provides yet another example of the government's lack of investment prowess. The results are typical of these types of large-scale endeavors. Lawmakers woefully underestimated the true costs of the war, whether through ignorance or for the sake of political expediency. As it unfolded, unanticipated and unintended consequences overwhelmed this large-scale endeavor. In hindsight, the benefits were of dubious value relative to the enormous cost. The results are distressingly similar in other government-sponsored endeavors, which include the government's inability to rein in the runaway costs of Social Security, health care, and municipal labor unions. Where can we find government-run projects whose results were on budget, on time, and better than we expected? Why would we trust politicians to get it right the next time?

If government investments don't pan out, we have not only wasted valuable resources that could have been put to better use, we have also led highly skilled workers to yet another mid-career change. Subprime mortgage investments did exactly that—they diverted a large number of skilled resources to unsustainable endeavors. The economy depends on the productivity of its most talented workers. Career changes permanently set back that productivity.

The government is ill-equipped to replace risk taking and investment in a way that truly avoids losses and bankruptcies and successfully transitions the economy to a more optimal allocation of resources. Many of these losses are unavoidable anyway. In the end, Florida homebuilders need to go bankrupt and move to new endeavors whether politicians intervene or not.

Even without special interests vying for control of the allocation process, lawmakers tend to choose projects, not for their economic viability, but for their ability to garner votes. This results in undertakings that reallocate value from small blocks of voters to large blocks—chiefly from a small number of investors to a large number of consumers. Lawmakers reallocate value rather than create it. It's almost impossible to create value; it's easy to reallocate it.

Most voters consume virtually everything they earn. They save next to nothing, invest even less, and seldom underwrite any risk. What politician seeking reelection is going to demand voters reduce consumption so that their government can increase investment? Instead, politicians cater to the demands of voters in order to get reelected—largely by reallocating income from investors to them. Voters like that!

Liberal lawmakers seek to increase consumption by providing government services to voters, paid with the taxes of rich investors. Conservative lawmakers seek to increase consumption by cutting taxes, but without reducing government services. The latter caters to the taxed, the former to the untaxed.

If stimulus spending borrows to increase consumption rather

than investment, as Obama's stimulus package did, and if the resulting future tax increases are more likely to be borne by successful risk takers, which group is most likely to reduce risk taking in response to increased government spending? The very investors underwriting the myriad risky experiments needed to find new endeavors and redeploy idle workers.

Ironically, Christina Romer's own research adds credibility to the theory that tax increases tomorrow from increased expenditures today dampen investment today. In her November 2008 study, "The Macroeconomic Effects of Tax Changes: Estimates Based on a New Measure of Fiscal Shocks,"[8] she concludes, "Tax increases are highly contractionary. The effects are strongly significant, highly robust, and much larger than those obtained using broader measure . . . The most striking finding . . . is that tax increases have a large negative effect on investment." That's especially worrying because investment is the expenditure with a high multiplier effect.

Government programs that borrow or print money to increase consumption or fund ineffective investment projects are ultimately tax increases. What difference does it make whether the government borrows money today from a taxpayer, or taxes them? Either way, the taxpayer has less money today. If the government later increases their taxes and pays back their loan, it's a wash. When the taxpayer receives the money from the repayment of the debt, he has to hand it back over for the new higher taxes. The increased taxation and expenditure occurred today, not in the future, no matter how confusing the accounting scheme. Taxes increase precisely when the post-Crisis economy needs to transition to a new allocation of resources.

Borrowing from the Chinese rather than from rich American investors is scarcely any different from borrowing from ourselves; the borrowed money still represents a future tax increase. According to Romer's research, taxpayers should respond rationally by dialing back investment today. If the quantity of dollar-denominated offshore funds available to borrow is fixed—if offshore producers choose to run trade surpluses independent of prevailing interest rates—then increased government borrowing necessarily displaces current or future private-sector borrowing. This is no different from the government borrowing from domestic lenders directly. If interest rates influence the size of the trade deficits, then increased government borrowing, which raises interest rates and encourages offshore producers to expand trade surpluses, pushes jobs offshore to increase the quantity of dollar-denominated offshore funds available to borrow. It doesn't subtract from a fixed amount of available debt as it does in the first case, but it doesn't stimulate domestic job growth, either. It stimulates offshore growth. The empirical evidence of near-zero multipliers on increased government consumption in countries with open trade borders may be indicative of that effect.

Another way to boost consumption is by cutting the taxes of poor consumers. But, as with increasing government expenditures, the gains in consumption come at the expense of rich taxpayers. If the economy uses tax cuts to increase consumption rather than investment, it yields no increase in the tax base to pay for the increase. Rich taxpayers should cut investment in anticipation of future tax increases.

Cutting the taxes of rich investors, however, can have the opposite effect when investors are willing to take risk and invest their tax cuts. When the government cuts taxes, it must then borrow from risk-averse surplus exporters to fund expenditures. In effect, the government borrows cheap funds from the Chinese to loan rich investors their taxes. The taxpayer underwrites the risk of investing a portion of the proceeds as equity. In that case, the government has turned risk-averse debt into equity. That grows equity, risk taking, and the economy. Again, wage earners and consumers are the chief beneficiaries. Unlike an increase in consumption, increased investment grows the future tax base needed to repay the increased debt. In a recession, when investors are reluctant to take a risk, this effect is diminished. (In truth, we can't really cut the taxes of the rich. They pay too high a share of the taxes. In the end, all we can do is lend them their taxes.)

It's no surprise, then, that the effect of fiscal and monetary stimulus on the U.S. economy has not been encouraging, either. Unless the Obama administration greatly underestimated the extent of the recession and its effect on unemployment, the stimulus appears to have had a much smaller effect on employment than expected (see Figure 8-1). Obviously, any administration would have a strong incentive to overestimate the severity of the recession and its impact on employment in order to claim credit when things turned out better than expected. At the time of the stimulus, the administration's outlook was so pessimistic, it drove the Dow down to a low of 6,547, despite the fact that the Dow rapidly recovered to 10,000 soon afterward. That strongly suggests that the recession was not as bad as painted in the administration's dire forecast. Nevertheless, unemployment has been far worse than the administration's expectations. While the interpretation of the results is ambiguous, it's hard to look at the outcome relative to the likely biases in the forecast and conclude that the stimulus worked as well as advertised.

Nor can we look at the economy's reaction to the stimulus in a vacuum. Considering the government's enormous response to the Financial Crisis, it's surprising how unresponsive the economy has

FIGURE 8-1: Actual U.S. Unemployment vs. Forecasted Unemployment

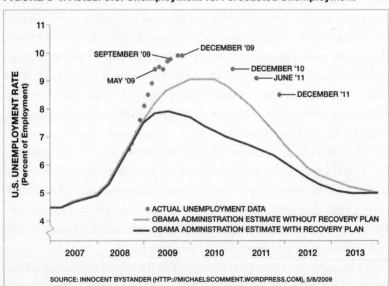

SOURCE: INNOCENT BYSTANDER (HTTP://MICHAELSCOMMENT.WORDPRESS.COM), 5/8/2009

been. When economic activity slackened, progressive tax rates automatically cut taxes in the current recession. The Congressional Budget Office estimates these tax cuts were even larger than the stimulus (see Figure 8-2).[9] Federal taxes fell from 18.5 percent of GDP before the recession to less than 15 percent afterward. Also, the Fed printed money and used it to make short-term loans and to buy newly issued Treasuries to fund increased spending. It was able to do this without causing price inflation. Without offsetting inflation, monetary expansion should stimulate increased risk taking if rational expectations don't offset these increases. The Fed also purchased over $1 trillion of risky mortgages to reduce the private underwriting of risk and to inject money into the economy. Under "QE2" (a second round of "quantitative easing," or injection of funds), the Fed bought another $600 billion of long-term securities. The government also made first explicit and now implicit guarantees of asset-backed and commercial paper and bank deposits. These guarantees shifted risk from the private sector to the public sector. As well, mortgage defaults and delinquencies have contracted mortgage payments at the expense of bank equity, which banks have now replenished largely with offshore investments that added to the economy's resources. Despite all these actions to stimulate the economy in addition to the fiscal stimulus, employment has been anemic. If the economy truly responds to government policies, as Keynesians predict, without the offsetting effect of rational expectations, it's hard to believe the economy wouldn't have responded more vigorously to this strenuous combination of monetary and fiscal stimulus. Frankly, it's hard to detect any response at all.

It is likely that circumstances surrounding this recession strengthened adverse investor reaction to increased government consumption beyond what is typical. Where the government has substantial unused debt capacity, or recession stems from a temporary setback in confidence rather than the need for structural changes, a temporary increase in government expenditures might logically lead to less concern that spending and taxes will rise in the future. In the current situation, the opposite is true. Government

FIGURE 8-2: U.S. Federal Spending and Revenues Relative to GDP

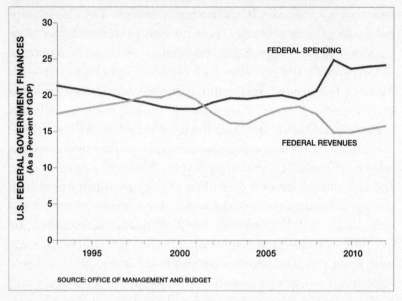

SOURCE: OFFICE OF MANAGEMENT AND BUDGET

spending, deficits, and debt were already high and taxes low relative to spending, making the risk of tax increases greater. A filibuster-proof majority of Democrats added to the risk of further increases in expenditures and taxes, which proved true with the Patient Protection and Affordable Care Act. The same Democratic majority also increased the risk of disproportionately higher taxes on rich investors—tax increases that the expiration of the Bush tax cuts portended. The economy also required structural changes to compensate for the risk of panicked withdrawals, which changes, at least so far, have not mitigated. A reduction in risk taking to compensate for that risk slows the transition to a more sustainable allocation of risk taking, which slows growth. That makes increased government spending, without tax increases, that much more unsustainable. The popularity of entitlements makes spending cuts unlikely. Diminished unused debt capacity increases the chances of unexpected monetary inflation to meet spending needs or to fulfill implicit guarantees, like those extended to European banks in the face of Greece's sovereign debt crisis. All of these circumstantial factors likely increased the offsetting effects of rational expectations.

An *Economist* article, "Much Ado About Multipliers,"[10] sums up the problem. The article concludes that "policymakers looking for precise estimates [of the multiplier] are deluding themselves." The "truth is that economists are flying blind." In his *Wall Street Journal*[11] review of Robert Skidelsky's book, *Keynes: The Return of the Master*, Greg Mankiw reaches a similar conclusion. He admits that "mathematics is fundamentally the language of logic. Modern research into Keynes's theories—I have conducted research myself—tried to put his ideas into mathematical form precisely to figure out whether they logically cohere. It turns out that the task is not easy." That's hardly the kind of certainty upon which trillion-dollar investments should be justified—especially in these already risky times. It is likely that uncertainty surrounding the true benefits of the stimulus only adds to the offsetting fears of investors and consumers.

Even worse, policymakers have unwittingly failed to distinguish a temporary reduction in risk taking from a permanent one. The need for structural change renders the effect from the stimulus temporary at best; when the stimulus ends, the structural problems remain, and once again, the economy dials back risk taking to compensate. Meanwhile, government intervention distorts the allocation of resources and slows the transition to sustainable alternatives. The stimulus exhausts precious resources, scares off productive risk taking, leaves structural problems unresolved, and accumulates a mountain of debt in its wake. If taxpayers failed to realize that the stimulus would leave a bill without producing permanent results, it's hardly lost on them now.

IMMIGRATION AND TRADE POLICIES

If we won't take the steps necessary to protect our economy from another bank run, and if fiscal stimulus doesn't create a permanent increase in employment, then what else can we do to reduce unemployment in the near term?

Recall that risk-averse savings leave us caught on the horns of a dilemma. We can leave risk-averse savings sitting idle and available to fund withdrawals, in which case we will have low but stable growth and lower employment. Or we can put those funds to work and have faster but more volatile growth and more employment. We have logically chosen the latter. Who are the chief beneficiaries of this policy? Immigrants and offshore workers. Who then should bear the risk of this increased volatility?

In the future, when we have learned to manage our economy more effectively, immigrants will begin life in America as temporary guest workers before we give them permanent residency. We'll skim the cream from the rest of the world's workforce and replace the less skillful and less reliable with an unlimited flow of temporary workers eager for their chance to make more money. We'll save a lot of money managing our workforce that way, by avoiding retiree benefits, for example. In a recession, we'll send unreliable workers home to reduce the volatility of our domestic employment.

If we don't idle temporary guest workers instead of our permanent residents, we'll idle offshore workers instead—or more likely, both. We can do that by either restricting their imports in a recession or by demanding they buy more of our goods as a condition of our buying theirs. When the economy is hoarding, as it is in a recession, we don't need their risk-averse short-term savings; we need them to buy goods that employ our less-skilled workers. These restrictions will prevent stimulus spending from merely stimulating the growth of imports.

It's concerning to imagine well-intentioned but misguided lawmakers holding the power to control imports. They would surely make a mess of it. Long-lasting restrictions on imports would slow our growth. They would suboptimize capital investment and unnecessarily consume high-cost domestic resources that could have been used more productively elsewhere.

And let's not underestimate the cost and difficulty of implementing such policies. Yanking away hardworking immigrants who perform jobs Americans are reluctant to fill could quickly damage businesses, and damage them permanently. Unreliable workers and workers who demand more pay than they are worth relative to alternatives are more prone to layoffs. It may be difficult to replace reliable hardworking immigrants with these workers. Unemployed workers may be reluctant to move to where available but short-lived jobs are located. Product prices would need to rise to pay wages necessary to attract workers. Price rises and subsequent declines take time, and the resulting changes are uncertain and disruptive. Businesses would need time to adapt to a more uncertain supply of immigrant labor. Reckless policies here could easily do more harm than good and the harm could be long lasting.

Nevertheless, thoughtful trade and immigration policies could reduce the volatility of domestic employment at a cost to the economy that's less than the cost of unemployment. Where we have production capacities that overlap with offshore producers—in automobiles and paper, for example—temporarily slowing trade deficits would better utilize our temporarily slack capacities. Why boost demand with ineffective fiscal stimulus, a portion of which merely stimulates foreign production, instead of forcing offshore economies to help fix our problem directly? Surely, the latter is more cost effective.

A long-term policy that uses risk-averse savings to accelerate growth is valuable to America. If we don't employ the world's army of cheap labor and capital, the rest of the world will. And the rest of the world is, first and foremost, China, which is rapidly catching us. Forgoing the value of low-cost labor widens their competitive advantage. If we make goods with high-cost labor that we could have made with low-cost labor, we've wasted the opportunity to redeploy our labor to more productive endeavors. Again, if off-shore labor is free, how much of it should we buy? All of it! At seventy-five cents an hour, it's effectively free.

But let's not kid ourselves about where this strategy leads. Risky innovation and access to cheap offshore goods and capital will drive our growth. The economy will distribute income unequally to a handful of lucky risk takers. The value of innovation will drive up demand and wages in the local service economy. We will need confidence in that growth to borrow and redeploy risk-averse offshore savings. It's a risky, volatile, high-growth strategy.

Well-intentioned populists will attack the unequal distribution of income and our open trade borders. They won't see that taxing lucky risk takers reduces risk taking, which slows innovation and, ultimately, the growth of domestic wages and employment. Nor will they see that closing trade borders will similarly slow our growth relative to the rest of the world. Their mistaken demands will grow more urgent in recessions, when unemployment is high and wages are falling. All things considered, it will cost less and be less risky politically to restrict international trade and immigration in a recession in order to reduce unemployment than to cling to policies that only maximize growth in the long run. Pragmatic immigration and trade policies could contribute significantly to reducing unemployment in recessions.

ALTERNATIVE COURSES OF ACTION

If fiscal stimulus under the current set of circumstances is temporary at best, and if our lawmakers can't or won't take steps to strengthen the government's guarantees of short-term debt nor use trade and immigration policies to our advantage, what else can we do to reduce unemployment?

The theory of rational expectations asserts that risk takers—both consumers and investors—will take more risk today if they see a brighter future tomorrow—a future with more equity to underwrite risk, better chances of success if they take risk, and higher payoffs if they succeed. Unless risk taking increases, efforts to improve the economy will merely shift economic activity from one endeavor to another.

To increase risk taking, lawmakers must do everything they can to bolster confidence. They need to demonstrate their clear understanding of the contemporary economy, the Financial Crisis, and the limitations of the government to increase employment permanently. They must take responsibility for passing this understanding on to their constituents. Falsely blaming predatory lending and fraudulent securitization when the problem is a buildup of hair-triggered short-term savings, unreliable government guarantees, and default-prone mortgages causes risk takers to lose confidence in the effectiveness of lawmakers to solve the problem.

Lawmakers also need to minimize the number of changes needed to strike at the heart of the problems. Failing to do so forces risk takers to adapt to unnecessary changes with unintended consequences. This increases risk and slows risk taking. Dodd-Frank is a prime example. Its more than 2,300 pages of regulation impose far-reaching rule changes on the economy, which affect everything from consumer protection to commodities' futures to corporate proxy rules that had little if anything to do with the Crisis. It leaves 235 rule makings unresolved pending extensive additional work and negotiation by regulators, including rules that have a major impact on critical issues such as proprietary trading by banks and margin requirements for swaps and futures. It increases the risk of damage from withdrawals rather than reducing it; reduces short-selling by restricting proprietary trading, which increases systematic risk; and threatens credit default swaps with unresolved rule changes at a time when we need more equity to underwrite risk. These radical, unnecessarily far-reaching, unresolved, and, in some instances, misguided rule changes slow rather than accelerate lending at a time when lending is already tentative.

In the absence of stronger government guarantees, the Fed attempts to accelerate growth by reducing short-term interest rates by expanding the money supply. In effect, it dares anyone to use hair-triggered short-term debt. So far, no one is biting. But the risk of inflation this causes, which threatens to unpredictably reallocate assets from lenders to borrowers and from the private sector to the public sector, increases uncertainty and slows risk taking.

If lawmakers hope to stimulate growth with fiscal stimulus, they must do it in a way that bolsters rather than lessens confidence. That requires spending money in ways that put government expenditures on a more sustainable trajectory. Investing in high-cost green energy or lengthening unemployment benefits rather than hiring displaced workers to create value increases the fear of future tax increases. A more logical expenditure would fund otherwise laid-off municipal workers, but only if they agreed to increase future contributions to their medical insurance and retirement benefits. That solves both near-term and long-term problems.

The Obama administration and its filibuster-proof congressional majority did the opposite. They passed an $800 billion stimulus that handed money to the states and their workers without demanding anything in return. They funded investment projects with little chance of success and extended unemployment benefits that increased rather than decreased the incremental cost of hiring idle workers. These unproductive and unsustainable expenditures increased rather than decreased the threat of future tax increases.

Even ultraliberal economist Paul Krugman agrees. "Public policy designed to help workers who lose their jobs can lead to structural unemployment as an unintended side effect."[12] Harvard economist Robert Barro estimates that the Obama administration's extension of unemployment benefits from twenty-six weeks to ninety-nine weeks has increased unemployment from 6.8 percent to 9.5 percent.[13] The longer we extend unemployment benefits the more they slow rather than accelerate the necessary reallocation of labor and capital. Unless idle workers create value for their government pay, the likelihood of future tax increases.

In the midst of the Financial Crisis, Democrats also used their filibuster-proof majority to divert the legislature's agenda to garnering a trillion dollars of income redistribution over the next ten years for their constituents through the Patient Protection and Affordable Care Act without first agreeing behind closed doors to compromises with Republicans to rein in health care usage. The difficulty with controlling health care cost today is that the usage of health care is wasteful because it is ungoverned by cost. Insurance is like going to dinner with friends who agree to split the bill evenly no matter what each person orders. This arrangement incentivizes everyone to order lobster and caviar. They demand all the health care they can get regardless of the cost. This is especially problematic with government-supplied health care because the recipients of that health care, namely, retirees and the poor, aren't the voters who pay the costs. Rationalizing the usage of health care based on the cost of services is the single biggest obstacle to long-term economic growth. Why would Democrats—the representatives of poor consumers—champion health care usage based on costs? They wanted exactly the opposite, and they achieved it. The law expands coverage without first controlling usage. This just puts a bigger burden on future tax payers without stimulating much if any increase in consumption during the current recession. That might be clever politics, but it's reckless economic policy. Investors recognize that they won't be able to buy Democratic support for rational health care usage without paying for their support with another trillion dollars. That kind of reckless legislating weakens investors' confidence and increases expectations of future taxes.

Because of this enormous shortcoming, Massachusetts voters tried to stop the passage of the health care bill by handing Ted Kennedy's senate seat to Republicans in order to defeat the Democrats' filibuster-proof majority and block the bill's passage. Democrats used the legislative process of reconciliation in an unprecedented way to pass the bill despite losing their filibuster-proof majority and the support of a majority of voters, even Massachusetts voters who reliably vote for Democrats. The Democratic Party's disregard—even contempt—for voters, and determination to ram far-reaching health care legislation through Congress further undermined voter confidence. Clearly, the priority of Democrats was to take advantage of their once-in-a-lifetime opportunity to pass health care, not accelerate growth.

The Obama administration, in addition to showing little willingness to work with Republicans on health care reform, has also refused to rein in popular but unrealistic entitlement promises. Sadly, there doesn't appear to be enough concern among retirees and near-retirees for the generation that follows. The threat of future draconian tax increases on successful young risk takers—a credible threat, given the political clout of retirees and the unwillingness of Democrats to join Republicans in opposing them— should increasingly dampen risk taking today. Ironically, successful risk taking today is the only shot we have at funding growing

entitlements without wrecking our economy. The alternative—
immigration—increases the likelihood of heavy taxes on successful risk takers by increasing the number of low-income voters.

Social Security and Medicare should be solvent for years to
come because they have taken in more tax revenue than they distribute; and they would be if politicians had truly saved and
invested those surpluses. But they used them to fund government
expenditures. With baby boomers beginning to retire in the next
several years (see Figure 8-3), expenditures now ramp up quickly.
To fund growing entitlements we must now raise taxes, increase
our rate of borrowing, or cut other government expenditures.
Grandfathering the benefits of near-retirees and agreeing to cut
future benefits does not solve this problem. Neither party can lead
the way on their own without the other party undermining them
with false promises of future benefits without additional taxes. A
compromise that increases growth probably requires preserving
near-term social-security benefits at the expense of reduced
end-of-life medical care.

FIGURE 8-3: Projected Social Security Outlays Relative to GDP

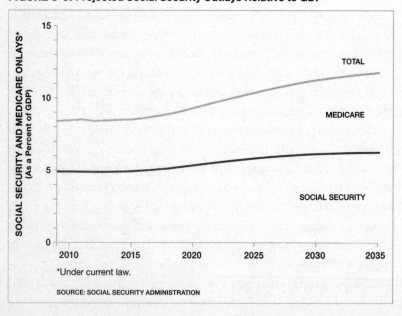

To encourage risk taking and accumulate equity more rapidly, lawmakers needed to lower the marginal tax rate permanently on successful investors. The failure of temporary stimulus to create permanent employment in the face of unresolved structural problems and the passage of expensive new health care coverage increases rather than decreases the threat of future taxes and dampens risk taking. Even if it's impractical to lower the income taxes on risk underwriters at this time, lower U.S. corporate taxes would encourage more risk taking.

American corporations face one of the highest tax rates in the world—39 percent, including state taxes. Germany's corporate tax rate is 30 percent; Korea's is 24 percent. A high corporate tax rate makes domestic businesses less competitive with competitors from countries with lower tax rates. At the same time, high domestic corporate tax rates make multinational companies reluctant to invest in the United States instead of basing operations in countries with low corporate taxes and exporting to the United States from places like Ireland, which has only a 12 percent corporate rate. Opponents of lower corporate taxes claim corporations pay low taxes even though U.S. rates are high, so lower rates will have a minimal effect. It's true that American corporations avoid paying U.S. taxes, but they often avoid them by moving operations offshore. Ireland, with one of the lowest corporate tax rates, had one of the fastest growing economies in recent years. Like the United States, Ireland also failed to utilize the influx of foreign investment prudently. But in hindsight, controlling a gusher of offshore capital is a nice problem to have.

Where domestic producers avoid international competitors with lower tax rates, in construction, for example, consumers ultimately pay corporate taxes in the higher price of goods. The reason politicians prefer higher corporate taxes is because most consumers don't recognize that they are being taxed. And in the eyes of their naïve followers, high corporate tax rates make populist politicians look like they aren't simpatico with "greedy" corporations and rich investors. In addition to making U.S. companies more competitive internationally and the United States more attractive to investors, lowering corporate taxes lowers the price of goods and services to consumers. Lower prices should also help stimulate consumer demand.

Repatriating offshore corporate profits and distributing them to shareholders may convert short-term capital that currently sits idle into long-term capital or consumption. It's misleading to claim offshore profits sit offshore, unavailable for use in the United States; they do not. U.S. companies deposit their offshore cash in U.S. banks.* That cash is available for domestic borrowing. Unfortunately, in a recession, short-term funds sit idle. Distributing these funds to shareholders may convert a large portion of them from short-term debt to equity, or into consumption.

All these mistakes by the Obama administration—the failure to take actions that would have increased rather than decreased investor confidence, the failure to reduce the risk of damage from withdrawals by strengthening government guarantees of short-term debt, and the failure to use immigration and trade policies to increase employment—dampened growth significantly. In 1982 and 1974, the United States suffered severe recessions with levels of unemployment similar to the 2008 recession. In the 1982 recession, the economy fell 2.8 percent† and unemployment rose to 10.8 percent. In the seven quarters that followed the end of that recession, the economy grew 11.8 percent, a 9 percent increase over its previous peak. In the 1974 recession, the economy fell 3.2 percent; unemployment reached 9 percent and the economy rebounded 8.3 percent in the seven quarters that followed—a 5.1 percent increase over the previous peak. In the 2008 recession, the economy fell 4.1 percent; unemployment reached 10.1 percent but the seven-quarter rebound through the first quarter of 2011 has only

---

*   or they purchase Treasuries, which pushes risk-averse savings that would otherwise buy Treasuries into bank deposits.

†   All percentages are cumulative and real, not nominal, except where noted.

increased GDP 4.9 percent, a 0.8 percent increase over the previous peak. A post-2008 rebound in the historic range of 8.3 percent to 11.8 percent instead of 4.9 percent would have increased GDP by $0.5 trillion to $1 trillion per year by the first quarter of 2011. A 5 percent to 9 percent increase over the previous peak, instead of the 0.8 percent increase, would have added $0.6 trillion to $1.2 trillion per year of GDP at a similar point in the recovery. The magnitude of the difference and its toll on the unemployed has been enormous.

It's no surprise, then, that when the Obama administration and Democrats won a filibuster-proof majority in the November 2008 election, the Dow dropped from about 9,000—the level at which it had stabilized in the wake of the widespread financial panic during September and October of that year—to 7,552 on November 20. When the Obama administration continued the emergency measures initiated by the Bush administration to mitigate panicked withdrawals, the Dow once again recovered to 9,000 at the end of 2008. But six months later, when the administration laid out its legislative agenda, the Dow plunged to a low of 6,547 on March 9, 2009 (see Figure 8-4). That's an astonishing 27 percent drop in value. Clearly, those downward market spikes were not indicative of an administration that inspired investor confidence in the wake of the Financial Crisis—in hindsight, rightly so. In contrast, after Reagan laid out his administration's agenda, the Dow rose from about 800 to over 1,000 in 1982, a 27 percent increase.

If voters want economic policies that increase risk taking, accelerate growth, and reduce unemployment, they must elect lawmakers who respect and encourage risk takers. The alternative is lawmakers who believe the increased risk of damage from withdrawals, increased government spending (which demands higher taxes), and far-reaching regulatory changes filled with unintended consequences has little, if any, impact on risk taking, economic growth, and increased employment. So far, the anemic economic rebound has proven them wrong.

FIGURE 8-4: Effect of Democratic Filibuster-Proof Victory on the Dow Jones Average

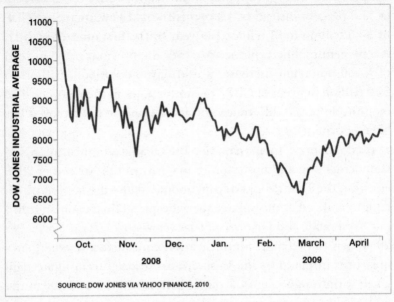

SOURCE: DOW JONES VIA YAHOO FINANCE, 2010

CONCLUSIONS

Strengthening government guarantees of short-term debt and using trade and immigration policies to reduce the volatility of U.S. employment were the two most effective policies the government had at its disposal to dampen the economy's contraction and accelerate its recovery. Strengthening government guarantees of short-term debt would have encouraged its increased usage. Instead, risk-averse capital sits idle. Restricting the trade deficit would have increased domestic employment in the short run. A guest-worker program would have allowed us to export unemployment. Given that our pro-growth and employment economic policies increase immigration and offshore employment, pushing unemployment to these beneficiaries in a recession, rather than to our own citizens, is logical and necessary.

Failing to utilize those options left significant structural issues unresolved. The now-recognized risk of damage from withdrawals dampens risk taking in both consumption and investment. Open trade borders allow fiscal stimulus to stimulate offshore production at the expense of our own. Open immigration allows marginal employment to expand rapidly when times are good. This employment is fragile in a recession.

A one-time increase in fiscal stimulus in the face of these permanent structural problems produces a temporary increase in employment at best. Rational expectations reduce temporary gains. Leakage of the stimulus to offshore producers reduces its effect further. We're left with an $800 billion tab, but little, if any, permanent increase in employment.

The Obama administration's disregard for the expectations of risk takers added further to the recession. It diverted blame for the Crisis to bankers and used the resulting public sentiment to pass unnecessarily far-reaching regulatory changes filled with unintended consequences that slowed lending. It fought to prevent foreclosures, which added to withdrawals and still-idle savings. It rammed through health care legislation over the objection of voters that redistributed income without truly containing health care usage. It wasted opportunities to use the stimulus to reduce long-term expenditures. It fought hard to prevent Republicans from using Congress's authority to increase the debt ceiling to cut cost. And it refused to address long-term entitlement reform despite near-suicidal willingness on the part of Republicans to support reductions. These positions threatened every working American with higher taxes.

Even if we fail to address our structural problems, it's not too late to address most of these other issues in a way that will bolster confidence and contribute to growth rather than dampening it. We just need voters who will elect lawmakers who understand the importance of these changes.

CHAPTER NINE

REDISTRIBUTING INCOME

REDUCING THE THREAT of higher taxes on successful risk takers may benefit the economy overall by increasing risk taking and accelerating the accumulation of equity needed to underwrite risk, but even if consumers and wage earners capture most of the value from investment, the rich still capture a disproportionate share of that value. According to the U.S. Census Bureau,[1] the lowest 20 percent of wage earners and their families only capture 5 percent of disposable income* properly adjusted to include government transfer payments, imputed real estate rents, and untaxed fringe benefits. Because of tax credits and transfer payments, this is slightly more than the 2 percent of the taxable income they earn. This doesn't include the value of indirect government services they receive, such as schooling for their children, police protection, and the like, which is substantial. The middle 40 percent of wage earners earn about a third of the income. Considering the amount of income recaptured by rich investors, is investment good for the poor and the middle class, or would they be better off if we taxed the rich and redistributed their income? Must we really allow the rich to consume so much when the poor are in need?

---

* Pretax income, plus imputed rents and non-taxed health care benefits, less taxes, plus transfer payments.

MORAL TRADE-OFFS

Typical of the argument for the view that advocates taxing the rich is Peter Singer's *The Life You Can Save*.[2] While wearing an expensive suit, you come upon a pond where a child is drowning. Would you ruin the suit by jumping into the water to save the child? If so, why did you buy the suit in the first place when you could have spent the money saving a child in poverty? The value of a dollar to a poor child is far greater than a dollar consumed by the rich. A rich man's suit is arguably worth nothing to society.

If the choice were merely a matter of the tradeoff between the needless consumption of rich investors relative to the much needier consumption of the poor, the decision would be easy. It would be beneficial to society overall to choose the poor. But the trade-off is hardly that simple.

Even if we place no value on the consumption of the rich, we must recognize that the rich invest rather than consume a portion of their income. That investment creates enormous value for consumers and wage earners *over and above* the value it creates for investors. The poor and the middle class capture a portion of that value, even if it's a small portion. At the very least, we must compare the value captured by the poor and the middle class from investment relative to the value they capture from a dollar of redistributed income. If the value they capture from investment is greater, they would be better served in the long run by lower taxes.

Several parameters factor into this trade-off. In Chapter 4 we saw that an incremental dollar of income earned by the rich yields only sixty cents of apparently worthless consumption. It also yields forty cents of valuable investment. That investment is valuable to society far beyond its value to investors.

In Chapter 2, we also saw that workers, not investors, capture 70 percent of the value of investment as wages (see Figure 2-1). They also capture the value of products over and above their price, the so-called buyers surplus. This value can be substantially larger than a product's price. For example, the value of Google,

Facebook, and Microsoft to users relative to their price, which is nearly free, is enormous. Bill Gates and Mark Zuckerberg might get rich, but they capture only a fraction of the value created by their innovations. If goods and services are worth twice their price—and they are surely worth far more than that—non-investors will capture 85 percent of the value from investment—the value as buyer surplus and 70 percent of half as wages. They would capture 5.7 times more value than the remaining 15 percent captured by investors.* As we saw in Chapter 2, the true ratio could easily top 20:1.

Historically, investment has produced a 7.5 percent per year real return† for investors.[3] An investor who demanded a 7.5 percent per year return (which economists call a "discount rate," a "hurdle rate," and the "time value of money") would be indifferent between receiving $1.00 today, which is certain, or receiving $1.075 a year from now from a risky investment. For the same reason, they would be indifferent between receiving a $1.00 today and seven-and-a-half cents a year forever from a risky investment or owning a risky investment worth $1.00 today that kept increasing in value at 7.5 percent a year for as long as they own it (economists call this "accretion"). Less risky investments, such as investments in inventory, typically begin paying annual returns almost immediately and continue to pay for a long time, whereas riskier investments in innovation usually accrete in value over their life. Investments in things such as plant and equipment take time to build and reach their full potential. They accrete in value and then eventually pay annual dividends.

Economists often use a 2 percent discount rate to justify social investments, such as investments to arrest global warming. Again, from Chapter 2, 1 percent to 2 percent per year is the return capital

---

* 85% = [70% × 50%] + [100% × 50%]; 5.7x = 85% / 15%; within this conceptual framework, a case can be made for 0.70 of buyers' surplus rather than $1.00.

† Real return is the return over and above inflation. Some economists use a slightly lower equity return. They argue that a 7.5% per year return is unsustainable because a one-time expansion in historic stock market price-earnings ratios generated a portion of that return. I use the historical returns because I contend that an ongoing unaccounted-for shift to intangible investment (described in Chapter 2) accounts for this expansion in P/E ratios.

would earn if investment were optimized. Highly progressive taxes on investors and businesses redistribute income from investors to consumers, including the government. The top 5 percent of income earners, for example—the principal owners of risk-bearing capital—pay close to 50 percent of all federal taxes (see Figure 9-1). This reduces the capital available for investment. Deficit-funded government spending unrestrained by taxation pushes up the growth in government spending, at the expense of investment, higher still. The reluctance of the current generation to save and invest on behalf of the next generation—as evidenced by our unwillingness to rein in government spending—adds to the shortage of capital as well. It makes little sense for society to discount the value of investment more than they otherwise would because of a shortage of capital.

FIGURE 9-1: Share of U.S. Taxpayers, Income and Taxes Paid by Income Percentiles (2007)

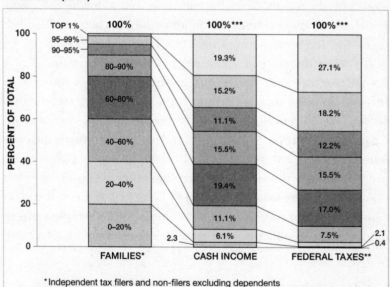

* Independent tax filers and non-filers excluding dependents
** Income, payroll, corporate and estate taxes
*** Segments adjusted to total 100%

SOURCE: TAX POLICY CENTER, URBAN INSTITUTE AND BROOKINGS INSTITUTE; RACHEL M. JOHNSON AND JEFFREY ROHALY, "THE DISTRIBUTION OF FEDERAL TAXES, 2009–12"; USED WITH PERMISSION OF THE URBAN INSTITUTE.

Investors also face far more risk of capturing value from their investments than society does. For this reason, investors logically demand a higher return from investment than society. Competition between investors drives down the returns they capture to near-zero. It wipes out competitive advantages quickly. And it distributes returns somewhat randomly between competing investors. AOL trumps Prodigy; Yahoo trumps AOL; and Google trumps Yahoo. Society faces far less risk. Competition between investors ensures that consumers and wage earners capture almost all the value and that the captured value is long-lasting. It scarcely matters to non-investors whether they capture 90 percent or 95 percent of the value, whereas small differences in the amount consumers capture make a big difference to the returns left over for investors. Society is also largely indifferent to which competing investors succeed and which fail. Society gets the benefit from social networking whether Facebook or MySpace succeeds. And the value of innovation builds on itself ad infinitum. Each breakthrough innovation—electricity, the telephone, radio, television, and so forth—is foundational to the advancements that follow—the Internet, email, search capability, and social networking. Their benefits last forever.

If society demands a 2 percent per year return instead of a 7.5 percent per year return and captures 5.7 times more from investment than investors, then forty cents of investment that accretes at 7.5 percent a year for ten years, or one that pays out 7.5 percent a year for twenty years (and gradually returns the original forty cents), is worth about $3.65 to society today. This assumes products are worth twice their price, including the buyers' surplus; therefore $3.65 of value equates to $1.80 of cash.* If non-investors capture $1.80 of value from forty cents of other people's investment and the middle class (the middle 40 percent of income earn-

---

* $1.82 of cash buys $3.65 of value—the good priced at a $1.82 and a $1.82 of buyers' surplus. The text rounds $1.82 to $1.80. Note the assumed amount of buyers' surplus both increases the return on investment captured by non-investors but then diminishes the cash equivalence of that value by a similar amount. One effect largely offsets the other. This makes the conclusion less sensitive to this assumption than it may appear.

ers) captures a third of that value (see Figure 9-1) then sixty cents in cash is captured by the middle class.* If the government had taxed the rich and redistributed a dollar of their income—both the forty cents of investment and the sixty cents of consumption— and if the middle class had captured their proportional 40 percent share of that dollar, they would have received forty cents of redistributed income. Income redistribution leaves the middle class significantly worse off. They give up sixty cents from investment to gain forty cents of redistributed income. It's especially bad for their children, who will share disproportionately in future benefits from investment.

The lowest 20 percent of wage earners only capture 5 percent of the $1.80, or nine cents of value. To garner that nine cents, they must forego 20 percent of the dollar of redistributed income, or twenty cents. The poor, therefore, would rather forgo investment.

It's no surprise that the poor capture so little of the value from investment. Of the 44 million people in poverty in 2009, according to the Census,[4] very few work. They largely garner value through income redistribution, not through the economics of investment, which creates value through wages and the consumption it buys. Sixteen million of the 44 million are children. They're in poverty because their caregivers are poor. Of the 28 million adults in poverty, only 2.6 million work full time. Almost no one with a full-time job lives in poverty. Of the remaining 25 million adults, 75 percent don't work at all, and 3.7 million are disabled. Approximately 4 million represent an increase in unemployment from 2006, when unemployment was essentially zero and anyone who truly wanted a job could have one. Single mothers number 4.4 million adults in poverty. Most are not supported by the fathers of their children. Those single mothers are caregivers to two-thirds of the 16 million children living in poverty.

Today, the bottom 20 percent of households supply only fifteen hours per week of work, on average. Their incomes don't reflect the economic wages of the working poor; they reflect benefits paid

---

* $0.60 = $1.80 / 3; more, if middle-class expenditures skew toward consumption.

by the government. A 2005 study published by the National Bureau of Economic Research[5] shows that "structural changes in wages, largely regarded as the major culprit of the increase in income inequality, explain less than a quarter of the rise in the measure of family income inequality." In fact, 70 percent of income inequality between the top and bottom deciles of wage earners comes from a decline in the income of the lowest decile relative to the median wage and "only 8% of the [70 percent] increase in the measure of inequality was attributable to wage changes." The study concludes, "Changes in labor supply [i.e., hours worked] and other income [government benefits] were the principal causes of the growing distance between the poor and the middle-income families." More accurately then, income redistribution and its detrimental effect on investment is harmful to anyone who works or seeks work—even Hispanic immigrants and offshore workers who seek work at low wages.

The middle class is no better off taxing the rich and distributing a share of their income to the poor than they are paying the poor's share themselves. As noted, leaving the dollar with the rich and letting them invest it on behalf of the economy is worth sixty cents to the middle class. If the middle class allowed the rich to continue investing, rather than redistributing their money, and paid the poor the share of the income redistribution they would have received—twenty cents—it would leave the middle class with forty cents, the same amount they would have gotten from redistribution. Taxing the rich and redistributing their income comes at the expense of the middle class.

Even worse, when rich people like Warren Buffett and Bill Gates give away one dollar of their income, it costs middle-class workers and their families $1.35 (of cash),* substantially more than sixty cents. Unlike the top 5 percent of workers, who consume 60 percent of their income and invest 40 percent, the richest families consume very little of their income, perhaps 10 percent or less in the case of Buffett and Gates, and invest the rest. Their income is

---

* $1.35 = [$0.90 / $0.40] × $0.60

so large that their extravagant consumption barely dents it. The dollar they give away largely would have funded investment and underwritten the risk necessary to create new products, lower costs, and long-lasting jobs. Accumulating more equity to underwrite more risk is the very thing the economy needs to grow employment. Who really paid for the dollar donated by the ultrarich? Workers did.

Had the rich continued investing, the demands of consumers would have dictated the success and failure of their investments. Investors would have run experiments to find new products that uncover those demands. When the rich give the dollar away, they take away consumers' control over that dollar of investment and give it to a charitable foundation. Again, who really gave up control? Consumers did.

In truth, workers make an even bigger sacrifice. The top 30 percent of workers and their families also capture their share of the returns from investment. They earn their share in three parts—their share as workers (no different than middle-class workers); the premium they garner as workers that are more talented; and the premium some of them earn for having successfully taken risk. Ignoring the latter two premiums, and only granting the top 30 percent of workers their share of investment as if they were middle-class workers enlarges the cost to all workers and their families by an additional 75 percent.* From this perspective, it costs workers and their families $2.35 when the ultrarich give away a dollar where 90 percent would have been invested and $1.05 when we redistribute a dollar of income where 40 percent would have been invested.† The dirty little secret behind taxing the rich is that it really taxes the middle class and workers generally.

Some may look at the assumptions—a 40 percent savings rate, 50 percent buyers' surplus, a 2 percent discount rate, and a ten-to-twenty-year investment life—and claim they are too favorable to

---

*   1.75 = [40% + 30%] / 40%

† $2.35 = 1.75 × $1.35; $1.05 = 1.75 × $0.60

investment. But to make investment more valuable to workers and their families than income redistribution, investment need only be worth $1.20 of cash* value (excluding buy surplus), not $1.80 of cash value.

Rather than using an even more conservative set of assumptions, a strong case can be made for the opposite. Buyers' surplus is likely higher than 50 percent, and the benefit of innovation to society lasts nearly forever. These assumptions would make the value of investment more than twice as large as $3.65.

HIDDEN COSTS AND MISTAKEN LOGIC

A host of additional real-world considerations favors investment over income redistribution as well. It is likely, for example, that the possibility of increased future consumption motivates investors to forgo current consumption and take risk. They take risk and responsibility to increase consumption and use their income to display their success and status to others. It's extremely conservative to assume that rich investors' consumption has no value to society. It's like arguing that feeding the rich has no value; only their investment and risk taking have value!

In truth, the U.S. economy is full of underutilized talent. Many liberal-arts majors choose selfish solipsism over the burden of shouldering the risk and responsibility critical to increasing economic growth. They study literature and art history rather than computer programming and engineering. To add insult to injury, these people often cite a lack of fulfillment from Richard Easterlin's never-ending aspirational treadmill as their reason for choosing not to take risk or shoulder responsibility. They recognize that working hard won't make them happy. Yet they claim hard-working business leaders, problem solvers, and risk underwriters are the

---

* $1.20 = [70% × $1.00] / 58%; 58% = [70% / 40%] × 33%; 33% is the share captured by the 40% middle class

selfish ones, and that higher marginal tax rates and income redistribution are the true moral course.

Ironically, the unwillingness of talented people to shoulder greater responsibility drives up the cost of talent. On one side of the equation, opportunities go unrealized for want of supply. As the value of forgone opportunities rises, investors can afford to pay talented employees more to realize these opportunities. The rising price of talent reveals the extent to which valuable investment opportunities go unrealized for want of supply. On the other side of the equation, an employee can only capture the share of an opportunity that a competing employee is willing to take to perform the same job. The greater the supply of talented employees willing to suffer the cost of increased responsibility and risk, the lower their pay. The cost of inducing another talented worker to bear the pain of increased responsibility sets the pay of talented workers. With a shortage of willing talent relative to a growing number of unrealized investment opportunities, the price for talent has risen (see Figure 2-5).

Given that investors—who capture only a small portion of the value from investment—find it economical to pay talented innovators to harvest unrealized investment opportunities, it must be even more valuable for wage earners and consumers, who capture almost all the value from investment, to allow investors to pay talented workers in order to achieve these returns. Given the relative shortage of willing talent, the high price for talent is essential to properly allocating what limited supply of willing talent we do have to the most valuable investment opportunities.

Given their enormous contribution, it should be obvious that small increases in the supply of talented risk takers will produce significant increases in GDP. The top 1 percent of income earners produces about a fifth of U.S. gross domestic income; the top 10 percent produces almost half the GDP (see Figure 9-1). The contribution of talented risk takers is critical to growing the prosperity of the world, its working poor, and its growing middle class.

Given the vast quantity of underutilized talent, it's clear that the economy is capable of enormous growth in productivity and wages—if it can motivate this underutilized talent to shoulder greater responsibility for its growth and take the personal risks necessary to achieve it. We should demand their leadership and risk taking as a moral responsibility—no matter their happiness— and declare as selfishly immoral the unwillingness of talented people to shoulder the burden of contributing this supply. University professors—who lead our children—should be in the front lines in this campaign. They often preach the opposite, promoting liberal arts over engineering, computer programming, and business administration. Without an overwhelming moral imperative, we ought to recognize the critical role that outsized pay plays in motivating the supply of talented risk takers.

One might also think of consumption as the cost of motivating investment for the benefit of society. For every dollar earned by a successful innovator or lucky risk taker, society captures forty cents of investment. Were society to pay the incremental dollar of income to a middle-class consumer, he would charge society ninety to ninety-nine cents of consumption for every penny of investment—a steep price. It's cheaper for society to allocate income to the rich.

To offset this truth, some advocates of income redistribution have proposed replacing progressive income taxes with progressive consumption taxes to discourage consumption and encourage work and investment. Taxpayers would report and verify their incomes and investments to the government, the difference between the two being consumption. Tax rates would rise as consumption grows. This would raise the cost of consumption—by taxing it more heavily—and lower the cost of investment—by eliminating the tax on invested income.

But again, if increased consumption and displays of status motivate risk taking, then consumption *is* the return for investment and risk taking. A heavy tax on consumption will discourage increased investment by making it harder to display status. With diminished payoffs for risk taking, workers might head to the beach rather than bearing the burden of increased risk and responsibility, as they have in Europe. It's a mistake to assume the sixty cents of consumption by the rich has no value. Its value is critical to economic growth and the long-term welfare of society.

In addition to reducing investment and the motivation that drives it, redistribution of income by the government decouples the full cost of labor from its market price. An employer who no longer has to bear the cost of an employee's health care might allocate that employee to a job that doesn't produce enough value to cover the employee's full cost. This is precisely how an economy ends up skewed toward a nation of burger-flippers! Customers will race to buy products priced below cost. A company that misprices some portion of its product offerings below cost and another portion too high above cost, to compensate—which happens routinely in business—ends up with demand and market shares unsustainably skewed toward the unprofitable offering. The same thing will happen to an economy that misallocates the cost of its labor. If offshore consumers buy these subsidized products, we end up subsidizing their consumption the way they are currently subsidizing ours. If we want employees covered by health care, they must produce goods and services valuable enough to cover the cost.

If companies don't bear the full cost of employees, employees will end up earning more than they contribute. They will earn wages proportional to their economic contribution from business plus government benefits unrelated to their economic contribution. One need only go to Detroit to see the long-term effects of this misallocation. It reduces investment, erodes competitiveness, slows growth, and leaves the economy fragile to downturns. It leaves young adults underemployed, as it has in cities like Detroit and throughout Europe. It destroys the value of local real estate. And it increases rather than decreases poverty. In the end, it doesn't matter whether labor achieves unsustainable pay through labor unions that monopolize the supply of labor or by electing politicians that force taxpayers to provide government benefits in excess of workers' taxes. In either case, misallocation diverts scarce resources from more productive endeavors to less productive endeavors. Investment declines and growth slows. The costs of these misallocations are not included in the calculations.

Some argue that redistribution to the poor is social insurance that protects all of us from misfortune. What's wrong with social insurance where the unfortunate receive payouts? Nothing. The problem, of course, is creating insurance with payouts suitable for a population with high incomes and then applying it to a population only able to produce low incomes. In that case, transfer payments masquerade as insurance. Insurance is only insurance if the demographics covered by the insurance can afford the true cost of the premiums.

Providing government services—health care, for example—that are somewhat proportional to each person's economic contribution is critical to the country's long-term success. Otherwise, we must tax successful risk takers, which slows growth and employment. The country is becoming—by necessity—a highly divergent economy. At one end of the spectrum, successful innovators make enormous contributions valued by a growing world. On the other end, young Hispanics without high-school educations and poor English skills risk their lives to slip across the border to find employment and send their children to our schools. We will not be as prosperous in the long run if we pour taxes on lucky risk takers to provide the same benefits to all Americans regardless of their economic contribution.

Divorcing morality from economics hurts the poor. Ironically, we build fences at the border to keep Hispanic immigrants out and we keep hardworking immigrants illegal to deny them economically illogical benefits designed for a richer America—all because of our demand for equally distributed benefits. Instead, we must accept and embrace wide differences in contributions. We must scale government benefits to economic contributions. Charge users for the services they consume. Design insurance to maximize the benefits for every level of contribution. And provide subsidies where needed. If we did that, poor immigrants would be the chief beneficiaries. And we would be largely indifferent to their legal status.

An international perspective reveals the problem of divorcing morality from economics. From a moral standpoint, one could argue that we should treat the U.S. poor as if they, too, were rich. About 1.4 billion of the world's 6.6 billion people live on less than $1.25 a day.[6] Compare that to the wealth of the U.S. poor in Figure 9-2. From a moral perspective, should we drain the United States of investment to help the world's poor, even if doing so hurts the middle class? Given the scale of world poverty, driving U.S. investment to zero would scarcely provide any sustainable benefit to the world's poor. Future generations would be poorer still. Historically, innovation and investment, especially innovation produced by the United States, is the only thing that has gradually pulled the world out of poverty.

FIGURE 9-2: Relative Wealth of U.S. Poor

CONSUMER DURABLE	PERCENT OF ALL HOUSEHOLDS (1971)	PERCENT OF POOR HOUSEHOLDS (2001)
Car or truck (one or more)	79.5	72.8
Air conditioner	31.8	75.6
Color TV (one or more)	43.3	97.3
Refrigerator	83.3	98.9
Clothes dryer	44.5	55.6
Microwave	>1.0	73.3
DVD or VCR	0	98.0
Personal computer	0	24.6
Cell Phone	0	26.6

SOURCE: REYNOLDS, *INCOME AND WEALTH*, 2006

To avoid this truth, proponents of income redistribution counter with "Our poor before others'." But surely, morality doesn't recognize geographical boundaries. If we are merely paying the richest poor in the world as a way to mitigate social unrest rather than to fulfill our moral obligation, then our moral obligation is to prevent unrest in the least expensive way.

A 2002 study for the World Bank across a wide sampling of economies, however, finds strong evidence that "growth is good for the poor."[7] It shows that the income of the poorest 20 percent of an economy tightly correlates to the economy's per-capita income—

with an astounding 88 percent correlation (see Figure 9-3). The study finds that this relationship "holds across regions, time periods, growth rates and income levels, and is robust to controlling for possible reverse causation from incomes of the poor to average incomes." The researchers conclude that "we are unable to uncover any . . . evidence that [pro-poor policies systemically] raise the share of income of the poorest in our large cross-country sample."

FIGURE 9-3: Effect of Median Income on Lowest Quintile Income

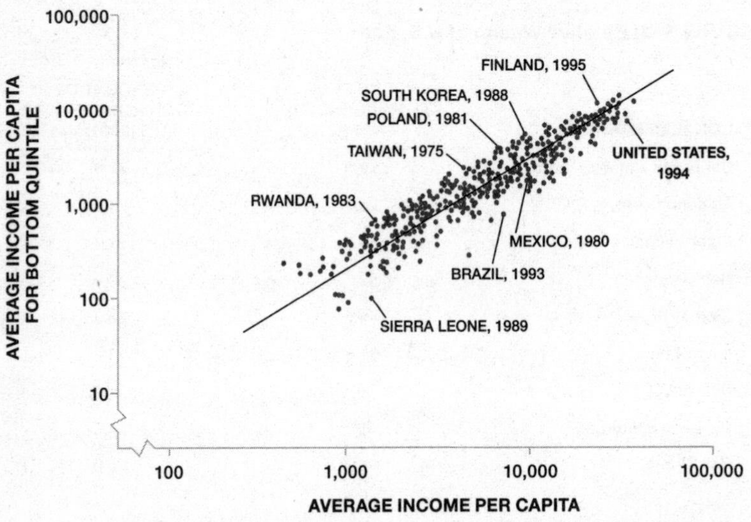

SOURCE: WEIL, DAVID N., *ECONOMIC GROWTH*, 1ST EDITION, © 2005, PP. 373. REPRINTED BY PERMISSION OF PEARSON EDUCATION, INC., UPPER SADDLE RIVER, NJ.

The United States added 40 million jobs from the 1980s to 2007—a 40 percent increase. Close to half those jobs employed immigrants, often poor Hispanic immigrants. Europe and Japan grew less than half as fast. The U.S. economy also employed tens of millions of offshore workers, largely poor Mexicans and Asians. Now that's helping the poor! Where are the robust examples where policies that more equally distributed income led to gains by the poor that are more significant than the post–*Roe v. Wade* growth of the United States?

Clearly, innovations, like polio vaccines and the Internet, help everyone, as well as all future generations. They accelerate economic growth, too. One need only look at history to see that a rising standard of living is the only thing that has truly helped the poor. The United States and its cutting-edge economy leads the world with its contribution to innovation. Its contributions are critical to the world and its poor. A dollar of aid may temporarily soothe a small portion of the world's pain. But it soothes that pain at the expense of less innovation and slower long-term growth—the very thing pulling the world out of poverty. Factories, investments, and innovation are gradually pulling Asia out of poverty, not charity. Commerce is the true salvation of the poor.

Charity may even hurt the poor more than it helps them. The long-term results of aid to Africa are so poor that experts such as Dambisa Moyo, one of *Time*'s "100 Most Influential People," concludes that the "evidence overwhelmingly demonstrates that aid in Africa has made the poor poorer, and growth slower."[8] Similarly, expenditures to reduce U.S. poverty may have contributed to a greater number of children born out of wedlock, reduced hours of labor supplied by poor families, increased dropout rates, increased drug use, and elevated crime rates—perhaps a greater cost to society and the poor than the value of their increased consumption.

Teenage pregnancy in the United States, for example, exploded in the 1960s as we increased welfare for unwed mothers, and peaked in the early 1990s at sixty-two births per 1,000 teenagers prior to welfare reform in the 1990s, before falling to forty-one births per 1,000 teenagers prior to the Financial Crisis.[9] That's still three and a half times more than France, four times more than Germany, and seven times more than Japan.[10] A poor girl in the United States with dismal economic prospects—a high-school dropout or the child of an illegal immigrant—might find welfare to be a viable alternative relative to a girl with more attractive economic prospects. It's no surprise that teenage pregnancy rates remain shockingly high among U.S. minorities who have less-promising financial futures. The rates are double those of white teenage girls.[11]

The cost of redistribution is likely higher still. We also know that lawmakers never actually distribute much of the income taken from rich investors to poor consumers. Instead, they use the money to curry favor with middle-class and even upper-middle-class voters. They use tax revenues to pay monopoly rent to municipal labor unions, to make social-security payments to richer-than-average senior citizens, and as tax breaks and subsidized financing to richer than average home owners and college graduates. Unfortunately, politicians demand their ransom.

The original comparison assumed the consumption of the rich had no value to society but that the redistributed income had full value to the recipients. But where the government redistributes income from the rich to the middle class or upper middle class, the value of their consumption to society is not dissimilar in value to the consumption of the rich. In truth, both are very rich. The original assumption, which only compares the rich to the poor and assumes that consumption of the rich has no value, exaggerated the difference.

Even worse, middle-income workers, who are unable to use income to differentiate themselves, have worked less as they have grown richer (see Figure 1-2). Redistributing income likely reduces middle-class output. That loss offsets some of the value created by income redistribution. My assumptions don't capture that loss.

Singer's example might better reflect reality constructed in the following way. You are driving an ambulance filled with critical hospital supplies, which, if you arrive on time, will save many people. On the way, you see a child break his leg. Should you stop to soothe the child's pain or drive on to arrive in time to save many more people? Yes, you might feel bad if you don't stop, but isn't that the burden society needs you to bear? Feel bad, but do the right thing—keep investing.

Some proponents of income redistribution counter that the difference between liberals and conservatives is simply a matter of the time value of money. The poor have higher discount rates—they put more value on the present relative to the future than the poor rich, who can afford to invest in the future. It's true that the poor probably have higher discount rates, than the economy as a whole. But at high societal discount rates, which value the present much more than the future, society uses scarce resources to support adults at the expense of children—to support social security rather than to invest in education. It supports unsustainably high union wages at the expense of long-term job growth. And it pollutes the earth with little, if any, regard for the future.* Perhaps the desperate poor prefer a scorched-earth investment policy—one that sacrifices the future for the present—but the future of our children depends on a lower discount rate than that.

Failing these arguments, some proponents of income redistribution counter by arguing that the effect on growth and innovation from a small amount of redistribution is immeasurably small. Then they leap logically but fallaciously from "small" to "zero." But that logic begs the question: is increased consumption at the expense of decreased investment worth more to society, or less? All that matters is the direction of the trade-off at the margin. Either an additional dollar of redistribution soothes more pain than the value of the lost innovation, or the lost innovation is worth more to society than the soothed pain. Ultimately, we are at a point on a line. The only thing that matters is the slope of the line at that point. The strategic question then is straightforward. With politicians now directing more than 40 percent of the economy's resources (see Figure 9-4), are we better off letting politicians control more or less of the economy's resources?

The political allocation process is not one in which thoughtful economists dictate the investment decisions; far from it. Large numbers of voting consumers array themselves against a very small number of investors. Numerous political factions demand

---

* Ironically, liberals tend to justify income redistribution at the expense of investment with higher discount rates than conservatives, but then justify investment to reduce global warming with discount rates that are lower than conservatives. Conservatives demand the same risk-adjusted hurdle rate for all investments.

FIGURE 9-4: U.S. Government Spending Relative to GDP

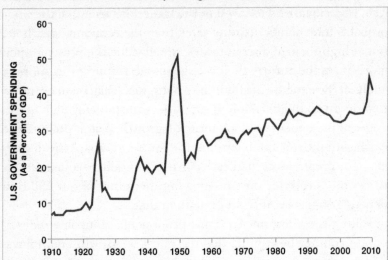

SOURCE: USGOVERNMENTSPENDING.COM

increased consumption, no matter the expense. These include workers who perpetually seek pay raises, special interest groups such as municipal labor unions that seek to thwart what would otherwise be logical outcomes from private markets, moralists bent on improving the lot of the poor without regard to costs, and politicians eager to curry favor with all of the above. On average, it's hard to believe this allocation process outperforms the private sector.

CONCLUSIONS

Proponents of redistribution believe they hold the moral high ground. Most of them demand *more* but have no perspective about where *more* becomes suboptimal. They mistakenly assume that redistribution consumes only the incremental consumption of the rich. They don't consider whether payouts for lucky risk taking motivate risk taking. They don't realize that consumers and wage earners capture almost all the value from investment and that

GDP only partially captures this value in measures of income. They draw little distinction between the effectiveness of the political allocation process relative to Darwinian survival of the fittest that prevails in private enterprise. They take it as a given that large political interventions will work as planned. At the very least, they need to "swallow the red pill" and recognize that the moral and economic trade-offs are more complex than they realize.

Innovation creates so much value that society as a whole would be better off allowing the need for status, and the consumption it demands, to motivate talented employees and successful investors to take the risks necessary to produce it. Even if the poorest 20 percent of families benefit from the redistribution of rich investors' income, the opportunity cost of the forgone investment comes at the expense of the middle class. Frankly, it would be better for the middle class if they paid for the poor's share of income redistribution themselves. It would be better still to do everything in our power—whether with money or moral suasion—to recruit more investors or talented workers to take the risk and responsibility necessary to create more innovation.

Many conservatives complain that government deficits burden future generations with debt. What burdens future generations is not debt per se but government-induced consumption whose increase comes at the expense of reduced investment. A reduction in investment and risk taking slows growth and diminishes the future for our children. Better that we fund consumption with cheap Chinese debt rather than with our precious equity—equity that could have been used to grow the economy. Better still, cut back government-induced consumption.

We needn't extend the argument philosophically to all government spending. All that matters is the incremental dollar of spending at the margin. Does an additional dollar of government spending and higher taxes on either the rich or the middle class benefit the middle class more than a dollar of spending cuts and lower taxes? It's hard to believe additional spending and taxes benefit the middle class more. And harder still to believe it benefits our children.

We should start by recognizing that fiscal and monetary stimuli have had, at best, only a temporary effect on the economy, and a tepid one at that. A temporary boost in economic activity might help to offset a temporary lull in risk taking that follows some recessions. But in a recession such as ours, which stems from a structural problem—the now-recognized risk of damage from withdrawals, which the trade deficit magnifies—the long-term cost of the stimulus is greater than its short-lived benefit. Unless we tax the middle class to pay for the increased spending, the resulting reduction in investment and risk taking costs far more than the benefit.

CONCLUSION

THE U.S. ECONOMY was on fire prior to the Financial Crisis. U.S. employment grew from 100 million workers in the mid-1980s to 140 million workers at its peak in 2007. While Europe went to the beach and Japan stagnated, America went to work.

This growth pulled tens of millions of immigrants into the U.S. workforce. Many were young Hispanic workers without high-school educations and with poor English skills. Real median incomes (the highest income of the lowest 50 percent of workers) increased substantially within every demographic of the workforce. Shifting demographics disguises this growth. The United States also put tens of millions of Chinese and other offshore workers to work on our behalf. No other high-wage economy has done more for the poor.

Despite popular belief, the United States poured more investment into innovation than the rest of the world. Intangible business investments rose steadily from about 7.5 percent of non-farm output in the mid-1970s to an unprecedented 15 percent today. Our manufacturing-based accounting expenses these investments as cost rather than recognizing them as investments. U.S. productivity soared as a result, while Europe's and Japan's stagnated. The American standard of living rose relative to that of Europe and Japan despite a workforce with lower academic test scores. American know-how and risk taking created companies like Google,

Facebook, Microsoft, Intel, Apple, Cisco, Adobe, Oracle, Wikipedia, YouTube, Twitter, Amazon, and eBay. The rest of the world created next to nothing.

The United States would have grown faster had it not been for a shortage of talent. In the 1980s, less than 25 percent of the jobs were the most technical jobs at the top of the wage scale—doctors, lawyers, scientists, and managers. But 50 percent of the 40 million jobs created by the economy were high-skilled jobs. Computers, cell phones, email, and the Internet increased the productivity of the most productive workers. Household staffs, restaurant workers, and logistics workers also contributed to their productivity. Unlike their European and Japanese counterparts, talented U.S. workers used time saved at home to increase hours spent at work while the hours worked by the rest of the United States and Europe declined.

All other things held constant, an increase in the relative supply of one factor of production—in this case, the productivity-enhanced supply of thinkers—would reduce its price relative to other production factors. But the pay of talented innovators grew faster than that of the rest of the economy. This happened because a growing universe of valuable investment opportunities went unrealized for want of supply. The top 1 percent of workers are paid relatively more in the United States, not because the other 99 percent earn less but because they contribute far more than their counterparts in other countries.

A shortage of talent exists, in part, because a large number of college graduates refuse to take the risk and responsibility necessary to bring unrealized investment opportunities to fruition. Art history and Elizabethan poetry don't employ workers; the arduous and tedious application of business sciences such as computer programming and accounting does. The rising price for successful business talent represents the incremental cost of motivating reluctant talent to step up and contribute—often, ironically, the very ones who lament rising income inequality. For the sake of those less fortunate, we must persuade our vast supply of underutilized talent that they have a moral obligation to lead and innovate.

Without the power of moral suasion, higher payouts are the only motivator we have to increase participation.

The growing value of innovation has been beneficial to the rest of the U.S. workforce. The prosperity of lucky innovators not only drives up the demand for employment and wages in the rest of the economy, it also pays a growing share of the taxes. Companies like Google, Facebook, and Microsoft provide critical training that other economies cannot duplicate. The resulting accumulation of equity underwrites more risk taking. High payoffs for lucky innovators motivate others to duplicate their success and avoid loss of status from failing to do so. Rather than lamenting the disparity of U.S. wages, we should cherish our good fortune.

The trade deficit also contributed to growth by eliminating capacity constraints. Clearly, the U.S. economy was running at or near full capacity prior to the Crisis. Unemployment dropped to a historically low 4.6 percent. Workforce participation stretched to 67 percent. We moved low-value-added "plastic widgets" manufacturing offshore to seventy-five-cents-an-hour Chinese labor and redeployed our highly skilled workforce to innovation and our skilled and unskilled workers to relatively more valuable domestic services, which now comprise 80 percent of the U.S. economy—doctors, lawyers, teachers, truck drivers, waiters, salesclerks, etc. These are jobs offshore companies can't easily fill.

Net imports ramped to 6 percent of GDP at their peak in 2007. That may be small relative to the overall economy, but it's large relative to the capacity it freed for increased investment. That investment grew the economy. Had the Chinese bought U.S. goods instead of U.S. assets, increased investment in innovation would not have been possible without cuts elsewhere. Had surplus exporters bought equity instead of debt, the purchase would have reduced incentives to increase investment and risk taking.

Despite the drumbeat of scaremongers, who insist Americans have borrowed and consumed too much and saved too little, increased investment grew household assets faster than debt, and household net worth increased even at post-Crisis valuations—values dampened by the threat of an emerging Financial Crisis in

Europe. Growth in the trade deficit, household debt, *and* assets are the mathematical outcome of increased business investment in a capacity-constrained economy. Households, which otherwise would have competed with business investment for domestic resources to increase consumption, consumed imports instead, while businesses used domestic resources to ramp up intangible investments that accelerated growth. In effect, savings exported to the United States, which go hand-in-hand with the trade deficit, indirectly funded increased U.S. investment. Because of this investment, households are richer today than they would have been—at least the ones that borrowed prudently.

To maximize our growth relative to the rest of the world, we must continue to put the world's unskilled labor and capital to work on our behalf. Making products for $17 an hour that we could have purchased for seventy-five cents an hour wastes resources that we could have used elsewhere. That reduces U.S. competitiveness. In a world awash with unskilled labor, we will not succeed by returning to a manufacturing-based strategy that succeeded in the 1950s. Today, competitive manufacturing in high-wage economies requires so much automation, it doesn't employ many workers.

Without robust exports to offset imports, only successful innovation will drive up the demand and wages of domestic workers without reducing growth. To avoid high unemployment, we must find ways to put the world's risk-averse savings to work prudently. If these imported savings sit idle, unemployment will rise. This requires pouring investment into innovation. As long as the return is greater than the cost of capital, we can continue to do this forever. The higher the return on investment, the more of this debt we can consume rather than invest. The greater our success, the higher our wages and employment will be.

Yes, this strategy is risky. Unfortunately, growth and employment demand prudent risk taking. But it's not nearly as risky as it appears. For two decades, innovation has proven so valuable it pulled 20 million immigrants into the United States to meet its growing demands. It put increasing distance between America's and other high-wage economies. And it succeeded without reducing the unskilled wage rate despite a world awash in unskilled labor. Because innovation is hard to predict, forecasters tend to underestimate its expected impact, despite centuries of progress powered by unanticipated creativity. This underestimation leads to suboptimized risk taking.

Innovation and the Internet have given the United States a unique window of opportunity to distance itself from the rest of the world. There's plenty of opportunity left, but we must take advantage of this window before it closes. Technological advantages can be short-lived. Look at Kodak and Digital Equipment Corporation.

This uniquely American innovation-based strategy will not succeed if we reduce the payouts for successful risk taking. Like any game of chance, payouts for lucky success motivate and justify risk taking. If we lower the payoffs for luck, we will lower the willingness of investors to risk probable failure. That will slow economic activity and diminish the growth of wages. Lest we forget, consumers and wage earners, not investors, capture almost all of the value from risk taking.

Rapidly changing U.S. demographics will make it harder and harder to pursue an investment-based strategy. A declining share of thirty-five- to fifty-four-year-old U.S. savers will likely put downward pressure on asset prices and discourage investment. A demographic tsunami of retirees and voting-age children of poor immigrants will soon wash over the United States, demanding increased consumption through the redistribution of income. A majority of voters already laments the rising return from successful risk taking. They demand trillions of dollars of income redistribution dressed up as stimulus spending, health care reform, and the continued growth of government spending.

Employment won't grow unless we increase risk taking. Risk taking won't grow until we accumulate more equity per dollar of GDP to underwrite more risk or we start taking more risk with the equity we have. Equity accumulates slowly. To recover quickly, we must increase risk taking per dollar of equity. Unlike other recessions that stem from a temporary lull in risk taking, this recession stems from a permanent dial-back in risk taking to compensate for the now-recognized risk of damage from withdrawals. Risk taking will remain tepid if we leave this risk hanging over the economy.

To maximize growth and employment, policymakers have long known they must allow the economy to use risk-averse short-term savings to fund increased investment and consumption rather than leaving the savings sitting idle available to fund withdrawals. This is especially important in a world economy filled with a surplus of cheap unskilled labor and risk-averse savings. If savings sit idle, as they do in recessions, unemployment will remain high. It's illogical to suffer permanently high unemployment to avoid intermittently high unemployment in recessions. Hence, banking's raison d'être.

But allowing banks to borrow short and lend long exposes the economy to the risk of infrequent but highly unstable hair-triggered bank runs. Policymakers have known this for a long time. Contrary to popular belief, subprime defaults didn't render banks insolvent, withdrawals did. Withdrawals were five times the size of defaults despite nearly unlimited government loan guarantees.

This is no ordinary recession. A full-scale run on the banks hasn't occurred since 1929. Temporary withdrawals on the scale of 1929 and 2008 bankrupt the entire financial infrastructure. Historically, it takes years for the economy to recover. Letting the fire burn for the sake of market discipline destroys enormous value, especially given the relatively low cost of putting it out.

Well-intentioned but misguided housing policy exacerbated the risk of subprime defaults triggering a bank run. Instead of reining in default-prone subprime lending, lawmakers demanded it. And they allowed Fannie Mae and Freddie Mac to raise low-cost government-guaranteed debt from offshore lenders to buy mortgage debt. Competition with government-subsidized GSEs made it nearly impossible for banks to fund low-risk conventional mortgages with hair-triggered short-term debt. The growth of risk-averse offshore savings chasing a limited amount of government debt pushed risk-averse short-term debt into subprime mortgages. The resulting surplus of funds contributed significantly to the growth of subprime mortgage lending and a loosening of credit standards. Had eager demand pulled a reluctant supply of funds, the opposite would have occurred. Nowhere else in the world were subprime mortgages a substantial share of real estate loans.

Nevertheless, it's disingenuous to blame the government's housing policy alone for triggering the bank run. Securitization of mortgages likely would have grown default-prone subprime lending even without government intervention. When banks discovered that investors would eagerly underwrite the risk of subprime loans by effectively putting up home owner down payments, the floodgates opened.

At the same time, it's unfair to blame bankers, regulators, and credit rating agencies. They expected first-loss capital buffers to absorb losses from defaults and protect defaults from triggering a run on the banks, just as 20 percent home owner down payments had historically. They failed to see that defaults would trigger withdrawals despite capital buffers large enough to absorb losses. It's likely a 30 percent drop in real estate prices would have triggered a run even with traditional 20 percent down payments.

Nor is it reasonable to claim bankers, regulators, and credit rating agencies should have recognized real estate prices were high and foreseen a drop in prices. No serious economist believes asset prices are predictable beyond the price reflected by the market's consensus. U.S. residential real estate prices rose less than many other countries and fell more. No one could have systematically predicted that. In truth, the Financial Crisis does not stem from a lack of government regulation or a failure of free markets; it's a by-product of logical economic policy that puts risk-averse savings to work to maximize employment.

The Crisis reveals the enormous risk of damage from withdrawals and the impotence of implicit government guarantees to hold withdrawals in check. Investors and consumers have dialed back risk taking to compensate for the now-recognized risk of damage from withdrawals. Prior to the Crisis, borrowers and lenders barely considered this risk. Employment soared as consumers and investors financed consumption and investment with loans funded by short-term deposits. Now, risk-averse short-term savings sit unused to offset this risk. As a result, the economy has contracted, growth has slowed, and unemployment has risen. Until we put these short-term funds back to work, the recovery will remain anemic.

The Crisis also makes it clear that banks cannot hold enough equity to mitigate withdrawals. Fifteen to twenty trillion dollars of government guarantees failed to prevent $1.5 trillion of withdrawals. Had guarantees been smaller, withdrawals would have been much larger. Leaving equity sitting idle to underwrite the risk of withdrawals has enormous opportunity costs. Only the government can reduce the risk of withdrawals without holding equity idle to make its guarantees to fund withdrawals credible.

Nor will pricing convert short-term debt into risk-bearing equity and change their relative amounts. Risk-averse investors won't bear risk at nearly any price. If they would, prices would adjust and the economy would recover quickly.

The Crisis also reveals that the cost of government guarantees, excluding the future cost of moral hazard, was near-zero. In fact, the government expects to turn a profit on the assets it bought to mitigate withdrawals in the Crisis.

Unfortunately, angry voters and politicians demand that politicians hold banks accountable for both loan losses and withdrawals. But doing so only increases the risk of damage from withdrawals. That increases the likelihood of a dial-back in risk taking.

Ironically, demands to hold banks accountable for the cost of taxpayer-financed guarantees push those costs onto home owners and wage earners by increasing the cost of home ownership and reducing employment. It would be advantageous to home owners and wage earners to leave guarantees and their costs to the government and taxpayers since rich taxpayers pay a disproportionate share of the taxes. If the government makes the guarantees and earns a profit, the middle class and poor consumers and wage earners can still raise the taxes of rich taxpayers!

The Crisis also reveals that implicit threats to punish banks that took economic risk failed to rein in risk taking. Pretending to leave banks at risk without charging them for implicit guarantees will continue to distort the pricing of risk. We tried that; it was a disaster. We must charge banks for the incremental risks they bear.

Reducing the size of banks that are too big to fail will do little, if anything, to solve the problem. Financial crises stem from shocks, like a 30 percent drop in real estate, that affect the entire economy, not a select number of financial institutions. Savers can withdraw from a fragmented banking system as easily as a consolidated one. Letting a large share of a fragmented banking system fail would inflict enormous damage on the economy, too. Risk-averse savings will continue to sit idle in the face of this risk. Limiting the size of banks will only reduce U.S. competitiveness in an increasingly integrated global economy.

In order to put short-term savings back to work without idling more equity, lawmakers must reduce the risk of damage from withdrawals. To do that, they need to strengthen rather than weaken government guarantees of liquidity. They need to strengthen the Fed's now-politicized ability to act in a crisis to stem withdrawals by reducing the risk of misguided political interference—which Dodd-Frank facilitates. They also need to bolster rather than hinder the ability of lenders to foreclose on home owners who fail to pay their mortgages. How else can banks retrieve their depositors' money?

To reduce the resulting risk of moral hazard, regulators need to charge banks for government guarantees based on the risk banks bear. They need to increase visibility into the risks banks take so that markets can price that risk more accurately. They need to allow, rather than restrict, banks to take both long and short positions when pricing risk. They also need to increase capital adequacy reserves to hold banks more responsible for the risk they can control—loan losses. They could write regulations to encourage the use of credit default swaps to underwrite default risk, but not liquidity risk, at a time when the economy needs access to more equity to underwrite risk. They could also restrict the funding of default-prone low-down-payment loans with short-term debt.

Unfortunately, proponents of default-prone subprime mortgages have successfully deflected blame for the Crisis to secondary issues. They accuse bankers of predatory lending, despite low down payments that shifted default risk to lenders. They claim bankers fraudulently syndicated loans despite it being common knowledge that banks were making and syndicating risky no-money-down loans, which sophisticated investors including banks and the government eagerly and knowingly bought. They believe bankers gamed incentive systems despite schemes that typically subjected bankers to significant long-term risk whose consequences they suffered. They assert bankers engaged in regulatory arbitrage, which, so far, appears inconsequential. They blame credit default swaps that functioned nearly identically to loans. They insist on restricting proprietary trading that was not a factor in the Crisis, and they claim laissez-faire regulators looked the other way despite a substantial rationalization of capital adequacy requirements and increases to capital buffers largely held by non-bank investors. Misled voters will never demand logical improvements that strengthen the recovery.

If lawmakers won't make changes that reduce the risk of damage from withdrawals without idling inordinate amounts of capital, what else can they do to strengthen the recovery? To reduce unemployment in the aftermath of a crisis, they could use thoughtful immigration and trade policies to dampen unemployment by temporarily exporting it. They could lower corporate tax rates to encourage domestic employment. They could cut back regulations that don't increase employment. Dodd-Frank and the Patient Protection and Affordable Care Act are ripe with opportunities that increase uncertainty and slow, rather than accelerate, employment. Lawmakers could increase the expected payoff for successful risk taking and accelerate the accumulation of equity by lowering marginal tax rates. They could reduce tax deductions to lower marginal tax rates while maintaining progressive taxation. They could reduce unrealistic promises around long-term expenditures, like Social Security and Medicare, which threaten today's risk takers with increased taxes in the future. They could similarly cut back fiscal stimulus that threatens increased taxes but only has a temporary effect on employment at best and almost no effect at worst. They could use the money used to stimulate the economy in the near term to negotiate structural improvements to long-term spending. These improvements could include reductions to runaway municipal union pension benefits and reductions in health care usage ungoverned by cost. The Obama administration and the Democratic Party used its filibuster-proof majority to do nearly the opposite at every turn.

In the end, commerce is the salvation of the poor, not charity. Successful risk takers put Americans, immigrants, and offshore workers to work, not government handouts. Increases in government expenditures that threaten risk takers with higher taxes won't put them back to work, at least not permanently. That merely hampers our transition to a sustainable economy by slowing the accumulation of equity and discouraging risk taking.

When all is said and done, you're either for investment and risk taking as a solution for what ails the economy, or you're against it. The real world offers no middle ground. Yes, advocates of investment have to cobble together a coalition of odd bedfellows to reach a majority, and sometimes that requires ambivalent compromise. But if there ever was a time to step up and make the right choice, this is it.

ACKNOWLEDGMENTS

Success is the by-product of determination, risk taking, and luck. I'm fortunate to have met Bruce Greenwald thirty-two years ago. Our lunchtime debates are the genesis of this book. Without his teachings, I would have little to say. The arguments certainly would not be as carefully considered, much less worthy of publication.

I am also fortunate that Steve Levitt read the book early in the process and liked it. His support gave the book credibility. Without it, I don't believe this book would ever have been published.

I'm fortunate my wife is a talented and successful writer with a top-notch agent. Twice, David McCormick graciously read the manuscript long before it was publishable and gave me enough encouragement to keep me writing. Without David's help, I would not have landed my own first-rate agent, Cathy Hemming. Without her belief in the book and her relationships, this book would never have seen the light of day.

I'm fortunate Adrian Zackheim took a leap of faith. Even if the book had been published, it likely would have been relegated to a dusty corner. It might still be, but Adrian and the team that he has assembled at Portfolio have given it a better chance to reach a larger audience.

I am thankful for the help of Brooke Carey, my editor, and her editorial team at Portfolio, especially Julia Batavia and the outside assistance of Nancy Cardwell. The studio's cut is always better than

the director's. Their commitment to the highest standard of quality, their determination to achieve it, and their wisdom have made
the book a lot better.

I am also thankful for the support of Tiffany Liao, Allison
McLean, Rimjhim Dey, and Stephanie Marshall. Breaking through
the noise is much harder than writing a book! Rimjhim, you took
this to another level.

. . . and to Patrick Dorton and his team. Catching cars is nearly
impossible, but nothing like actually catching one! Thank you for
keeping me from getting run over—again and again.

I am especially grateful for the help and support of Rico
Michaels, my research assistant, and Michele Avallone, my admin-
istrative assistant. They both know that putting up with my
demands is harder than writing a book or breaking through the
noise! Even more so, their unwavering belief in the book has been
a continual source of encouragement. They pulled this book out
of the fire more than once!

I would be remiss if I didn't thank my partners and colleagues
at Bain Capital for giving me the wherewithal to pursue my
dreams, and Mitt Romney in particular, for giving me a chance
and showing me, by example, what responsibility to the community really means.

And lastly, to my wife, Jill, your belief in me is more valuable
to me than anything. Thank you. And to our daughter, Campbell,
my love for you is the true source of motivation for this book—to
leave the world a better place than I found it, for you and for all
children.

INTRODUCTION

1. David Leonhardt, "In Health Bill, Obama Attacks Wealth Inequality," *The New York Times*, March 24, 2010, A1.
2. Alan Heston, Robert Summers, and Bettina Aten, "Penn World Table Version 6.3," Center for International Comparisons of Production, Income and Prices at the University of Pennsylvania, August 2009.
3. Bruce Greenwald and Judd Kahn, *Globalization: The Irrational Fear that Someone in China Will Take Your Job* (New York: Wiley, 2009).
4. Federal Reserve Flow of Funds, http://www.federalreserve.gov/releases/z1/.
5. Joseph Stiglitz, Jonathan M. Orszag, and Peter Orszag, "Implications of the New Fannie Mae and Freddie Mac Risk-Based Capital Standard," *Fannie Mae Papers*, v. 1, no. 2 (March 2002).
6. Paul Krugman, "The Market Mystique," *The New York Times*, March 27, 2009, A29.
7. Paul Volcker, "Future of Finance Initiative," *The Wall Street Journal* conference (Horsham, England, December 9, 2009).
8. Thomas Philippon, "The Evolution of the US Financial Industry: Theory and Evidence," Stern School of Business (November 2008).
9. Douglas Bernheim, "Taxation and Saving," in A. J. Auerbach and M. Feldstein, eds., *Handbook of Public Economics*, vol. 3 (Amsterdam: Elsevier Science BV, 2002): Chapter 18.

CHAPTER 1: A BRIEF HISTORY OF THE U.S. ECONOMY

1. Claudia Goldin and Lawrence Katz, *The Race Between Education and Technology* (Cambridge, MA: Harvard University Press, 2008).
2. U.S. Census Bureau, "Place of Birth of the Foreign-Born Population: 2009," October 2010, http://www.census.gov/prod/2010pubs/acsbr09-15.pdf; The Federal Interagency Forum on Child and Family Statistics, "Indicator FAM4: Percentage of Children Ages 0–17 by Nativity of Child and Parents, Selected Years 1994–2009," http://www.childstats.gov/americaschildren/tables/fam4.asp?popup=true.
3. Robert J. Samuelson, *The Great Inflation and Its Aftermath: The Past and Future of American Affluence* (New York: Random House, 2008).
4. Alfred P. Sloan, Jr., *My Years with General Motors* (New York: Doubleday & Company, 1963).

5. Andrew Grove, *Only the Paranoid Survive* (New York: Doubleday & Company, 1996).

6. U.S. Census Bureau, "Business Dynamics Statistics," October 2011, http://www.ces.census.gov/index.php/bds/bds_database_list.

7. N. Gregory Mankiw, *Macroeconomics*, 6th ed. (New York: Worth Publishers, 2007), Table 8-3: 248.

8. Paul Romer, "Endogenous Technological Change, Part 2: The Problem of Development: A Conference on the Institute for the Study of Free Enterprise Systems," *Journal of Political Economy*, v. 98, no. 5, (October 1990): S71–102.

9. Matt Ridley, *The Rational Optimist: How Prosperity Evolves* (New York: HarperCollins, 2010).

10. U.S. Department of Labor, "A Chartbook of International Labor Comparisons," (Washington: Bureau of Labor Statistics, March 2009).

11. Ibid.

12. Lisa B. Kahn, "The Long-Term Labor Market Consequences of Graduating from College in a Bad Economy," Yale School of Management (August 13, 2009).

13. "Real Wages and Salaries vs. Real Cost of Benefits," graph, EconomPic Data website, http://econompicdata.blogspot.com.

14. Federal Reserve Economic Data, "Real GDP by Country," Federal Reserve Bank of St. Louis, U.S. Department of Labor: Bureau of Labor Statistics, http://research.stlouisfed.org.

15. "House of Horrors, Part 2," *The Economist*, November 26, 2011: 90; McKinsey Global Institute, "Global Capital Markets: Entering a New Era," September 2009, http://ww1.mckinsey.com/mgi/reports/pdfs/gcm_sixth_annual_report/gcm_sixth_annual_report_full_report.pdf.

16. Alexander Kowalski and Ilan Kolet, "Productivity Is Not the Savior You Think It Is," *Bloomberg BusinessWeek*, October 24-30, 2011: 15–16.

17. Federal Reserve Board, "Household Debt Service and Financial Obligations Ratios," December 13, 2011, http://www.federalreserve.gov/releases/housedebt/default.htm.

CHAPTER 2: THE ROLE OF INVESTMENT

1. Alan Greenspan, *The Age of Turbulence: Adventures in a New World* (New York: Penguin, 2007).

2. See for example, Ben Bernanke and Refet Gürkaynak, "Is Growth Exogenous? Taking Mankiw, Romer and Weil Seriously," in Ben Bernanke and Refet Gürkaynak, eds., *NBER Macroeconomics Annual 2001*, vol. 16 (Cambridge, MA: MIT Press, 2002).

3. Paul Krugman, "How Did Economists Get It So Wrong?" *The New York Times*, September 6, 2009, MM36.

4. Roger G. Ibbotson and Peng Chen, "Long-Run Stock Returns: Participating in the Real Economy." *Financial Analysts Journal*, January/February 2003: 88–98.

5. Carmen M. Reinhart and Kenneth S. Rogoff, *This Time Is Different: Eight Centuries of Financial Folly* (Princeton, NJ: Princeton University Press, 2009).

6. Charles Mulford, "Capitalization of Software Development Costs: A Survey of Accounting Practices in the Software Industry." Georgia Institute of Technology, May 2006, www.mgt.gatech.edu/finlab.

7. Carol A. Corrado, Charles R. Hulten, and Daniel E. Sichel, "Intangible Capital and Economic Growth." *Finance and Economics Discussion Series,* April 2006, www.aueb.gr/deos/seminars/Corrado_24-10-07.pdf.

8. Bart van Ark, Janet X. Hao, Carol A. Corrado, and Charles R. Hulton, "Measuring Intangible Capital and Its Contribution to Economic Growth in Europe." *European Investment Bank Papers,* v. 14, no. 1 (2009); Janet X. Hao and Charles R. Hulton, "What Is a Company Really Worth? Intangible Capital and the 'Market to Book Value' Puzzle," Working Paper #08-02, Economics Program of the Conference Board, Revised November 2008.

CHAPTER 3: THE ROLE OF THE TRADE DEFICIT

1. Ricardo J. Caballero, Emmanuel Farhi, and Pierre-Olivier Gourinchas, "An Equilibrium Model of 'Global Imbalances' and Low Interest Rates," *American Economic Review* 98, no. 1 (2008): 358–93.

2. John Taylor, *Getting Off Track: How Government Actions and Interventions Caused, Prolonged, and Worsened the Financial Crisis* (Stanford, CA: Hoover Institution Press, 2009).

3. Alan Greenspan, *The Age of Turbulence* (New York: Penguin, 2007); Alan Greenspan, "The Fed Didn't Cause the Housing Bubble," *The Wall Street Journal,* March 11, 2009, A15; Alan Greenspan, "The Crisis," *Greenspan Associates LLC,* April 15, 2010; Robin Harding, "Bernanke Says Foreign Investors Fuelled Crisis," *Financial Times,* February 18, 2011, http://www.ft.com/cms/s/0/eea1957c-3b5e-11e0-9970-00144feabdc0.html#axzz1NxKq4gLv.

4. Ben Bernanke, "Monetary Policy and the Housing Bubble," Annual Meeting of the American Economic Association, January 3, 2010.

5. Alan Greenspan, "The Fed Didn't Cause the Housing Bubble."

6. Alan Greenspan, *The Age of Turbulence* (New York: Penguin, 2007); Greenspan, "The Fed Didn't Cause the Housing Bubble"; Greenspan, "The Crisis."

7. Carmen M. Reinhart and Kenneth S. Rogoff, *This Time Is Different: Eight Centuries of Financial Folly* (Princeton, NJ: Princeton University Press, 2009).

8. Bruce Greenwald and Judd Kahn, *Globalization: The Irrational Fear that Someone in China Will Take Your Job* (New York: Wiley, 2009).

9. U.S. Bureau of Labor Statistics, "International Comparisons of Annual Labor Force Statistics, Adjusted to U.S. Concepts, 10 Countries, 1970-2010," U.S. Bureau of Labor Statistics, Division of International Labor Comparisons, March 30, 2011, http://www.bls.gov/fls/flscomparelf/employment.htm.

10. U.S. Bureau of Labor Statistics, *Monthly Labor Review* (March 2010).

11. "GDP: Feels Like It's 2008 All Over Again," *Bloomberg Businessweek,* December 6-12, 2010: 20.

CHAPTER 4: THE ROLE OF INCENTIVES

1. U.S. Bureau of Labor Statistics, "International Comparisons of Annual Labor Force Statistics, Adjusted to U.S. Concepts, 10 Countries, 1970-2010," U.S. Bureau of Labor Statistics, Division of International Labor Comparisons, March 30, 2011, http://www.bls.gov/fls/flscomparelf/employ ment.htm.

2. Randall Stross, "What Has Driven Women Out of Computer Science?" *The New York Times*, November 16, 2008. www.nytimes.com/2008/11/16/business/16digi.html.

3. Rachel M. Johnson and Jeffrey Rohaly, "The Distribution of Federal Taxes, 2009-12," Urban-Brookings Tax Policy Center, August 2009; "Table T06-0308: Current-Law Distribution of Federal Taxes by Cash Income Percentiles, 2007," Urban-Brookings Tax Policy Center, November 30, 2006, http://www.tax policycenter.org/numbers/displayatab.cfm?DocID=1390.

4. Richard Easterlin, "Does Economic Growth Improve the Human Lot? Some Empirical Evidence," in Paul A. David and Melvin W. Reder, eds., *Nations and Households in Economic Growth: Essays in Honor of Moses Abramovitz* (New York: Academic Press, 1974).

5. Robert Frank, "Darwin, The Market Whiz," *The New York Times*, September 18, 2011.

6. ———, "The Invisible Hand, Trumped by Darwin?" *The New York Times*, July 12, 2009, BU7.

7. Matt Ridley, *The Rational Optimist: How Prosperity Evolves* (New York: Harper Collins, 2010).

8. "Poverty Reduction and Equity," The World Bank, http://web.worldbank.org/WBSITE/EXTERNAL/ TOPICS/EXTPOVERTY/0,contentMDK:20 153855~menuPK:373757~pagePK:148956~piPK:216618~theSit ePK:336992,00.html; "Poverty," The World Bank, http://data.worldbank .org/topic/poverty?display= graph.

9. Edward C. Prescott, "Why Do Americans Work So Much More Than Europeans?" *Federal Reserve Bank of Minneapolis Quarterly Review* 28, no. 1 (July 2004): 2–13.

10. Bradley Heim, "The Elasticity of Taxable Income: Evidence from a New Panel of Tax Returns," Office of Tax Analysis, U.S. Department of the Treasury, August 2006; Emmanuel Saez, Joel Slemrod, and Seth Giertz, "The Elasticity of Taxable Income with Respect to Marginal Tax Rates: A Critical Review," *National Bureau of Economic Research*, Working Paper 15012, May 2009; John Gruber and Emmanuel Saez, "The Elasticity of Taxable Income: Evidence and Implications," *Journal of Public Economics* 84 (2002): 1–32.

11. Bradley Heim, "The Elasticity of Taxable Income."

12. Jens Arnold, "Do Tax Structures Affect Aggregate Economic Growth? Empirical Evidence From A Panel of OECD Countries," *OECD Economics Department Working Papers* No. 643, October 14, 2008, <http://dx.doi.org/10.1787/236001777843>.

13. Peter Kuhn and Fernando Lozano, "The Expanding Workweek? Understanding Trends in Long Work Hours Among US Men, 1979–2004,"

National Bureau of Economic Research, Working Paper 11895, December 2005, http://www.nber.org/papers/w11895.

14. Linda A. Bell and Richard B. Freeman, "The Incentive for Working Hard: Explaining Hours Worked Differences in the U.S. and Germany," *National Bureau of Economic Research, Working Paper* 8051, December 2000, http://www.nber.org/papers/w8051.

15. Robert Frank, "Before Tea, Thank Your Lucky Stars," *The New York Times*, April 26, 2009, BU5.

16. Kristin J. Forbes, "A Reassessment of the Relationship Between Inequality and Growth," *American Economic Review* 90, no. 4 (2000): 869–87.

17. Robert J. Barro, "Inequality and Growth in a Panel of Countries," *Journal of Economic Growth* 5 (March 2000): 5–32.

18. Karen E. Dynan, Jonathan Skinner, and Stephen P. Zeldes, "Do the Rich Save More?" *National Bureau of Economic Research, Working Paper* 7906, September 2000, http://www.nber.org/papers/w7906.

19. John Maynard Keynes, *The Economic Consequences of the Peace* (New York: Harcourt, Brace and Howe, 1920).

20. Alan Greenspan, *The Age of Turbulence* (New York: Penguin, 2007).

21. Bill Clinton, "Clinton Q&A: On Goldman Sachs and SEC," Peterson Institute Conference, April 2010, http://www.rationalwalk.com/?p=6669.

22. Robert J. Barro, "The Stock Market and Investment," *National Bureau of Economic Research, Working Paper* 2925, April 1989, http://www.nber.org/papers/w2925.

23. Ben Bernanke, "What the Fed Did and Why," *The Washington Post*, November 4, 2010.

24. Carmen M. Reinhart and Kenneth S. Rogoff, *This Time Is Different: Eight Centuries of Financial Folly* (Princeton, NJ: Princeton University Press, 2009).

25. Florian Pelgrin, Sebastian Schich, and Alain de Serres, "Increases in Business Investment Rates in OECD Countries in the 1990s: How Much Can Be Explained by Fundamentalists?" *OECD Economics Department Working Papers* No. 327, April 15, 2002, http://dx.doi.org/10.1787/688436342124.

26. Robert S. Chirinko and Huntley Schaller, "Business Fixed Investment and 'Bubbles': The Japanese Case," *Institute for Advanced Studies, Vienna*, Economic Series No. 28, March 1996.

27. Zuliu Hu, "Stock Market Volatility and Corporate Investment," *International Monetary Fund Working Paper* WP/95/102, October 1995, www.imf.org/external/pubs/ft/wp/1995/wp95102.pdf.

28. Wendy Carlin and Colin Mayer, "Finance, Investment and Growth," *Center for Economic Policy Research Discussion Paper* No. 2233, September 1999.

29. Malcolm Baker, Jeremy C. Stein, and Jeffrey Wurgler, "When Does the Market Matter? Stock Prices and the Investment of Equity-Dependent Firms," *The Quarterly Journal of Economics* 118, no. 3 (2003): 969–1005.

30. "Betting on Big Ben," *The Economist*, February 19, 2011.

31. "A Helping Hand For Start-ups," *The Economist*, October 8, 2011, 77–8; U.S. Census Bureau, "Business Dynamics Statistics," October 2011, http://www.ces.census.gov/index.php/bds/bds_database_list.

32. Rüdiger Fahlenbrach and René Stultz, "Bank CEO Incentives and the Credit Crisis," *National Bureau of Economic Research, Working Paper* 15212, August 2009, http://www.nber.org/papers/w15212.
33. "Special Reports: Global Heroes," *The Economist*, March 12, 2009, http://www.economist.com/node/13216025.
34. "Work Stoppages Involving 1,000 or More Workers, 1947–2009," Bureau of Labor Statistics, February 17, 2010, http://www.bls.gov/news.release/wkstp.t01.htm.
35. N. Gregory Mankiw, *Macroeconomics,* 6th ed. (New York: Worth Publishers, 2007), Table 8-3, 248.

CHAPTER 5: THE ROLE OF BANKS, CREDIT RATING AGENCIES, AND REGULATORS

1. "Briefing: The State of Economics," *The Economist,* July 18, 2009.
2. Financial Crisis Inquiry Commission, "The Financial Crisis Inquiry Report: Final Report of the National Commission on the Causes of the Financial and Economic Crisis in the United States," January 2011, 228–229.
3. Ibid.
4. Andrew Leventis et al., "Mortgage Markets and the Enterprises in 2007," The Office of Federal Housing Enterprise Oversight, February 2009, www.fhfa.gov/webfiles/1164/MME2007revised.pdf.
5. Viral Acharya and Matthew Richardson, eds., *Restoring Financial Stability* (New York: Wiley, 2009).
6. Stan Liebowitz, "New Evidence on the Foreclosure Crisis," *The Wall Street Journal,* July 3, 2009.
7. Christopher Mayer, Karen Pence, and Shane Sherlund, "The Rise in Mortgage Defaults," *Journal of Economic Perspectives* 23, vol. 1 (2009): 27–50.
8. Viral Acharya and Matthew Richardson, eds., *Restoring Financial Stability*.
9. Financial Crisis Inquiry Commission, "The Financial Crisis Inquiry Report," 228.
10. Ibid.
11. "House of Horrors, Part 2," *The Economist*, November 26, 2011, 90; McKinsey Global Institute, "Global Capital Markets: Entering a New Era," September 2009, http://ww1.mckinsey.com/mgi/reports/pdfs/gcm_sixth_annual_report/gcm_sixth_annual_report_full_report.pdf.
12. Financial Crisis Inquiry Commission, "The Financial Crisis Inquiry Report," 169.
13. Tobias J. Moskowitz and L. Jon Wertheim, "What's Really Behind Home Field Advantage?" *Sports Illustrated*, January 17, 2001, 65–72.
14. Bloomberg.
15. Floyd Norris, "It May Be Outrageous, but Wall Street Pay Didn't Cause This Crisis," *The New York Times*, July 31, 2009, B1.
16. Sue Kirchhoff and Barbara Hagenbaugh, "Greenspan Says ARMs Might Be Better Deal," *USA Today*, February 23, 2004.
17. Carmen M. Reinhart and Kenneth S. Rogoff, *This Time Is Different: Eight Centuries of Financial Folly* (Princeton, NJ: Princeton University Press, 2009).

18. "The Role of Ratings in Structured Finance: Issues and Implication," Bank for International Settlements, Committee on the Global Financial System, January 2005.

19. Charles W. Calomiris, "The Subprime Turmoil: What's Old, What's New, and What's Next," *International Monetary Fund*, October 2, 2008, http://www.imf.org/external/np/res/seminars/2008/arc/ pdf/cwc.pdf.

20. Stefan Morkotter and Simone Westerfeld, "Rating Model Arbitrage in CDO Markets: An Empirical Analysis," *International Review of Financial Analysis* 18 (2009): 21–33.

21. Ingo Fender and John Kiff, "CDO Rating Methodology: Some Thoughts on Model Risk and Its Implications," *Bank for International Settlements, Monetary and Economic Department, Working Papers No. 163*, November 2004.

22. See for example, Bethany McLean and Joe Nocera, *All the Devils Are Here: The Hidden History of the Financial Crisis* (New York: Penguin, 2010).

23. Financial Crisis Inquiry Commission, "The Financial Crisis Inquiry Report," 191–2.

24. Ibid., 203.

25. Ibid., 203.

26. Paul Krugman, "How Did Economists Get It So Wrong?" *The New York Times*, September 6, 2009, MM36.

27. John H. Cochrane, "How Did Paul Krugman Get It So Wrong?" John H. Cochrane's Web Page, September 16, 2009, http://faculty.chicago-booth.edu/john.cochrane/research/Papers/ krugman_response.htm.

28. Rüdiger Fahlenbrach and René Stultz, "Bank CEO Incentives and the Credit Crisis," *National Bureau of Economic Research, Working Paper* 15212, August 2009, http://www.nber.org/papers/w15212.

29. Michael J. Moore and Christine Harper, "Bank Pay Rules Won't Tame Wall Street," *Bloomberg BusinessWeek*, February 24, 2011.

30. Larry McDonald, *A Colossal Failure of Common Sense: The Inside Story of the Collapse of Lehman Brothers* (New York: Cross Business, 2009).

31. Michael Shnayerson, "Profiles in Panic," *Vanity Fair*, January 2009.

32. Michael Lewis, "The Man Who Crushed the World," *Vanity Fair*, August 2009.

33. Edmund Phelps, "A Fruitless Clash of Economic Opposites," *Financial Times*, November 2, 2009, http://www.ft.com/cms/s/0/f71cfc6a-c7e6-11de-8ba8-00144feab49a.html.

34. Financial Crisis Inquiry Commission, "The Financial Crisis Inquiry Report," 447.

35. U.S. Department of the Treasury, "Risk-Based Capital Guidelines; Capital Adequacy Guidelines; Capital Maintenance: Capital Treatment of Recourse, Direct Credit Substitutes and Residual Interests in Asset Securitizations; Final Rules," *Federal Register* 66, no. 230 (November 29, 2001).

36. Financial Crisis Inquiry Commission, "The Financial Crisis Inquiry Report," 99.

37. Viral V. Acharya et al., eds. *Regulating Wall Street: The Dodd-Frank Act and the New Architecture of Global Finance* (New Jersey: John Wiley & Sons, 2011).

38. Congressional Oversight Panel, "June Oversight Report: The AIG Rescue, Its Impact on Markets, and the Government's Exit Strategy," Washington: U.S. Government Printing Office, June 10, 2010.

CHAPTER 6: THE ROLE OF SHORT-TERM DEBT AND GOVERNMENT POLICY

1. Financial Crisis Inquiry Commission, "The Financial Crisis Inquiry Report: Final Report of the National Commission on the Causes of the Financial and Economic Crisis in the United States," January 2011, 228–229.
2. Tobias Adrian and Hyun Song Shin, "The Changing Nature of Financial Intermediation and the Financial Crisis, 2007–09," Staff Report No. 439, Federal Reserve Bank of New York, March 2010; Tobias Adrian, Karin Kimbrough, and Dina Marchioni, "The Federal Reserve's Commercial Paper Funding Facility," *Economic Policy Review*, Federal Reserve Bank of New York, May 2011; Ben Bernanke, "Correction of Recent Press Reports Regarding Federal Reserve Emergency Lending During the Financial Crisis," *Board of Governors of the Federal Reserve* System, December 6, 2011; "Monetary Policy and the Housing Bubble," Annual Meeting of the American Economic Association, January 3, 2010; Sewell Chan and Jo Craven McGinty, "In Crisis, Fed Opened Vault Wide for the U.S. and World, Data Shows," *The New York Times*, December 2, 2010, A1; Rebecca Christie, "Accounting for the Bailout," *Bloomberg BusinessWeek*, April 11, 2011; "Adding Up the Government's Total Bailout Tab," *The New York Times*, February 4, 2009, http://hytimes.com/interactive/2009/02/04/business/20090205 -bailout-totals-graph.html
3. Financial Crisis Inquiry Commission, "The Financial Crisis Inquiry Report."
4. Tobias Adrian and Hyun Song Shin, "The Changing Nature of Financial Intermediation and the Financial Crisis, 2007–09"; Tobias Adrian, Karin Kimbrough, and Dina Marchioni, "The Federal Reserve's Commercial Paper Funding Facility"; Sewell Chan and Jo Craven McGinty, "In Crisis, Fed Opened Vault Wide For the U.S. and World, Data Shows"; Rebecca Christie, "Accounting for the Bailout"; "Adding Up the Government's Total Bailout Tab."
5. Ibid.
6. Gary Gorton, *Slapped by the Invisible Hand: The Panic of 2007* (New York: Oxford University Press, 2010).
7. Ibid.
8. Stephen Schwarzman, "Some Lessons of the Financial Crisis," *The Wall Street Journal*, November 4, 2008, http://online.wsj.com/article/SB122576 100620095567.html.
9. Bethany McLean and Joe Nocera, *All The Devils Are Here: The Hidden History of the Financial Crisis* (New York: Penguin, 2010); Gillian Tett, *Fool's Gold: How the Bold Dream of a Small Tribe at J.P. Morgan Was Corrupted by Wall Street and Unleashed a Catastrophe* (New York: Free Press, 2009).

10. "Update on U.S. Subprime and Related Matters," transcript of teleconference, *Standard & Poor's*, November 1, 2007, as reported in Gary Gordon, "The Subprime Panic," *European Financial Management* 15, no. 1 (2009): 10–46.

11. Alicia H. Munnell, Lynn E. Browne, James McEneaney, and Geoffrey M. B. Tootell, "Mortgage Lending in Boston: Interpreting HMDA Data," *Federal Reserve Bank of Boston*, Working Paper 92-7, 1992.

12. "Closing the Gap: A Guide to Equal Opportunity Lending," Federal Reserve Bank of Boston, 1992.

13. "The National Homeownership Strategy: Partners in the American Dream," *U.S. Department of Housing and Urban Development*, May 1995, 4-4, 4-5, 4-10.

14. Robert Shiller, "Economist Robert Shiller: Is A Double Dip in Housing Ahead?" *Bloomberg BusinessWeek* interview with Charlie Rose, April 1, 2010, http://www.businessweek.com/magazine/content/10_15/b4173013214814.htm.

15. Emil W. Henry Jr., "How to Shut Down Fannie and Freddie," *The Wall Street Journal*, November 11, 2010.

16. Federal Housing Finance Agency, "Data on the Risk Characteristics and Performance of Single-Family Mortgages Originated from 2001 through 2008 and Financed in the Secondary Market," September 13, 2010, http://www.fhfa.gov/Default.aspx?Page=313.

17. "The Role of Government Affordable Housing Policy in Creating the Global Financial Crisis of 2008," Staff Report to the Committee on Oversight and Government Reform, U.S. House of Representatives, 111th Congress, July 7, 2009.

18. Fannie Mae Annual Report, 2007, 87–89, http://www.fanniemae.com/ir/pdf/annualreport/2007/2007_annual_report.pdf.

19. "The Role of Government Affordable Housing Policy in Creating the Global Financial Crisis of 2008."

20. Atif Mian and Amir Sufi, "The Consequences of Mortgage Credit Expansion: Evidence from the U.S. Mortgage Default Crisis," *Social Science Research Network*, December 12, 2008, http://papers.ssrn.com/sol3/papers.cfm?abstract_id=1072304.

21. Christopher Cox, "Speech by SEC Chairman: Opening Remarks at SEC Roundtable on Modernizing the Securities and Exchange Commission's Disclosure System," U.S. Securities and Exchange Commission, Washington, D.C., October 8, 2008.

22. Tobias Adrian and Hyun Song Shin, "The Changing Nature of Financial Intermediation and the Financial Crisis of 2007–09."

23. "FAQs: MBS Purchase Program," *Federal Reserve Bank of New York*, August 20, 2010, http://www.newyorkfed.org/markets/mbs_FAQ.HTML.

24. Rebecca Christie, "Accounting for the Bailout," *Bloomberg BusinessWeek*, April 11, 2011.

25. Michael S. Gibson, "Credit Derivatives and Risk Management," *FEDS Working Paper No. 2007-47*, May 22, 2007.

26. Bradley Rogoff and Michael Anderson, "DTCC Data Show Corporate CDS Fears Overblown," Barclays Capital Credit Strategy, November 6, 2008.

27. "Market Statistics: Other Data Sources," *ISDA CDS Marketplace*, http://www.isdacds-marketplace.com/market_statistics/other_data_sources.
28. Gary Gorton, *Slapped by the Invisible Hand*.
29. Peter J. Wallison, "Dissent from the Majority Report of the Financial Crisis Inquiry Commission," American Enterprise Institute for Public Policy Research, January 14, 2011, http://www.aei.org/paper/100190.

CHAPTER 7: PREVENTING ANOTHER BANK RUN

1. Congressional Committee on Oversight and Government Reform, "The Role of Government Affordable Housing Policy in Creating the Global Financial Crisis of 2008," July 27, 2009.
2. Nadezhda Malysheva and John R. Walter, "How Large Has the Federal Financial Safety Net Become?" *Economic Quarterly* 96, no. 3 (2010): 273–90.
3. See for example, J. Michael Harrison and David M. Kreps, "Speculative Investor Behavior in a Stock Market with Heterogeneous Expectations," *Quarterly Journal of Economics* (May 1978): 323–36.

CHAPTER 8: REDUCING UNEMPLOYMENT

1. Jon Hilsenrath and Ruth Simon, "Spenders Become Savers, Hurting Recovery," *The Wall Street Journal*, October 22-23, 2011, A1, A14.
2. N. Gregory Mankiw, *Macroeconomics,* 6th ed. (New York: Worth Publishers, 2007).
3. M. B. Snow, "$4.4 Trillion: The Spending Boom," *The Wall Street Journal*, August 22, 2010, http://sroblog.com/2010/08/22/4-4-trillion-wsj-com/.
4. Robert J. Barro and Charles J. Redlick, "Macroeconomic Effects From Government Purchases and Taxes," *National Bureau of Economic Research, Working Paper* 15369, September 2009, http://www.nber.org/papers/w15369.
5. Ethan Ilzetzki, Enqieu G. Mendoza, and Carlos A. Vegh, "How Big (Small?) Are Fiscal Multipliers?" National Bureau of Economic Research, Working Paper 16479, October 2010, http://nber.org/papers/w16479.
6. "American Recovery and Reinvestment Act of 2009," *Wikipedia*, http://en.wikipedia.org/wiki/American_Recovery_and_Reinvestment_Act_of_2009.
7. Peter Baker, "Education of a President," *The New York Times Magazine*, October 12, 2010, MM40.
8. Christina D. Romer, "The Macroeconomic Effects of Tax Changes: Estimates Based On a New Measure of Fiscal Shocks," *National Bureau of Economic Research, Working Paper* 13264, March 2007, http://www.nber.org/papers/w13264.
9. "The Effects of Automatic Stabilizers on the Federal Budget," *Congressional Budget Office*, May 2010.
10. "Much Ado about Multipliers," *The Economist*, September 26, 2009.
11. Greg Mankiw, "Back in Demand," *The Wall Street Journal*, September 21, 2009, A17.

12. Paul Krugman, *Macroeconomics* (New York: Worth Publishers, 2005).
13. Robert Barro, "The Folly of Subsidizing Unemployment," *The Wall Street Journal*, August 30, 2010.

CHAPTER 9: REDISTRIBUTING INCOME

1. U.S. Census Bureau, "Income, Poverty, and Health Insurance Coverage in the United States: 2010," January 5, 2011, http://www.census.gov/hhes/www/income/income.html; U.S. Census Bureau, "Table 1. Income Distribution Measures, by Definition of Income: 2009," 2010, http://www.census.gov/hhes/www/cpstables/032010/rdcall/1_001.htm; U.S. Department of Labor, "Labor Force Statistics from the Current Population Survey," Washington: Bureau of Labor Statistics, August 3, 2011, http://data.bls.gov/timeseries/LNS11300000.
2. Peter Singer, *The Life You Can Save: Acting Now to End World Poverty* (New York: Random House, 2009).
3. Roger G. Ibbotson and Peng Chen, "Long-Run Stock Returns: Participating in the Real Economy," *Financial Analysts Journal* (January-February 2003): 88–98.
4. Carmen DeNavas-Walt, Bernadette D. Proctor, and Jessica L. Semega, "Income, Poverty, and Health Insurance Coverage in the United States: 2010," U.S. Census Bureau, September 2011, www.census.gov/prod/2011pubs/p60-239.pdf.
5. Chulhee Lee, "Rising Family Income Inequality in the United States, 1968–2000: Impacts of Changing Labor Supply, Wages, and Family Structure," *National Bureau of Economic Research, Working Paper 11836*, December 2005, http://www.nber.org/papers/w11836.
6. "Poverty Reduction and Equity," The World Bank, http://web.worldbank.org/WBSITE/EXTERNAL/TOPICS/EXTPOVERTY/0,contentMDK:20153855~menuPK:373757~pagePK:148956~piPK:216618~theSitePK:336992,00.html; "Poverty," The World Bank, http://data.worldbank.org/topic/poverty ?display= graph.
7. David Dollar and Aart Kraay, "Growth Is Good for the Poor," *Journal of Economic Growth* 7, no. 3 (2002): 195–222.
8. Dambisa Moyo, "Why Foreign Aid is Hurting Africa," *The Wall Street Journal*, March 21, 2009.
9. "U.S. Teenage Pregnancies, Births and Abortions: National and State Trends by Race and Ethnicity," Guttmacher Institute, January 2010.
10. Rana Foroohar, "Whatever Happened to Upward Mobility?" *Time*, November 14, 2011.
11. "U.S. Teenage Pregnancies, Births and Abortions: National and State Trends by Race and Ethnicity."

Figure 1-1: U.S. Productivity Growth Relative to Other Developed Economies
Alan Heston, Robert Summers and Bettina Aten, Penn World Table Version
7.1, Center for International Comparisons of Production, Income and
Prices at the University of Pennsylvania, November 2012.

Figure 1-2: U.S. Hours Worked per Worker Relative to Other Developed Economies
Alberto Alesina, Edward Glaeser, and Bruce Sacerdote, "Work and Leisure
in the U.S. and Europe: Why So Different?" Harvard Institute of Economic Research, Discussion Paper Number 2068, April 2005: 62, http://
www.colorado.edu/Economics/morey/4999Ethics/AlesinaGlaeser
Sacerdote2005.pdf.

Figure 1-3: U.S. Hourly Productivity Growth Relative to Other Developed Economies
Bruce Greenwald and Judd Kahn, *Globalization: The Irrational Fear that
Someone in China Will Take Your Job* (New York: Wiley, 2009), Table 2.4, 35.

Figure 1-4: Effect of Economic Policies on Employment (2007)
U.S. Department of Labor, "International Comparisons of GDP Per Capita
and Per Employed Person: 17 Countries, 1960-2008," Washington: Bureau
of Labor Statistics, July 28, 2009; U.S. Department of Labor, "A Chartbook of International Labor Comparisons," Washington: Bureau of Labor
Statistics, March 2009.

Figure 1-5: Effect of Science Test Scores on Productivity
"Education: The Next Generation of U.S. Workers is Falling Behind,"
Bloomberg BusinessWeek, February 25, 2008, 17.

Figure 1-6: Growth of U.S. Income by Demographics
"Median Income by Race, Hispanic Origin, and Sex, 1947-2005," *The World
Almanac and Book of Facts: 2008* (New York: World Almanac Books, 2008),
46.

Figure 1-7: U.S. Household Saving Rates
Janet H. Kmitch, "Alternative Measure of Personal Saving," Survey of
Current Business, Bureau of Economic Analysis, October 2010, http://
www.bea.gov/scb/pdf/2010/10%20October/1010_saving.pdf.

Figure 1-8: U.S. Debt Relative to GDP
Simon Hilsenrath, "Spenders Become Savers, Hurting Recovery," *The Wall
Street Journal*, October 22-23, 2011: A14.

Figure 1-9: U.S. Stock Market Capitalization Relative to GDP
Ron Griss, The Chart Store website, www.thechartstore.com.

Figure 1-10: Real U.S. Household Net Worth
Federal Reserve Flow of Funds Accounts of the United States

Figure 2-1: U.S. Labor's Share of Income
Michael R. Pakko, "Labor's Share," National Economic Trends, Federal Reserve Bank of St. Louis, August 2004, http://research.stlouisfed.org/publications/net/20040801/cover.pdf.

Figure 2-2: U.S. Food Expenditures Relative to Disposable Income
United States Department of Agriculture, "Food CPI and Expenditures: Table 7," July 13, 2011, http://www.ers.usda.gov/briefing/cpifoodand expenditures/data/Expenditures_tables/table7.htm.

Figure 2-3: Effect of Investment on Productivity
David M. Weil, *Economic Growth* (Boston: Pearson, 2005), Figure 3.1, 49.

Figure 2-4: U.S. Intangible Investment Relative to Nonfarm Output
Carol A. Corrado, Charles R. Hulten, and Daniel E. Sichel, "Intangible Capital and Economic Growth," *Finance and Economics Discussion Series,* April 2006, www.aueb.gr/deos/seminars/Corrado_24-10-07.pdf.

Figure 2-5: U.S. College Graduate Wage Premium
Claudia Goldin and Lawrence Katz, *The Race Between Education and Technology* (Cambridge, MA: Harvard University Press, 2008), Figure 8-1: 290.

Figure 3-1: U.S. Foreign Borrowings Relative to the Trade Deficit
Carol C. Bertaut and Laurie Pounder, "The Financial Crisis and U.S. Cross-Border Financial Flows," *Federal Reserve Bulletin* (November 2009), A147-A167.

Figure 3-2: Effect of the Asian Financial Crisis on Non-China Asian Investment
"Invested Interests," *The Economist,* January 23, 2010, 74.

Figure 3-3: Effect of the Asian Financial Crisis on U.S. Exports
U.S. Census Bureau, "U.S. Trade in Goods and Services—Balance of Payments (BOP) Basis," U.S. Census Bureau, Foreign Trade Division, June 9, 2011, http://www.census.gov/foreign-trade/statistics/historical/gands.pdf.

Figure 3-4: M2 Relative to Nominal GDP
Ben Bernanke, "Monetary Policy Report to the Congress," Board of Governors of the Federal Reserve System, July 15, 2008, http://www.federal reserve.gov/monetarypolicy/files/20080715_mprfullreport.pdf.

Figure 4-1: Share of Income Earned by Top 0.1% of U.S. Workers
Jon Bakija, Adam Cole, and Bradley T. Heim, "Jobs and Income Growth of Top Earners and the Causes of Changing Income Inequality: Evidence from U.S. Tax Return Data," *Department of Economics Working Papers,* 2009, Figure 1: 72, http://web.williams.edu/Economics/bakija/BakijaHeimJobsIncomeGrowthTopEarners.pdf.

Figure 5-1: Home Price Appreciation Relative to Other Developed Economies
"House of Horrors, Part 2," *The Economist,* November 26, 2011: 90.

Figure 5-2: Volatility of U.S. GDP
John Taylor, *Getting Off Track: How Government Actions and Interventions Caused, Prolonged and Worsened the Financial Crisis* (Stanford, CA: Hoover Institution Press, 2009), Figure 14: 35.

Figure 5-3: U.S. Mortgage-Backed Securities Holdings by Type of Investor
Andrew Leventis et al., "Mortgage Markets and the Enterprises in 2007," The
Office of Federal Housing Enterprise Oversight, February 2009, www
.fhfa.gov/webfiles/1164/MME2007revised.pdf.

Figure 5-4: Banking's Share of U.S. Credit
Gerard Minack, "Downunder Daily: Does Money Matter?" *Morgan Stanley
Research,* January 28, 2009, Exhibit 4: 2.

**Figure 5-5: U.S. Bank Assets as a Percent of GDP Relative to Other
Developed Economies**
"The Devil's Punchbowl," *The Economist,* July 11, 2009, 55.

Figure 5-6: U.S. Banks Leverage Relative to Europe
Matt King and Hans Peter Lorenzen, "Addicted to Credit," *Citigroup Global
Markets Ltd,* April 2009, 9.

Figure 5-7: Shift in Riskiness of Bank Assets
Viral Acharya and Matthew Richardson, eds., *Restoring Financial Stability*
(New York: Wiley, 2009), Figure 2.3: 95.

Figure 6-1: Growth of U.S. Money Market Funds
"Sleep Therapy," *The Economist,* June 27, 2009, 81.

Figure 6-2: Percent of U.S. Homes Purchased with Low Down Payments
Financial Crisis Inquiry Commission, "The Financial Crisis Inquiry Report:
Final Report of the National Commission on the Causes of the Financial
and Economic Crisis in the United States," January 2011, Figure 4: 494.

Figure 6-3: U.S. Mortgages Owned by Fannie Mae and Freddie Mac
Viral Acharya and Matthew Richardson, eds., *Restoring Financial Stability*
(New York: Wiley, 2009), Figure 4.3: 126.

Figure 6-4: Dow Jones Average Following the Lehman Brothers Bankruptcy
http://www.dowjones.com/.

Figure 6-5: VIX Following the Lehman Brothers Bankruptcy
VIX (Chicago Board Options Exchange Volatility Index)

Figure 8-1: Actual U.S. Unemployment vs. Forecasted Unemployment
"The April Numbers Are In—It's Official," Innocent Bystander website,
May 8, 2009, http://michaelscomments.wordpress.com/2009/05/08/
the-april-numbers-are-in-its-official/.

Figure 8-2: U.S. Federal Spending and Revenues Relative to GDP
Office of Management and Budget, "Historical Tables: Budget of the U.S.
Government, Fiscal Year 2012," U.S. Government Printing Office,
Washington, DC, 2011, http://www.whitehouse.gov/sites/default/files/
omb/budget/fy2012/assets/hist.pdf; Office of Management and Budget,
"Budget of the U.S. Government, Fiscal Year 2013" U.S. Government
Printing Office, Washington, DC, 2012, http://www.whitehouse.gov/sites/
default/files/omb/budget/fy2013/assets/budget.pdf.

Figure 8-3: Projected Social Security Outlays Relative to GDP
Social Security Administration, "A Summary of the 2011 Annual Reports:
Social Security and Medicare Boards of Trustees," May 5, 2011, http://
www.ssa.gov/oact/TRSUM/index.html.

**Figure 8-4: Effect of Democratic Filibuster-Proof Victory on the Dow Jones
Average**

Dow Jones via Yahoo Finance, 2010.

Figure 9-1: Share of U.S. Taxpayers, Income, and Taxes Paid by Income Percentiles (2007)

Tax Policy Center, Urban Institute and Brookings Institution, "Table T06-0308. Current-Law Distribution of Federal Taxes By Cash Income Percentiles, 2007," November 30, 2006, http://www.taxpolicycenter.org/numbers/displayatab.cfm?DocID=1390; Rachel M. Johnson and Jeffrey Rohaly, "The Distribution of Federal Taxes, 2009-12," Urban-Brookings Tax Policy Center, August 2009.

Figure 9-2: Relative Wealth of U.S. Poor

Alan Reynolds, *Income and Wealth* (Westport, CT: Greenwood Press, 2006), Figure 4.2: 67.

Figure 9-3: Effect of Median Income on Lowest Quintile Income

David M. Weil, *Economic Growth* (Boston: Pearson, 2005), Figure 13.6, 373.

Figure 9-4: U.S. Government Spending Relative to GDP

Christopher Chantrill, "U.S. Government Spending As Percent of GDP," U.S. Government Spending website, http://www.usgovernmentspending.com/us_20th_century_chart.html.